Birds
by behaviour

Birds
by behaviour

Dominic Couzens

First published in 2003

Collins is an imprint of HarperCollins*Publishers* Ltd.
77–85 Fulham Palace Road
London
W6 8JB

The Collins website address is:
www.collins.co.uk

08 07 06 05 04 03

10 9 8 7 6 5 4 3 2 1

ISBN 0 00 711549 0

Edited and designed by Blackingstone Books

Colour reproduction by Saxon, England
Printed and bound by Printing Express, Hong Kong

Contents

Introduction

This book will help you identify the birds of Britain and Europe. There are many such books on the market: so why another one?

Birds by Behaviour differs from other 'field guides' (identification books that are supposed to be used outdoors, in the field) in one very important respect. It ditches all discussion of plumage and plumage patterns and concentrates instead on shape, behaviour and ecology. Such an approach leaves plenty of room to highlight details of lifestyle that might be missing from other books, yet can still be useful in identifying and appreciating birds. By leaving out much that clogs up other field guides (and tends to be endlessly repeated from book to book), the way is clear to concentrate only upon those aspects of shape and behaviour that might otherwise be overlooked.

Here's an example of how this book can be helpful. If a certain species of bird looks very similar to another but wags its tail in a completely different way, you will probably find it easier to locate that piece of information here than in another guide. The feature might well be mentioned in the text of a conventional guide, but it will be hard to dig out. In *Birds by Behaviour*, the tail-wagging will be given pride of place, and the difference will be hard to miss. That's not all, however, for we have also included other details that are simply not treated anywhere in other identification guides. If that certain tail-wagging bird also flies in a different way, feeds in a different way, or even exhibits more aggressive tendencies than its close relative, such characteristics will also be found here, so long as they are considered useful for identification.

You will also notice that the style of this book is slightly different. *Birds by Behaviour* is much more pictorial than other field guides: illustrations fill every page and are labelled only with annotations. There is no 'heavy' body of text as such, and there are no distribution maps. No mention is made of

the sounds that the birds make. We have truly pared the information down to concentrate on what we believe is less well-covered elsewhere.

It should become obvious that, by adopting this approach, we have taken the risk that everybody who buys this book will also own a more conventional field guide. *Birds by Behaviour* is best used to complement one of these, as a secondary source of information to a primary identification text. Although we have included illustrations of most plumages adopted by European birds, space has dictated that some have been left out, and we have made no attempt to help you tell one type of plumage from another, other than by labelling them. We are not pretending to give the whole identification picture, only a supplementary one.

But that is not to say that we have in any way sacrificed accuracy for overall impression. Thanks to the skill and dedication of our team of artists, I believe the illustrations all stand up for themselves. It is only the type of illustration, the behaviour depicted and the annotations that make this book different to the many other superbly illustrated identification books that are available. I would like to take the opportunity here to thank the artists most warmly for their fantastic efforts.

THE MATERIAL COVERED

When contemplating writing a bird identification guide free of discussion of plumage details, the first question to be asked was: 'What then should be included?' Although the first answer was always shape and posture, the next set of characteristics tended to be more difficult to decide.

Two points always emerged from this question. The first was that one person's idea of what is useful for identification would always differ from someone else's; what to include was a matter of opinion. The second point was that the most useful non-plumage identification pointers differ from bird group to bird group, and from species to species. What is useful for one might not necessarily be useful for another. For example, birds of prey are most usefully identified by their manner of flight, but for warblers this feature is largely meaningless – warblers don't differ much in the way in which they flit about. Conversely, warblers often sing at a particular height or in a particular posture, whereas for the largely silent birds of prey such considerations are irrelevant.

If presenting different features for different birds might lend *Birds by Behaviour* a rather arbitrary feel, we don't apologise for this at all. The variety is what has made the book both difficult and fascinating to

produce, and on the material selected it stands or falls.

An important jargon word that pervades the world of bird identification is 'jizz'. Jizz is understood as that combination of shape and behaviour that marks a bird out even at great distance, usually without a dot or a stripe of its plumage being observed. The Treecreeper, hug-creeping up a tree with its jerky, preoccupied style is a good example; its colours don't need to be seen for the bird to be identified. Much of what is included in this book really comes down to this, the combination of shape and mien that is encompassed in the word 'jizz'.

Another very important point about the material covered needs to be highlighted. In a conventional plumage-based field guide there are always plenty of incontrovertible facts. Bird identification has become quite an exact science – you can tell a Firecrest from a Goldcrest because it always has a black stripe through its eye, for example. In shape, however, differences are often quite subjective, and in behaviour and ecology birds often exhibit tendencies rather than rules. Out of necessity we have included much detail that is useful but not necessarily incontrovertible.

A good example concerns the difference in motion between the Snipe and the Jack

Snipe (p115). When standing or feeding, Jack Snipes tend to exhibit a very distinctive up-and-down rocking motion, as if they were on springs. Birdwatchers have used this feature to distinguish the two species for many years, and it is part of the standard protocol for identifying them. Yet Jack Snipes don't always bounce up and down while they are being observed, and Snipes occasionally do. In 90 per cent of cases it is a useful distinction, but it is not a rule. Not all birds adhere to what they are supposed to do.

The waters are equally muddied in regard to habitat and ecology. Birds break rules, but exhibit tendencies. Little Ringed Plovers tend to avoid estuaries in favour of freshwater, but you will always find the odd one that stops off by an estuary on migration. Crossbills usually feed up in conifer trees, but the occasional maverick will fly down to feed upon the seeds of a herbaceous weed. This book does not make allowances for such unusual behaviour, and we request that you treat many of our behavioural tips as useful rather than set in stone.

HOW TO USE THIS BOOK
We hope that many users will simply sit down and browse through this book, looking at the plates and reading the notes. Those who are reasonably familiar with the birds

Birds swimming on the sea

Most *ducks* are plump-bodied with large head and bill, and a short neck. They ride higher in the water than divers, cormorants or grebes. Most *ducks*, including *Goldeneye, Common Scoter, Scaup* and *Red-breasted Merganser* dive with wings closed into the body, often with a jump clear of the water.

When diving *Eider, Velvet Scoter* and *Long-tailed duck* sink down with wings partially open.

Scaup

Goldeneye – very plump, head, seems too large for neck

Red-breasted Merganser

Velvet Scoters

Long-tailed Duck – short body, long neck, rounded head.

Red-breasted Merganser (female) – size of large grebe, shorter neck, sharp stern, steeper forehead, 'uncombed hair' at back of head, darker look.

Goldeneye

Common Scoter

Eider – large, short body, huge head.

Slavonian Grebe – small grebes dive with plop into water wings tightly closed to body. Smaller grebes resemble auks, but have rounded, sometimes fluffy sterns.

Red-throated Diver – (below) smallest diver but larger/longer bodied than any grebe, with thicker neck.

Diver – as Cormorant/Shag, but round end to back. Dagger-like bill, rounded hindcrown. Often seen 'snorkelling', placing head in

Great Crested Grebe – largest grebe, but smaller than any diver, with longer neck. All grebes have 'round stern', with blunt-ended, completely tailless look.

water to look around prior to dive; cormorants and grebes tend not to.

Cormorant/Shag

Common Scoter – ducks have shorter, more compact bodies than divers and cormorants, with relatively bulbous heads and blunt bills.

Divers rarely form flocks, but are well spread over the sea.

Example of general family pages

and the order in which they are customarily listed will find no difficulty in working out the plates and gleaning information for themselves. For others, though, there is a particular way in which this book is best used, which is as follows.

If you come across an unknown bird:

1. Determine what family or group the bird is in by looking at one of the general pages.
2. Find the relevant section, using the index.
3. Browse through the plates covering the family or group you have chosen.
4. If the family or group is a large one, such

as ducks, check the plates with broader subject matter (e.g. 'Feeding in freshwater') first, to help you focus in on the bird you are interested in.
5. Refer to the plate featuring your bird (e.g. 'Pochards').
6. Check all references to the bird you think it is, using the index again.

By then we hope you will have enough information to confirm the identity of your bird in tandem with a conventional field guide.

You can of course enter this 'progression route' at any time. However, if you should enter at point 5, please note that many species are featured on more than one plate. For example, the Skylark is mentioned and illustrated on 'Larks, Pipits and other small brown birds', 'Seed-eating bird families', 'Larks: Song-flights and habitats' and 'Larks: Other Larks', so don't forget to include point 6 when you are checking a species out.

The following is a list of the general comparison pages:

Birds swimming on the sea (pp12–13)
Birds flying over the sea (pp18–19)
Long-legged wading birds (pp28–29)
Raptors: Types (pp60–64)
Waders: Families of Waders (p96)
Gulls vs Terns (p131)
Pigeon-like birds (pp142–143)
Aerial birds (p154)
Larks, Pipits and other small brown birds (pp162–163)
Small brown birds of woodland and garden (pp178–179)
Thrushes, Warblers and Flycatchers (p180)
Seed-eating bird families (pp230–231)

As a final suggestion, check the plates carefully to find out all the information given for a particular bird. Many of the plates are very 'busy', meaning that some notes can be fairly hidden away in all corners of the page.

THE NAMES OF THE BIRDS

There has been much discussion recently about the names of European birds, and at the same time scientific research has broadened our understanding about how certain species are related to each other. The result of the former has been a change in some names of familiar birds, and the latter has led to some extra species being included in the roll call of European representatives.

In this book we have taken a relaxed view on both. We have only labelled the plates with English (vernacular) names, although the scientific names are included in the index, and we have tended towards using names that have been in use for some time. The updated names, however, are mentioned in the index within [square brackets].

We have included some of the new 'splits' – Taiga and Tundra Bean Goose, the Redpolls, some of the gulls – but have omitted others for fear of making complicated distinctions even more complicated (e.g. Crossbills, Chiffchaffs). We do appreciate that they might be worthy of inclusion if future editions are called for, when their identification criteria become clearer and more widely accepted.

GEOGRAPHICAL SPREAD

This book includes all the breeding birds of Europe east to European Russia and most of the common migrant visitors. We have excluded the birds of the Middle East and North Africa, even though many other guides do feature them, and we have also left out most birds that could be considered as rare or 'accidental' visitors. We have limited ourselves in this way for two reasons. Firstly, it has been a problem to squeeze what information we have into a book of manageable size. Secondly, some of the Middle Eastern and North African birds are much less well-known than their European counterparts, especially in certain aspects of their behaviour and ecology covered by this book. So we have left them out until a greater body of relevant information becomes available.

TECHNICAL TERMS

It is inevitable that we have had to use some technical terms, particularly for parts of the bird. There is no short cut to learning what all these are. Most are given here, but please also refer to the Glossary for further explanation.

PARTS OF A BIRD

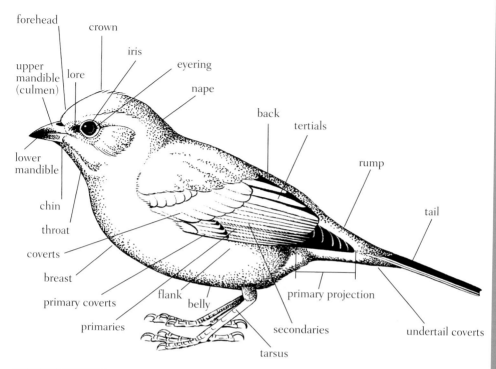

forehead

crown

iris

eyering

upper
mandible
(culmen)

lore

nape

back

tertials

rump

lower
mandible

tail

chin

throat

coverts

breast

primary coverts

flank

belly

primary projection

primaries

secondaries

undertail coverts

tarsus

BUZZARD UNDERWING

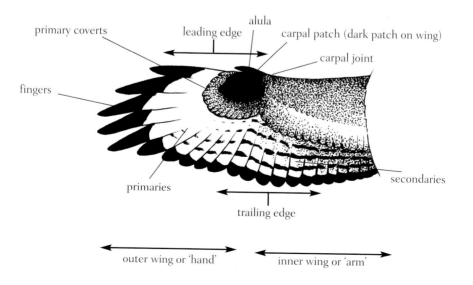

primary coverts

alula

leading edge

carpal patch (dark patch on wing)

carpal joint

fingers

primaries

secondaries

trailing edge

outer wing or 'hand'

inner wing or 'arm'

Birds swimming on the sea

Most Ducks are plump-bodied with large head and bill, and a short neck. They ride higher in the water than Divers, Cormorants or Grebes. Most Ducks, including *Goldeneye*, *Common Scoter*, *Scaup* and *Red-breasted Merganser* dive with wings closed into the body, often with a jump clear of the water.

When diving *Eider*, *Velvet Scoter* and *Long-tailed Duck* sink down with wings partially open.

Scaup

Goldeneye – very plump, head, seems too large for neck.

Velvet Scoters

Red-breasted Merganser

Long-tailed Duck – short body, long neck, rounded head.

Red-breasted Merganser (female) – size of large grebe, shorter neck, sharp stern, steeper forehead, 'uncombed hair' at back of head, darker look.

Goldeneye

Common Scoter

Eider – large, short body, huge head.

Slavonian Grebe – small grebes dive with plop into water, wings tightly closed to body. Smaller grebes resemble auks, but have rounded, sometimes fluffy sterns.

Red-throated Diver (below) – smallest diver but larger/longer body than any grebe, with thicker neck.

Diver – as Cormorant/Shag, but round end to back. Dagger-like bill, rounded hinderown. Often seen snorkelling, placing head in water to look around prior to dive; Cormorants and Grebes tend not to.

Great Crested Grebe – largest grebe, but smaller than any diver, with longer neck. All grebes have 'round stern', with blunt-ended, completely tailless look.

Shag

Common Scoter – ducks have shorter, more compact bodies than divers and cormorants, with relatively bulbous heads and blunt bills.

Divers – rarely form flocks, but are well spread over the sea.

Grebes and Auks tend to form small parties, or are well-spaced. Ducks, Gulls, Fulmars, Shearwaters and Storm Petrels habitually swim on the sea in dense clusters.

Guillemot/Razorbill – auks have pointed ends and very short necks.

Great Crested Grebe – large grebes usually slip below the water without a leap.

Manx Shearwater – smaller head than auk, thin bill and abrupt forehead; wings much longer than tail. Often hunts at surface, head down, but will also submerge with wings partly open.

Phalarope – tiny. Needle-thin bill. Very buoyant/cork-like on water, feverishly picks at water surface, often turning in circles as does so.

Tern – only occasionally settle on water, usually on migration.

Storm Petrel – tiny body, thin bill.

Black Guillemot (winter) – relatively long body, dagger-like bill.

Guillemot (winter)

Shearwater

Little Gull – larger than Phalarope, with longer wings, bigger head, thicker bill.

Fulmar – looks like gull, but chunkier, with shorter, thicker bill; patters on surface to take off.

Herring Gull – longer bill and neck; lifts effortlessly from the water.

Cormorant/Shag leaps before diving, shows tail.

Diver – 'rolls' smoothly into water, no tail.

Cormorant/Shag – long body, low in water, head up, smooth slope to back, thick blunt bill, angled back of head.

Gannet (immature) – like goose but with long, pointed tail. Rides buoyantly.

Divers

Great Northern Diver – sometimes in short-term, loose gatherings.

Black-throated Diver – bulge in neck often obvious from behind.

Black-throated – in winter plumage, is starkly and smartly light and dark.

Black-throated – often in small, well-dispersed groups.

Great Northern – thick bill held horizontally; black. Dagger-like bill shape.

Black-throated – usually much smaller than Great Northern. Well proportioned, with snake-like neck. Crown can be high, with slight bump to forecrown, but head and neck look smoothly rounded.

Great Northern – in winter plumage, less contrasting than Black-throated. Looks a bit messy.

Red-throated Diver – smallest diver. Uptilted head/bill.

Red-throated – sometimes dives with slight jump (others do not).

White-billed Diver – largest diver. Uptilted head and bill.

Red-throated – often in small, well-dispersed groups.

Cormorant – long body, low in water, head up, smooth slope to back, thick blunt bill, angled back of head.

Red-throated – usually uptilted head/bill. Bill looks rather thin. Gently sloping forehead/flat crown. Neck held straight, with fairly straight drop down from neck to chest.

Great Crested Grebe – abrupt stern.

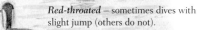

Great Northern – bulkier than Black-throated, broad-beamed, with thicker bill. Thick neck, large head. Always with high crown. Often large 'bump' on head; crown flatter, giving angular look to head/neck.

White-billed – thick bill/head held at upward tilt; ivory-coloured. Exotic bill shape. Slightly broader-based than Great Northern's bill. Lower mandible angled upwards. Often large lump on head. Slightly larger overall than Great Northern.

Black-throated – bill held horizontal. Thicker bill than Red-throated. Crown curved. Forehead sometimes steep. Neck held smoothly rounded in S-shape, chest protrudes.

Great Northern Diver – very slow, smoother wing-beats, flexible, rather goose-like action.

Black-throated Diver – slower, stiffer, shallower wing-beats than Red-throated.

Red-throated Diver – fast wing-beats, deeper than Black-throated, higher upstroke.

White-billed Diver – wing-beats even slower than Great Northern, if only slightly.

Great Crested Grebe

Cormorant

Black-throated – head/neck, as well as bill, held straighter than Red-throated. Wings placed centrally. Feet project visibly.

Red-throated – head can sag almost alarmingly in flight. Bill often held upwards, giving rather curious shape. Wings appear to be slightly backswept and behind centre of body. Feet small, don't project much beyond tail.

Great Northern – centrally placed wings. Thick-necked, bulky. Broader wings than Red- or Black-throated. Large feet, often spread in flight.

White-billed – large feet.

Red-throated – often makes goose-like cackle in flight. Others silent in flight.

Red-throated is only diver that can take off without running start. This is a Black-throated.

All divers found on sea in winter. Most are widespread, but White-billed Diver mainly found in Arctic waters.

Red-throated (breeding plumage) – often breeds on small, shallow pools in moorland/tundra regions, sometimes close to sea. Commutes to larger lakes or sea to fish, hence often seen flying.

Great Northern (breeding plumage) – breeds mainly in Iceland, on large lakes.

Black-throated (breeding plumage) – on large lakes, usually far from sea. Obtains fish on home lake. Fewer aerial excursions.

White-billed (breeding plumage) – doesn't breed in Europe.

Grebes

Red-necked Grebe – much less skinny than Great Crested, shorter neck/wings.

Great Crested Grebe – remarkably skinny outline. Long thin neck drooped below body line.

LARGER GREBES

Red-necked – second largest grebe; stockier and more compact than Great Crested, with shorter neck. In ones or twos at the most. Has greater tendency than Great Crested to dive with leap out of water.

Red-necked – has front-heavy appearance, especially at distance. Often recalls Slavonian Grebe in jizz rather than Great Crested.

Red-necked – less clean cut, dingier. Bill shorter than Great Crested, thicker and blunt-looking.

Great Crested – largest grebe, slimmest and most elegant.

Red-necked (breeding plumage) – prefers more vegetated lakes and marshes than Great Crested, to suit retiring habits. Often hides on small lakes, sometimes those surrounded by forest. Tends to shy away in vegetation.

Great Crested – stark black-and-white. Bill long and sharp.

Great Crested – display.

Great Crested – usually dives with smooth roll, without leaping.

Great Crested (breeding plumage) – on lakes with some, even little, vegetation; in marshes, on slow-flowing rivers. The grebe most often seen in open water; not at all shy.

Little Grebe – flies more than most grebes. Rushes over surface, half-running/half-flying, very fast.

Slavonian Grebe – only grebe to fly with body/neck inclined upwards.

SMALLER GREBES

Slavonian – small version of Great Crested, long neck, long body, flat crown. Stern not markedly 'fluffy'.

Black-necked Grebe – small and skinny-necked, neck held straight out, not raised.

Slavonian – very clean-cut black-and-white grebe (like Great Crested in full winter plumage). Red eyes. Bill straight/stubby; forehead slopes gently; flat crown.

Black-necked – less contrasting in plumage than Slavonian, especially on cheeks; black on crown has 'riding hat' shape. Red eyes. Bill small/slightly uptilted, sharp 'chiselled' point; forehead steep; crown rounded and highest above eye, not at back.

Black-necked – slightly smaller than Slavonian, with thinner neck, shorter body, rounded crown. Tends to ride higher in water, exaggerating 'fluffy' stern.

Black-necked – on highly productive shallow weedy ponds. Often uses seasonal waters/floods.

Little – brown-and-white, not black-and-white, with little contrast in plumage. Dark eyes. Very small straight bill, usually with obvious gape patch. Head rounded.

Black-necked – takes much food on water surface, immersing neck, without diving. Only grebe to form breeding colonies. Tends to nest among gulls or terns.

Little – smallest grebe, plump body, short thin neck. 'Floating rabbit' with pronounced fluffy rear end.

Slavonian – usually on small, weedy pools/ marshes, with some open water.

Little – often submerges with only head/neck showing, checking for danger.

Little – small, with prominent green gape patch.

Little – almost any shallow freshwater with plenty of fringing vegetation, however small. Skulks beneath banks of rivers, canal and ditches.

Slavonian – tufts give 'horned' look.

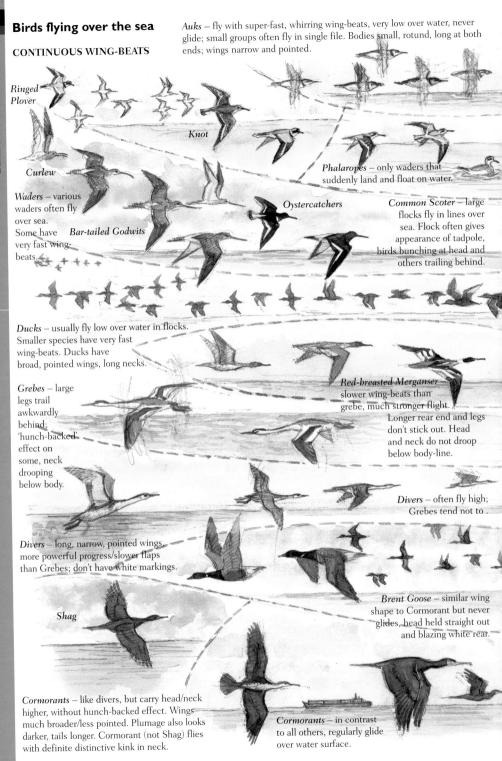

Birds flying over the sea

CONTINUOUS WING-BEATS

Auks — fly with super-fast, whirring wing-beats, very low over water, never glide; small groups often fly in single file. Bodies small, rotund, long at both ends; wings narrow and pointed.

Ringed Plover

Knot

Curlew

Phalaropes — only waders that suddenly land and float on water.

Waders — various waders often fly over sea. Some have very fast wing-beats.

Bar-tailed Godwits

Oystercatchers

Common Scoter — large flocks fly in lines over sea. Flock often gives appearance of tadpole, birds bunching at head and others trailing behind.

Ducks — usually fly low over water in flocks. Smaller species have very fast wing-beats. Ducks have broad, pointed wings, long necks.

Grebes — large legs trail awkwardly behind; 'hunch-backed' effect on some, neck drooping below body.

Red-breasted Merganser — slower wing-beats than grebe, much stronger flight. Longer rear end and legs don't stick out. Head and neck do not droop below body-line.

Divers — often fly high; Grebes tend not to .

Divers — long, narrow, pointed wings, more powerful progress/slower flaps than Grebes; don't have white markings.

Brent Goose — similar wing shape to Cormorant but never glides, head held straight out and blazing white rear.

Shag

Cormorants — like divers, but carry head/neck higher, without hunch-backed effect. Wings much broader/less pointed. Plumage also looks darker, tails longer. Cormorant (not Shag) flies with definite distinctive kink in neck.

Cormorants — in contrast to all others, regularly glide over water surface.

FLAPS ALTERNATE WITH GLIDES

Large Shearwater (*Great*) – much smaller than Gannet, shorter tail/narrower wings. Often holds wings slightly bowed, hugging waves, banking from side to side.

Gannet (juvenile) – very large, far bigger than any shearwater. Distinctive 'pointed at all angles' shape, with long, sharply pointed wings, pointed head, pointed tail.

Fulmar – species of shearwater, with usually stiff-winged flapping and gliding. Similar to gull, but flies with rigid wings held straight out, not flexed.

Small Shearwater – rapid, shallow wing-beats almost as fast as auk/duck, always followed by tell-tale glide. Banks from side to side.

OTHER FORMS OF FLIGHT

Skuas – fly like gulls, but usually have more sharply pointed wings and faster, more powerful and 'purposeful' flight.

Gulls – long, narrow wings that bend back slightly at carpal joints. Slow, shallow wing-beats with smooth, relaxed action. At times soar and wheel, with long periods of gliding.

Terns – more pointed wing-tips than gulls; tend to fly with wings angled further backwards. Light flight action with elastic wing-beats; in contrast to gulls, do not soar/glide.

Storm Petrels – tiny seabirds fly with fast flapping but irregular progress, rather like Swallow or House Martin.

PLUNGE-DIVING

Gannet – gives away identity, even at long range, with spectacular plunge-dives from height.

Terns – plunge-dive with splash.

Gulls – may attempt plunge-diving but enter water with awkward, open-winged posture.

Shearwaters

Fulmar – nests in open on cliffs. Attends nest during day.

Fulmar – chunky shape, large head, thick neck. Wings quite blunt. Has broader tail than other shearwaters.

Cory's – holds wings bowed.

Cory's Shearwater – nests in burrows or in open. Only visits nest at night.

Fulmar – at distance, unusual colouration cannot be seen, and pale underwing is similar to other shearwaters.

Cory's – lethargic, laboured flight on flexible wings. Few slow, deep wing-beats, long glides. The rest – busy, purposeful flight, bursts of stiff, shallow wing-beats followed by glides.

Cory's – large, long-winged. Slightly blunt wing-tips, angled backwards a bit. Looks large-headed. Pale bill.

Great Shearwater – wings not bowed. Stiffer wing-beats than Cory's.

Sooty Shearwater – larger than Mediterranean, longer wings.

Great – smaller than Cory's, and sharper wing-tips. Looks small-headed. Dark bill.

Mediterranean Shearwater – nests in burrows, visits at night.

Sooty – heavy body, long wings that look too small. Wings distinctly angled back. Small head, dark bill.

Manx Shearwater – cross-shaped at distance.

Manx – nests in burrows, visiting at night.

Mediterranean – larger than Manx, looks heavier (especially at rear); pot-bellied, almost duck-like.

Manx – quick flaps/glides low over water, often veering from side to side, one moment showing black, the next white.

Manx – slender.

Bulwer's Petrel – usually seen singly. Doesn't fly more than 2m above waves.

Little – faster, more whirring wing-beats than Manx, with very obviously longer series of flaps between glides. Smaller than Manx, shorter wings with rounded tip. Thin bill, rounded head.

Little – often raises wings over back and patters over surface, like Storm Petrel, but unlike others here.

Bulwer's Petrel – bursts of rapid wing-beats followed by unusual twisting/turning glides. Erratic flight. Deep wing-beats, glides with wings slightly bowed.

Little – uniquely, head often raised slightly in flight.

These species often follow ships:
Cory's Shearwater
Great Shearwater
Little Shearwater
Fulmar

These species do not follow ships:
Sooty Shearwater
Manx Shearwater
Mediterranean Shearwater
Bulwer's Petrel

Fulmar – in rough seas, reverts from wing-flaps/glides to glides only. Quite effortless impression, rides wave crests with ease.

Cory's Shearwater – rises high over waves in steep arcs.

Great Shearwater – turns angled on wing-points, steep rises.

FLIGHT IN WINDS AND ROUGH SEA

Little Shearwater – glides/banks, but reverts to fluttering in troughs of waves.

Sooty Shearwater – swept-back wings even more obvious. Less steep bounding than Cory's or Great.

Manx Shearwater – abandons flaps and relies on gliding, flies low over wave-roughs then rises steeply, up to 10m.

Storm Petrels

European and *Wilson's Petrel* – regularly follow ships; others don't.

European – 'bat-like' flight pattern, uniquely weak and fluttering, almost continuous flapping with short glides. Hugs surface of water. Often buffeted by wind/hurled about.

European – when feeding, wings raised over back in sharp V, short legs patter surface.

European – smallest Storm Petrel, only two-thirds size of Leach's. Short wings, held fairly straight out. Square-ended tail.

Wilson's (below) – when feeding, wings raised over back in shallow V, long legs trailing. Bounces, skips, dances over surface.

Wilson's Petrel (below) – 'swallow-like' flight pattern, strong/fluttering, vigorous wing-beats with short glides. Often flies much higher than other Storm Petrels, to as much as 3m. Very direct, purposeful flight.

Wilson's – only Storm Petrel in which legs project beyond tail in flight.

Leach's Petrel – doesn't follow ships but is occasionally seen around trawlers.

Wilson's – slightly larger than European, broader/more rounded wings, held straight. Almost straight trailing edge. Square-ended tail.

Leach's (below) – largest Storm Petrel, long wings, obviously angled back, very pointed. Long, forked tail.

Leach's – 'Nightjar-like'/'tern-like' flight pattern, uniquely bounding, relatively slow, deep wing-beats interspersed with longish glides on bowed wings. Irregular changes in speed/direction.

Leach's – when feeding, hangs still over water surface, wings just raised above horizontal/slightly bowed. Gives butterfly-like impression.

Leach's – rarely rests on surface.

Madeiran – 'Shearwater-like' flight pattern, faster wing-beats than Leach's, longer glides/characteristic shearing over water. Not as bounding as Leach's. Characteristic zigzag path, bursts of wing-beats then shearing on flat wings. When feeding, wings raised just above horizontal, as in Leach's, not bowed.

Madeiran Petrel – in between Wilson's and Leach's in size, slightly shorter and broader wings than Leach's. Wings angled back slightly less than Leach's. Slightly notched tail.

Pelicans

Soaring pelicans well-organised and co-ordinated. Flap in time or sequence with leader. Lines.

Storks – faster moving, in swarm.

Both flap then glide, look heavy.

Dalmatian Pelican

White Stork   *White Pelican*

Dalmatian Pelican – usually in smaller colonies, similar habitat to White, but also at altitude. Tends to fish alone more often. Much less sociable. Can take to smaller waters.

White Pelican – often in large colonies, spending much time in communal fishing. Colonies are in deltas, islands of large lakes etc., in lowlands. Two species can be found in same colony.

Dalmatian – 'grubby' plumage.   *White* – cleaner looking.

Dalmatian – slightly larger than White, only obvious when together.

White – skin tapers to point on forehead.

Swan – more elegant neck.

Pelicans – swim high in water, wings loose.

Dalmatian – adult has 'bad hair day' curly nape feathers, longer and more untidy in breeding season.

White – shaggy, downward-hanging crest.

Dalmatian – broad forehead, concave where abuts bill.

Dalmatian – pale iris, small area of surrounding skin.

White – dark iris, large area of pink skin.

Cormorants

Different to geese:
Cormorants combine flaps with glides, geese don't glide.
Cormorants have shallower wing-beats.
Cormorants have longer tails.
Cormorants fly in silent flocks; geese noisy.
Cormorants' flocks are less organised.

Cormorant – slow wing-beats, many glides. Often flies high.

Goose

Shag – thin, straight neck, held horizontally.

Shag – often in rougher water around rocks.

Shag – has crest when breeding.

Shag – blunter wings, less angled back. Wings slightly further back. Tail heavy. Pot-bellied. Fast wing-beats, almost as fast as large duck. Fewer glides. Lower flight-path, close to water. Rarely over land.

Cormorant – skin around eye, Shag has little.

Cormorant – sharper wings, attached in middle. Flat tummy.

Cormorant – thick, kinked neck.

Cormorant – leaps or slinks into dive.

Shag – thinner bill, higher crown. Bill could be snapped off. Thinner neck.

Cormorant – heavy bill sunk into head. Thick neck.

Shag – more often springs into dive. Higher leap than Cormorant.

Cormorant – larger than Shag.

Cormorants – nest on cliff ledges.

Cormorants – often roost on piers, jetties and sand-bars. *Shags* – only on rocks.

Cormorant – angular head, *Shag* – rounded head.

Cormorants nest inland on trees. *Shags* don't.

Shag – nests in small colonies, rock crevices or cave.

Pygmy Cormorant – among vegetation in marshes, deltas.

Shags not inland on freshwater.
Cormorants regular all year on freshwater.

Pygmy Cormorant – short bill and neck, cute expression, long tail.

Egrets

Cattle Egret – small, rather stocky. Often hunched. Shorter yellow bill.

Great Egret – large, elegant, size of Grey Heron. Long yellow bill (blackish for short time in breeding season).

Great Egret – least sociable egret, usually alone. Sedate.

Great Egret – back plumes in breeding season.

Cattle Egret (*above*) – rounded head with much feathering on the chin, making for a characteristic jowl. *Little Egret* (*below*) – flat head and long bill. Neck plumes in breeding season.

Little Egret – black legs with yellow feet. Small, elegant. Long, narrow black bill.

Cattle Egret – stocky in flight, looks stub-nosed. No obvious coiling of the neck. Feet hardly project beyond tail.

Great Egret – very slow wing-beats (like Grey Heron). A large version of Little Egret, although wings seem attached further forward. Feet project a long way.

Cattle Egret/Little Egret – fast wing-beats (about pace of crow).

Little Egret – elegant, long bill, obvious neck-keel.

Squacco Heron – looks like egret in flight, with white wings. Small/stocky, feet hardly projecting beyond the tail at all.

Great Egret – usually feeds by water. Stands/waits for prey to appear, or walks slowly, before striking.

Cattle Egret – most sociable egret, always in groups. Dashing.

Little Egret – dashes after fish that it has spied in the water, often raising wings as runs; others do not. Places one foot on surface of water and trembles it, to stir up foot; others don't.

Cattle Egret – usually feeds in drier places than others. Also rides the backs of large animals. Other egrets have quite different behaviour.

Bitterns and Herons

Grey Heron – bill thick/powerful.

Grey Heron – large, long-necked. Often feeds in open, beside rivers/lakes.

Grey Heron (juvenile)

Purple Heron (juvenile) – bill longer, thinner, sharper. Seems to fit seamlessly into head, accentuating snake-like appearance of head and neck.

Bittern – smaller than Grey or Purple Herons, with shorter, much thicker neck. Very difficult to see, feeds deep in reed-beds.

Purple Heron – slightly smaller/darker than Grey Heron, with thin, snake-like neck. Usually feeds concealed in vegetation.

Bittern – rounded wings give distinctly owl-like appearance, apart from trailing feet! Semi-nocturnal habits.

Grey Heron – slow, almost lumbering wing-beats. Wings are held in distinctively bowed manner.

Purple Heron – long neck retracted to give more obvious 'neck keel' in flight.

Long-eared Owl

Purple Heron – in flight, shows more splayed toes than Grey Heron.

Bittern – faster wing-beats than large herons. More stocky and front-heavy.

Grey Heron – all year round in all watery places. Nests in colonies in tall treetops.

Bittern – all year round only in thick, extensive reed-beds (dense enough for it to hold on to several stems while clambering). Nest is pile of reeds at ground level. Single nests.

Purple Heron – summer visitor to extensive reed-beds, where nests placed near the ground. Singly or small groups.

Night Heron – medium-sized heron with a short, thick bill. Hunched posture.

Night Heron (adult)

Purple Heron

Bittern

Night Heron (juvenile)

Little Bittern

Squacco Heron

Night Heron – juveniles have spotted plumage, like Bittern, but smaller, with shorter neck/legs. Mainly feeds at night. Waits motionless for food to appear, with quick strike, or walks slowly along.

Night Heron – more often seen in the open than Bittern, often perches in trees; Bitterns never do. Mostly nocturnal. During the day roosts in treetops in small groups. Sociable. (Bittern solitary.)

Night Heron – flies with bill pointing downwards, feet only just projecting beyond tail. Shallow wing-beats. Bittern flies with bill pointing forwards, feet projecting. Fuller wing-beats.

Little Bittern (*below*) – very skulking/secretive. Semi-nocturnal. Actively climbs to top of reed stems; even up trees/bushes.

Squacco Heron

Squacco Heron (adult) – feeds during day and at dusk. Mainly stands in wait for prey.

Little Bittern – flight with fast, clipped wing-beats on rounded wings. Ends in glide.

Little Bittern – truly tiny heron, perhaps more likely to be confused with Water Rail or Moorhen than another heron.

Moorhen

Squacco Heron (immature) – when on ground, crouches down.

Little Bittern – often feeds at dusk or dawn. Makes quick strike from standing position, or walks along slowly, stalking. Usually remains hidden in reeds.

Long-legged wading birds

Crane – tall, longer legs/smaller bills than storks. Common Crane has 'bushy tail' effect, like Ostrich.

Stork – huge birds. Massive, colourful, dagger-like bills. Long legs, long necks, heavier bodies than herons.

Cranes – feed by probing/picking from land/water. In contrast to the other tall wading birds, eat much plant material, especially in winter.

Storks – feed by walking about, striking at prey, often in more open areas than herons.

Glossy Ibis – smaller than Storks/large herons, only the size of Curlew. Long, very curved bill. To feed, walks along slowly/probes its bill into water/mud.

Herons – stand motionless, waiting for food to come into range, and then make a rapid strike.

Egret – small white members of heron family.

Bittern – skulking, brownish member of heron family.

Spoonbill – feeding method is give-away.

Curlew

Glossy Ibis

Flamingo – unique pinkish-white birds with oddly bent bills, plus exceptionally long legs/thin neck.

Places bill in water, sweeps it from side to side as walks.

Heron – dagger-like, straight bill.

Great Egret

White Stork

Crane

Greater Flamingo – usually feeds by walking slowly over shallow water, with head immersed, filtering small invertebrates with unusual bill. Like Spoonbills, tend to sweep head from side to side

Spoonbill – large, white, extraordinary spatula-shaped bill.

Cranes – on migration, very high in V-formation.

Cranes – graceful flight, slow, imperious flaps/glides. Long wings.

Stork – generally silent in flight.
Crane – longer legs, longer neck, repeated calling in flight.

Grey Heron

Great Egret – slow, steady flaps, no real glides, retracted neck.

Purple Heron

Herons – steady flaps on rounded wings.

Squacco Heron

All *herons* fly with their neck retracted, to form so-called 'keel'. Rest fly with neck extended.

Spoonbill – faster flaps than Great Egret, every few flaps followed by a glide; extended neck.

Herons, Glossy Ibis, Spoonbill – wing-tips don't show obvious fingers. **Storks** and **Cranes** – primary feathers well-spaced when wings extended to show 'fingers'.

Glossy Ibis – flaps interspersed with glides. Flies in ragged lines.

Stork

Greater Flamingo – extraordinary elongated shape in flight. Often in long lines.

Bittern

Glossy Ibis – uncommon marshland species, mainly Eastern Europe. Breeds in colonies, in trees with heron species, or in reed-beds.

Little Bittern

Greater Flamingo – colonies on salt-flats and mud, with curious mud nests. Not among other birds.

Storks

White Stork – huge in flight. Slow wing-beats, much gliding with neck outstretched.

White – forms large migratory gatherings, wheeling about on thermals.

Egyptian Vulture – could be confused with White Stork at distance. Short neck, short legs, wedge-shaped tail.

Black – typical 'prehistoric look' of storks. Very slightly smaller than White.

White – open country bird, often in farmland. Usually close to rivers/marshes, prefers to feed in marshy ground.

Black Stork – migrates in smaller flocks than White, and much less dependent on thermals for migration.

White – feeds in fields or marshes, taking mammals, amphibians, insects, few fish.

White – small colonies, often close to people. Fearless. Endless bill-clattering at nest upon greeting, head thrown back.

Black – forest bird, feeding in marshy areas/rivers in forested areas.

Black – no bill-clattering greeting; breathy, vocal sounds.

White – nests on buildings, telegraph poles.
Black – nests solitarily in crown of tree. Shy of people/disturbance. Rare.

Black – tends to feed in water, especially rivers. Eats mainly fish, plus few insects and amphibians.

Swans

Only **Mute Swan** carries young on back.

Mute – often swims or perches with bill pointing downwards. Bewick's and Whooper Swans look straight ahead.

Mute – long neck, bill has prominent knob.

Mute Swan (*far left*) – nests in temperate lakes/rivers, even town parks, also sea.

Whooper Swan (*centre*) – on lakes and rivers, also small pools. Mainly northern forests, in Iceland in tundra zone.

Bewick's Swan (*left*) – in far north, on pools, lakes, rivers in tundra.

Mute Swan in Britain all year.
Whooper Swan in wintering grounds (including Britain) Sept–Apr.
Bewick's Swan in wintering grounds (including Britain) Nov–Mar.

Only **Mute Swan** makes celebrated 'sighing' sound with wing-beats.

Whooper and **Bewick's Swans** make bugling calls in flight:

Only **Mute Swan** has threat display with wings raised. Others remain tight-winged.

Whooper – very long neck, head looks small. Bill long, wedge-shaped.

Mute – has long, pointed tail. Others don't.

Mute – head looks cut off.

Whooper – has long 'Roman nose'.

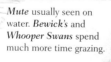

Mute usually seen on water. **Bewick's** and **Whooper Swans** spend much more time grazing.

Bewick's and **Whooper Swans** perform head-forward displays.

Bewick's – shorter neck. Faster wing-beats.

Bewick's – lands at steeper angle than others, looks more agile.

Bewick's (*right*) – shorter neck, head looks larger. Shorter bill, gentler expression. **Whooper** and **Mute Swan** very full-breasted. **Bewick's** smaller/slighter, breast doesn't bulge. More compact body shape, goose-like.

Geese: Breeding habits

Barnacle Geese

Brent Goose – in far Russian Arctic.

White-fronted Goose – only in Arctic Russia.

Red-breasted Goose – does not breed in Europe.

Lesser White-fronted Goose – northern Scandinavia and Arctic Russia.

Tundra Bean Goose – tundra of northern Scandinavia and Russian Arctic.

Pink-footed Goose – Iceland.

Taiga Bean Goose – taiga of Scandinavia and Russia.

Canada Goose – mainly Britain, the Low Countries and Scandinavia (introduced from North America).

Barnacle Goose – a few islands in Baltic. Mainly in Arctic.

Greylag Goose – widespread in Europe.

Greylag – breeds in warmer climates than other geese. Requirements include undisturbed grazing land/large expanses of water. Tends to be found in large marshes and reed-fringed lakes.

Egyptian Goose – parkland with large lakes. Introduced to southern Britain.

Canada – breeds in temperate open country with lakes/rivers, often in close proximity to people.

Pink-footed Goose – often breeds along river gorges, on inaccessible ledges.

Barnacle Goose – often on steep cliffs in High Arctic, nesting on inaccessible ledges.

Barnacle – on low, grassy islands. Sometimes colonial.

Tundra Bean Goose – breeds on damp tundra.

Pink-footed – sometimes on open tundra, especially if predator-free. Colonial.

White-fronted Goose – breeds on open lowland tundra, often on hummock, usually beside marsh/lake.

Brent Goose – on High Arctic coastal tundra.

Lesser White-fronted Goose – marshes/ bogs among willows/birches.

Taiga Bean Goose – unusual; breeds within thick coniferous forests or birch scrub, in boggy patches.

Geese: Where Geese winter

Greenland White-fronted Goose – Ireland and South-west Scotland, Oct–Apr.

Canada Goose – mostly resident. (Swedish birds migrate south to Germany in Nov, return in Mar.)

Egyptian Goose – resident.

Pink-footed Goose – Britain, Low Countries, Denmark, late Sept–Apr.

Dark-bellied Brent Goose – temperate Western European coasts, Sept–Apr.

Barnacle Goose – Ireland, Scotland, Holland, Oct–Apr.

Greylag Goose – widespread in Europe, including North, East and Central Scotland, Oct–Apr.

Red-breasted Goose – western Black Sea, including Romania and Bulgaria, Nov–Mar.

Pink-footed Goose – roosts on lakes/estuaries. Long, spectacular movements between roost/feeding sites, up to 30km apart.

Light-bellied Brent Goose – Denmark, North-east England, Ireland, Sept–Apr.

All geese are vegetarians, obtaining food by grazing, usually on land. In winter most species feed over agricultural fields/grassland, taking grass, leaves, roots, seeds.

Brent Goose – in contrast to other geese, feeds mainly on mudflats/saltmarshes, also coastal fields. Roosts on estuarine waters, according to tide.

In the evening geese must find somewhere safe to overnight. Fields are usually too dangerous, so birds travel to large lakes, marshes or estuaries. Being sociable, movements of geese between feeding/traditional roosting grounds can involve thousands of birds – a spectacular sight against pale skies of sunset or dawn.

Barnacle Goose – feeds over coastal pasturelands. Roosts on estuaries, on sandbanks/open water.

Bean Goose
(both Taiga and Tundra forms) –
feed on fields, steppes, flood meadows.
Roost on large bodies of water, such as
lakes. Not estuaries. Don't normally
travel far to roost, max 5–10km.
If suitable places available, will roost
next to feeding grounds.

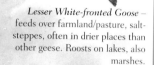

Bean (both Taiga and Tundra
forms) – West and Central Europe
late Sept–Mar; in Britain not
normally until at least Nov.

Lesser White-fronted Goose –
feeds over farmland/pasture, salt-
steppes, often in drier places than
other geese. Roosts on lakes, also
marshes.

White-fronted Goose – North-west coasts
of Europe (including South-west England),
plus Central Europe and western Black
Sea, Oct–Mar.

Lesser White-fronted – Balkans and
western Black Sea region; a few in
Holland, Oct–Mar.

Greylag Goose – roosts
on estuaries/lakes.
Many populations
prefer to spend night
near feeding grounds.

**Pink-footed, White-
fronted** and **Greylag
Goose** – feed over
agricultural fields
and grassland.

White-fronted (both
forms) – roosts on
estuaries/floodlands,
close to feeding sites.

Red-breasted Goose –
feeds over steppes/
crops, often quite dry
habitats. Roosts
on lakes.

Canada Goose – feeds over grass, lawns and
parkland. Roosts on lakes/mud banks.
Undertakes short commuting flights at low altitude.

Egyptian Goose – feeds over lakeside pastures.

Geese: Feeding on the ground

Canada Goose – very large and long-necked.

1st year

Greylag Goose – thicker neck than Bean, larger head, thicker, broader-based bill.

White-fronted Goose – slightly larger/longer-necked than Pink-footed; characteristically deep-chested. Head square, high forehead with white blaze.

Taiga Bean Goose – large, long neck, wedge-shaped bill.

Tundra Bean Goose – smaller, with shorter neck/bill. More black on bill.

Bean Goose (1st year)

White-fronted – legs orange-red.

Pink-footed Goose – faster rate of feeding than Bean.

Pink-footed – pink legs/pink-and-black bill, stubby and triangular. Small/comparatively dainty overall. Shorter neck and rounder head than Taiga Bean.

Bean (both forms) – triangular head.

Pink-footed – relatively tiny head/bill (compared to Greylag).

Greylag Goose – probes in mud for food.

Egyptian Goose – unusual plumage, very long pink legs. Bulky body.

Bean (both forms) – holds hea characteristically upright, almost swan-like. Hea wedge-shaped, long bill. Bill orange and black. Orange legs.

Greylag – legs dull pink.

Greylag – regularly feeds in water, especially by upending (in contrast to mainly land-feeding Bean, White-fronted and Pink-footed Geese).

Canada – regularly feeds in water. Head-dipping, like swan, is characteristic.

Greylag Goose – large/bulky, long thick neck and massive head/bill.

White-fronted Goose – probes in mud for roots/tubers. Smaller species don't.

'Russian' White-fronted Goose – smaller bill, pink.

White-fronted (1st year)

Greenland form of White-fronted Goose – longer bill, orange. Slightly larger overall, longer neck.

Lesser White-fronted Goose – adults (near right) and juveniles (far right) have yellow eye-ring. Shorter neck, rounder head than White-fronted, wing-tips project beyond tail.

Lesser White-fronted – noticeably faster feeding rate than White-fronted.

Lesser White-fronted – almost always smaller/daintier than White-fronted.

White-fronted – wing-tips reach tail.

Barnacle Goose – smaller than Canada Goose, shorter neck.

Barnacle – usually flocks only with own species. Dense gatherings, more bickering than other geese. Flocks dense on field, more spread out when feeding on mudflats.

Red-breasted – colourful plumage, easy to miss among flocks of others.

Red-breasted Goose – thick neck, tiny bill.

Red-breasted – often associates with Brent and White-fronted Geese.

Barnacle – short, thick neck, rounded head. Small bill. Quite plump.

Brent Goose – similar size to Lesser White-fronted.

Brent – slimmer/darker than Barnacle.

Brent – often feeds in water, upending.

'Dark-bellied' Brent Goose (above).

'Light-bellied' Brent Goose (above left).

Brent – doesn't normally flock with other geese; often associates with Wigeon.

Geese: Flying

Pink-footed Goose – neck shorter than most species; thin neck/ small bill. Fluid wing-beats quicker than those of other 'grey' geese.

Greylag Goose – very thick neck/huge bill. Broad wings, blunt wing-tips.

White-fronted Goose – looks deep-chested. Narrow wings.

White-fronted – square head, in adults with white blaze.

Lesser White-fronted Goose – very difficult to distinguish from White-fronted in flight; smaller/shorter-necked. Faster wing-beats.

Bean Goose (both forms) – long wings.

Taiga Bean Goose – very long neck.

White-fronted (above) – thicker neck, larger head.
Pink-footed (below) – head blob on thin neck.

Greylag – looser flight formations.

White-fronted – bunched flight formations.

Pink-footed – usually neat V-formations.

Bean (both forms) – shier than most other geese, taking flight at slightest hint of danger. Flocks tend to be smaller than others.

Pink-footed – incessant noise.

Greylag

White-fronted

Bean (both forms) – not especially noisy.

Bean

Greylag – flight powerful but, at times, appears hard work. Rises with some difficulty, taking longer run than other geese.

Lesser White-fronted

Pink-footed

Greylag – noted for twisting, so-called 'whiffling' descents (also seen in other species, especially Pink-footed).

White-fronted – 'jumping' take-off, twisting descent.

Canada Goose – longer neck than any other geese. Slow, swan-like wing-beats. Magnificent flight, normally not much above treetop height.

Brent Goose – narrower wings than other geese, much quicker wing-beats (as rapid as Mallard).

Barnacle Goose – less shy than many other geese. Distinctly pointed wings. Slower wing-beats than Brent.

Red-breasted Goose – small with short neck. Fast wing-beats.

Egyptian Goose – heavy flight on broad wings.

Canada

Brent (below) – flies in irregular lines, not V-formation. Often very tame.

Barnacle – often flies in lines or U-shape, not strict V-formation.

Brent

Barnacle

Red-breasted

Egyptian

Red-breasted – flies in irregular lines, like Brent.

Greylags

Egyptian – in small parties, usually low.

Ducks: Diving and flying

When identifying ducks it is important to establish whether they feed on the surface of the water or by diving. This is a useful first step.

Mallard

Shoveler

Wigeon

Surface-feeding, non-diving ducks have four main methods of feeding: dabbling, head-dipping, up-ending and land feeding.

Surface-feeding ducks occasionally dive, but with great effort/much splashing and pop up rapidly. Dives are usually escape responses to predators, e.g. this Teal is evading Marsh Harrier.

Land feeding (*Mallard*)

Head-dipping (*Garganey*)

a

b

Up-ending (*Mallard*)

Dabbling (*Teal*)

Surface-feeding ducks walk well on land. Their legs are placed in centre of body, giving horizontal stance. Diving ducks struggle awkwardly on land. Legs are set well back, giving an upright stance.

Smew – diver.

Mallard – surface-feeder.

Goldeneye – diver.

Surface-feeding duck (*Pintail*) – on water, tail points up.

Diving duck (*Tufted Duck*) – on water, tail often points down (some exceptions).

Shelduck – surface-feeder.

Diving duck (**Tufted Duck**) – black or white wing-bars and panels in flight.

Surface-feeding duck (*Mallard*) – brightly coloured 'speculum' in flight.

TAKING OFF

Surface-feeding ducks 'spring' from water, no running required (*Mallard*).

Back-set legs that enable diving ducks to propel them underwater make taking off difficult. Diving ducks often require 'runway', pattering over surface of water to gain speed to fly (*Red-breasted Merganser*).

FLYING

Although most ducks make swishing sounds with wings, following species are particularly noisy in flight.

Barrow's Goldeneye – similar to Goldeneye.

Goldeneye – singing of wings in flight.

Shoveler – distinctive rattle of wings on take-off.

Steller's Eider – singing tone similar to Goldeneye.

In addition to those illustrated, *Mallard* also makes obvious wing-swish.

Ducks: Breeding of surface-feeding Ducks

Here we show typical habitats in which surface-feeding Ducks breed
and place their nests. Duck displays can be seen from the first stages
of pairing in autumn until the following spring; many are communal.
A few displays are shown here if typical to species concerned.

Shelduck – forward-rush display.

Shelduck – nest is in hole; usually
in dune or field. Rabbit holes often
used. Usually near sea, also in
some inland areas.

Head-dipping display before copulation.

Ruddy Shelduck – does not breed
near sea.

Ruddy Shelduck

Ruddy Shelduck – nest in hole,
usually in cliff or bank. Less
dependent on water than other
ducks. Mainly breeds in steppe
country. South-east Europe only.

Marbled Duck – breeds on
shallow steppe lakes in warm
regions. Confined to small areas
in Europe.

Marbled Duck – nest is on ground
in thick vegetation.

Marbled Duck

Pintail

Pintail – breeds on lakes
surrounded by lowland
grassland and steppe.
Nest usually in short
cover, also in open.

Garganey – breeds by shallow freshwater lakes surrounded
by grass/steppe. Nest on ground by grassy tussock.

Garganey – unique display;
head lifted to rest on back.

Wigeon – male has diagnostic 'wing-lifting' display.

Wigeon – breeds on lakes/marshes surrounded by forest, also on tundra. Nest on ground in thick vegetation.

Mallard (*below*) – breeds on almost any body of freshwater, large or small, also by sea in some places. Nests on ground under bushes, also regularly in tree holes.

Mallard – communal courtship of males, seen autumn to spring. Many displays, including the 'head-up-tail-up' and 'water-flick'.

Mallard – nods head before copulation, then female solicits by lying flat on water.

Mallards

Shoveler (*left*) – breeds on very productive, shallow bodies of water, often small. Must have muddy margins. Nest on ground in grass.

Shoveler – in contrast to most surface-feeding ducks is territorial, and has threat display with bill held up.

Mandarin – display unmistakable.

Mandarin – usually on freshwater lakes surrounded by woodland. Nests in holes in trees.

Teal – breeds on small/large pools with rich fringing vegetation, usually in forested areas. Nest usually on ground under bushes.

Gadwall – in breeding season on shallow freshwater lakes, usually quite large. Nest on ground, among dense vegetation. Displays similar to Mallard. Pursuit-flights, involving a female/two or more males, common.

Teal – 'head-up-tail-up' display.

Ducks: Breeding of diving Ducks

Diving Ducks occupy a wide range of habitats for breeding.
Many species breed by freshwater, but retreat to sea in
winter. Several have very distinctive displays, illustrated
here. Note that duck displays can be seen throughout
winter, and on breeding grounds in spring.

Red-crested Pochard – breeds on fairly large
fresh/brackish lakes. Nest on
ground, often very deep in
vegetation.

Pochard –
head-throw
display typical
of several
diving ducks.

Pochard – breeds on productive,
vegetation-fringed lakes with plenty
of open water, particularly in steppe
regions. Nest is among vegetation,
often on small islands.

Ferruginous Duck

Ferruginous –
breeds in vegetation-fringed lakes/marshes,
often in steppe country. Nest may be on
ground, or floating vegetation.

Scaup – breeds on
freshwater lakes in tundra
and moorland. Nest on
ground, among
tussocks,
sometimes
on floating
vegetation.

Tufted Duck –
neck-stretch
display,

common
among
diving ducks.

Scaup

Tufted – breeds on clear lakes of all kinds, often
without much fringing vegetation. Often in
town parks. Nests on ground, on islands in
lakes, sometimes on floating vegetation.
Common Scoter – breeds on tundra and in
lakes among extensive forests. Nest well-
concealed in thick vegetation on ground.

**Long-
tailed
Duck** –
species of
tundra pools in
the Arctic. Nests
on ground in thick
vegetation.

Common Scoter – 'low rush' display.

Velvet Scoter – breeds in variety of
habitats, including mountain
regions/tundra, especially lakes
among boreal forests. Nest often
at foot of tree in wood.

Long-tailed –
displays undertaken with much calling,
musical nasal sound likened by some to
sound of bagpipes. Displays include
much head-shaking/head-tossing.

Goldeneye – breeds by lakes surrounded by forest. Nest placed in hole in tree, often quite far from water.

Harlequin Duck – only breeds in Iceland, on fast-flowing tundra streams. Nest is among dense scrub.

Goldeneye – most distinctive head-tossing display, often seen early spring.

Smew – breeds especially in thick lowland forest country, by rivers/clear lakes. Nests in holes in trees, especially those of Black Woodpeckers.

Smews

Goosander (below) – breeds mainly along rivers with deep, clear water. Also on lakes. Nests in holes in trees.

Goosander – typical display is vertical 'sky-pointing'.

Red-breasted Merganser – displays include a non-vertical 'salute' followed by a curtsey.

Red-breasted Merganser – breeds mainly along coasts, needs vegetation cover nearby. Does not nest in tree-holes but in hollows on ground, e.g. by tree roots.

Ruddy Duck – in display cocks tail vertically as White-headed, but beats its bill against chest feathers to blow bubbles.

Red-breasted Merganser – duckling.

White-headed Duck – displays include cocking the tail vertically, and making a sideways lurch.

Eider – head bill-tossing display, throwing head back.

Ruddy – breeds on shallow, reed-fringed lakes, platform of vegetation for nest.

Eider – breeds near sea, often placing nest in open among short turf, frequently in large colonies. Nest famously lined with insulating down.

Evocative, suggestive cooing.

Ducks: Feeding in freshwater

Gadwall – selects productive lakes with fringing vegetation. Feeds mainly on vegetable material. Favourite method is head-dipping in shallow water. Some up-ending, little dabbling.

The ducks here are more or less confined to freshwater. Opposite are species with more catholic requirements, including those that visit estuaries.

Gadwall – female dabbling.

Gadwall (male)

Coot

Gadwall (top, left and right) – often steals food from other birds, especially Coots (also Red-crested Pochard). Look for ducks apparently associating with Coots.

Shoveler – very shallow bodies of water, often quite small. Feeds on animal material by filtering. Main method is dabbling. Swims around with bill 'stuck' to water. Often in circles, each bird benefiting from foot stirrings of swimming bird in front.

Ferruginous Duck (below) – on lakes with much fringing vegetation. Dives among dense, floating vegetation with small areas of open water. Feeds much by dabbling/head-dipping, and diving.

Garganey – female dabbling.

Ferruginous

Garganey (above) – in shallows on water with much fringing vegetation, keeping close to cover. Main feeding methods head-dipping and dabbling, latter rather like Shoveler. Unlike Teal, doesn't often up-end.

Goosander (male)

Pochard (female)

Tufted Duck (female)

Pochard

Pochard – productive lakes with plenty of open water. Dives mainly for vegetable material. Also feeds from surface at times. Uniquely will sometimes paddle at surface with feet before submerging.

Tufted – lakes/ponds of various sizes, also rivers of varying depths. Common species, feeding mainly on animal matter. Dives for food.

Goosander – lives on lakes with deep, clear water, feeding on fish. Dives.

Shelduck – mainly estuaries, but also shallow freshwater. Feeds mainly on animal material

Shelduck – favoured feeding method is to scythe in mud or shallow water, swinging its bill from side to side.

Female **Mallard** up-ending (*left*) and feeding on land (*below*).

Mallard (*above*) – almost any body of water will do. Many feeding methods, especially dabbling/up-ending, will also feed from land. Does not scythe like Shelduck.

Pintail – on large, productive lakes/lagoons. Common on estuaries. Specialises in up-ending, reaching to greater depths than other surface-feeding ducks because of long neck.

Female **Pintail** dabbling while walking.

Wigeon (*right*) – open waters/floodlands. Also estuaries. Differs from other ducks in specialising on grazing on grass. Dabbles, rarely up-ends.

Female **Wigeon** grazing.

Teal (*below*) – shallow pools, often quite small. Mainly feeds on seeds, especially in winter. Dabbles in characteristic way by walking in shallow water.

Goldeneye (*left*) – mainly on deep lakes without much fringing vegetation. Equally at home on sea in winter. Feeds on aquatic invertebrates. Dives, often energetically, only short visits to surface.

Red-crested Pochard – large lakes and lagoons, often with fringing reed-beds. 'Diving' duck but most often seen head-dipping (as here) and dabbling.

Smew (female)

Goldeneye (female).

Smew – on fairly deep lakes. Also sheltered saltwater. Feeds on fish. Dives.

Ducks: Seaducks in winter

Velvet Scoter

Common Scoter – usually fly in large groups in characteristic lines over the water. Large flocks may form tadpole-like shape, dense 'head' followed by wavy 'tail'.

Velvet Scoter – medium-sized, well built, large head. Small flocks, well spaced out.

Common Scoter – smaller than Velvet Scoter, with smaller bill. Often in large (or huge) dense flocks.

Red-breasted Merganser – sociable, in medium-sized groups, fairly spaced out.

Red-breasted Merganser – common on sea.

Goldeneye – not gregarious. Small groups, doesn't associate much with other ducks.

Goosander – not usually found on sea.

Red-breasted Merganser – looks very long-bodied, slim and long-necked. Wings appear attached to end of body. Small groups.

Scaup

Scaup – rounded-head, medium-sized, bulky.

Wigeon – surface-feeding duck that often rests on sea.

Wigeon

Mallard (not illustrated) – often rests on sea.

Eider – dives by sinking with half-open wings.

Eider – characteristically slow wing-beats, almost like goose. Flocks always low over sea, form long lines, not much co-ordination.

Brent Goose – longer necked than Eider.

Long-tailed Duck – often in dense flocks on the sea. Can be very restless, lots of taking off and landing with splash.

Long-tailed – often winters further out to sea than others.

Long-tailed – very distinctive flight. On stiff wing-beats the wings never seem to rise above horizontal, look swept back. Swings from side to side in level flight, lands with splash.

Long-tailed – swims low when feeding. Dives with head-back, forward lunge, tail spread, wings slightly spread.

Long-tailed – small, dumpy, short-necked, small-headed.

Goldeneye – dumpy; large triangular-shaped head.

Goldeneye – looks plump, fast wing-beats. Small groups.

Velvet Scoter – white wing-panel always obvious.

Harlequin Duck – in small groups. Looks very dark.

Harlequin – on rough waters, mainly around Iceland. Immune to heaving seas.

Velvet Scoter – flies in small groups. Often feeds among rocks. *Common Scoter* – prefers open sea.

Harlequin – distinctive bob of head in time with each stroke of feet.

Harlequin – usually close to shore, by rocks.

King Eider (*below*) – tends to feed further out than Eider. (Eider usually in shallow, inshore waters.)

Eider

Velvet Scoter

Eider – heavy body, large wedge-shaped head.

Steller's Eider

Steller's Eider – feeds by upending as much as diving.

Steller's Eider – usually right by rocks close inshore. Shaped like surface-feeding duck.

Ducks: Shelducks

Mallard (male) – similar sized, but shorter legs/thinner neck.

Shelduck – large knob on bill.

Shelduck – male and female look similar.

Mallard – male and female quite different.

Mallard – no knob on bill.

Shelduck – large, long legs and neck.

Shelduck – 'disappear' late summer when majority of North-west European population concentrates at favourite moulting grounds, e.g. the Waddenzee, off northern Germany.

Shelduck – juvenile a confusing duck.

Shelduck – especially common on estuaries and coasts. Less common far inland; not at high altitude.

Egyptian Goose – larger, dark 'shades'.

Shelduck – takes mainly animal food. Favourite is estuarine snail Hydrobia. Usually feeds in water or mud.

Ruddy Shelduck – takes much plant material, often on land.

Shelduck – arched wings, slow wing-beats. (*Mallard* – wings not arched in flight, faster wing-beats.)

Ruddy Shelduck – pointed wings.

Ruddy Shelduck – South-east Europe only, in steppe country. Brackish water, mainly far inland, often at high altitude.

Egyptian Goose – more rounded wings, longer neck.

Goosander (male) – long, cigar-shaped, slim body.

Eider (male) – shorter neck, much larger head held slightly downwards.

Ducks: Strange Ducks

Mandarin and Ruddy Duck from China and North America respectively. Introduced; both breed in wild in Europe, especially Britain. White-headed Duck native but rare relative of Ruddy Duck. Marbled Duck, with strange, washed-out colouration, related to both surface-feeding ducks and Pochards..

Mallard (pale female) – larger, more heavily built.

Wigeon (female) – similar 'shades' around eye, but short bill/no crest.

Pintail (female) – larger, longer neck, no crest.

Marbled Duck – small, slim with long bill, slight crest or 'pony-tail'.

Marbled – often seen perched in shade, on branches/other vegetation on edge of marshes. Most active dawn/dusk. Often well-hidden by day.

Pintail (female)

Marbled – not energetic. Does not 'spring' from water like other surface-feeding ducks. Doesn't tend to fly far or high.

Marbled – found mostly on shallow, freshwater marshes/ lakes in steppe country. Rare.

Mandarin – feeds on surface only; does not dive, hardly ever up-ends. Often wanders into woodland at night, especially to take acorns from ground.

Mandarin –unmistakable. Quick take-off, rapid flight, twists and turns past trees.

Mallard (female) – larger body, larger bill, comparatively longer neck, smaller head.

Wigeon (female) – smaller head.

Mandarin (female) – short-necked, bushy-crested, small bill.

Tufted Duck (female) – shorter tail, more ample stern, high crown.

Teal (female) – straighter back, ample stern.

White-headed Duck (female)

Ruddy and *White-headed Duck* – often feed at night. Loaf on water with tail cocked at 45 degree angle.

Ruddy (female) – distinctly sloping back, sloping forehead giving 'perky nose'.

White-headed (male) – slightly larger, huge bulging bill interrupting forehead line.

Ruddy (male) – smaller than White-headed. Sloping forehead.

Ducks: Dabbing ducks

Mallard – large, heavy-bodied. Rounded back.

Mallard (male)

Gadwall – slightly smaller than Mallard. Flatter back. Neck held up to give 'regal' look compared to Mallard. Swims higher in water than Mallard, especially at stern.

Mallard (eclipse)

Mallard (female)

Gadwall (female)

Gadwall (eclipse)

Gadwall – tends to point tail up vertically when upending.

Gadwall (male)

Mallard – tends to point tail at angle when upending.

Gadwall – rounder head; smaller, thinner bill. Female's bill has clear-cut orange sides.

Mallard – large bill, flat crown.

Pintail – swims high, often raising its tail.

Pintail – very elongated duck (even female), with long neck, long tail.

Pintail (eclipse)

Pintail – small head, rounded crown.

Wigeon – quite large head, steep forecrown.

Wigeon – swims with neck retracted.

Wigeon – quite long tail, but short neck. Plumper than Pintail.

Shoveler – bill held down, often appears 'stuck' to surface of water. Slouches down. Mallard also has large bill, but usually holds it upright.

Wigeon (male)

Shoveler – quite small, but large head and enormous bill. Front-heavy.

Shoveler (female)

Wigeon (eclipse)

Wigeon (female)

Shoveler (eclipse)

Teal – often upends. Garganey rarely does.

Garganey – larger head, more angular crown than Teal, longer bill.

Garganey (female)

Teal (female)

Teal (eclipse)

Teal – very small, neckless. More rounded crown than Garganey. Bill often has orange at base.

Garganey – slightly larger than Teal, longer bodied, stern floats higher. Tail slightly longer. Only Mar–Sept.

Mallard – upcurled tail feathers of breeding plumage make male obvious in flight.

Mallard – wings broad-based, less pointed than other ducks' wings.

Gadwall (female)

Pintail – very elongated, head 'stuck' on to thin neck.

Wigeon – pointed tail like Pintail, but shorter. Tends to fly high, often in large flocks.

Gadwall – narrower based wings in flight. Faster wing-beats than Mallard.

Pintail – long pointed tail. Wings look to be positioned far back on body.

Wigeon – less elongated than Pintail, shorter neck.

Pintail – often in neatly organised flocks. Often fly high.

Shoveler – front-heavy. Wings look to be positioned towards back of body. Short tail. Faster wing-beats than Mallard, wings slightly narrower and more pointed. Often flies high.

Wigeon/Teal – flocks often tumble/twist down upon landing.

Garganey – longer neck and larger body than Teal.

Teal – narrow, sharply pointed wings.

Teal – distinctive, fast-flying flocks, so tightly packed and acrobatic that often look like waders.
Garganey – flocks make fewer twists and turns than Teal flocks.

Ducks: Pochards

MALES

Pochard – gently sloping forehead, but with peaked head like Ferruginous.

Ferruginous Duck – peaked head, long neck.

Tufted Duck – distinctive head shape, steep forehead, flat crown giving perky, rounded look. Tuft or crest, although can be little more than a bump.

Tufted – tip of bill black.

Scaup – head smoothly rounded, no hint of a crest.

Scaup – only nail of bill black. Broader bill than Tufted.

Ferruginous – shorter body than Tufted. White eye (male, *above*), brown eye (female, *below*).

Pochard – red eye (male, *above, second from left*), brown eye (female, *below second from left*).

Red-crested Pochard – large body, long neck, large rounded head. Distinctive. Swims higher in water than other Pochards.

FEMALES

Pochard – sloping, 'ski-jump' forehead, smooth transition from forehead to bill.

Red-crested Pochard (female)

Scaup – large/broad-beamed.

Ferruginous – peaked head, as if bump had formed after being struck on the head. No tuft.

Rare *Ring-necked Duck* – occasional visitor from America, especially to Britain.

Tufted – yellow eye.

Tufted – squared-off head, tuft; smaller than Scaup. High forehead, angle between bill/forehead.

Ring-necked – bill with white band. *Tufted* – no band.

Tufted – squared-off head, tuft.

Pochard – sloping forehead, no bump on back of head.

Ferruginous – retiring, skulking in dense vegetation.

Ring-necked – longer tail than Tufted, often cocked. Peaked hindcrown at angle to nape, giving very distinctive head shape (as if extra piece of head added on top).

Although *Tufted* and *Pochard* have rather different plumage, can be hard to distinguish in poor light. Striking differences in head shape between these two common freshwater ducks are most useful guide.

ECLIPSE MALES

Ferruginous Duck – longer bill than Tufted but shorter body.

Tufted Duck – shorter body than Scaup, tail can be more obvious.

Scaup – long rear body slopes down to water. Fuller-breasted than Tufted.

Ferruginous – usually in small groups (others often in large parties).

Pochard – tends to be seen sleeping in groups during day. **Tufted** (*second from left*) tends to be more awake during day.

Red-crested Pochard – in contrast to other Pochards, diving not preferred feeding method. Tends to dabble and dip neck, in manner of surface-feeding duck. Often feeds on land.

Tufted – common, mainly on freshwater.
Scaup – on sea in winter.

Scaup (female)

Scaup – often dives with more of leap than Tufted.

Tufted – smaller than Scaup.

Tufted – fast, straight flight.

Pochard – heavy body, wings look too short to lift it.

Scaup (female)

Ferruginous – smaller body, faster wing-beats.

Ferruginous – rises from water more easily than other Pochards.

Tufted – rises more quickly than Pochard.

Red-crested Pochard (female)

Pochard – makes effort to rise.

Red-crested Pochard – big effort to rise. Powerful flight on broad wings.

Ducks: Eiders

Eider widespread as breeding bird on North-west European coasts, including Baltic and Arctic Ocean. King Eider breeds only in far north, in Russia. Wanders southward in winter, but mainly above Arctic Circle.

Steller's Eider doesn't breed in Europe. Winters mainly in Arctic waters.

Eider – dives at moderate depths, especially for mussels. Prefers shallow water. *King Eider* deeper.

King Eider (male) — head shape quite different to Eider, has small 'sails'on back.

King Eider (male)

Eider – breeds on coasts.
King Eider – breeds inland, on tundra pools.

King Eider – stragglers often found among Eider flocks.

Eider (male) – large, longer bodied than King Eider.

King Eider (female) – shorter bill than Eider. Forehead bulges. Feathering makes rounded incursion on to bill.

Steller's Eider – smaller, less bulky than others. Same size as Goldeneye.

Eider (female) – wedge-shaped head with 'Roman' nose. Flat crown. Uninterrupted slope from forehead to bill. Feathering makes sharp angle on to bill.

Steller's Eider – long wings, long tertials.

Steller's Eider – square head, bill shaped like surface-feeding duck's. *Eider* has triangular head, wedge-shaped bill.

Steller's Eider (female)

Eider (eclipse male)

Eider (female) – bill often points slightly downwards.

King Eider (2nd-winter male) – slightly shorter neck than Common Eider. Holds head up when swimming.

Steller's Eider – usually close inshore, even up-ending among rocks.

Eider (eclipse male)

Steller's Eider (eclipse male)

King Eider (eclipse male)

King Eider – curious 'smiling' expression.

Steller's Eider – much easier take-off than other Eiders, long wings, quick wing-beats.

King Eider – shorter neck, faster wing-beats.

Eider – heavy take-off, short wings, slow wing-beats.

Ducks: Sawbills

Sawbills are ducks with specially adapted bills for catching/holding fish, with saw-like serrations on upper and lower jaw.

Red-breasted Merganser – winters on sea, habit of 'beaching' regularly. Forms flocks even in breeding season.

Goosander (male) – bulbous head.

Red-breasted Merganser (male) – 'punk hairdo'.

Goosander – breeds/winters on freshwater. Usually seen in pairs.

Smew (male) – much the smallest sawbill, shorter bill and neck than others.

Smew (female)

Goosander (female) – considerably larger/bulkier than Red-breasted Merganser, large-headed appearance, thicker neck. 'Hair' hangs down 'in a bob'.

Red-breasted Merganser (female) – looks much slimmer than Goosander, with smaller head and thinner neck. 'Hair' is spiky with two peaks.

Goosander (male) – thicker bill than Red-breasted Merganser.

Goosander – very elongated in flight.

Red-breasted Merganser (male) – narrower bill than Goosander, thinner at base, slight upcurve.

Red-breasted Merganser (female) – slightly less bulky than Goosander.

Goosander (female)

Smew

Smew (far left) – very agile in flight. Takes off quite easily, in contrast to Red-breasted Merganser and Goosander. Flocks in flight have curious habit of separating.

Red-breasted Merganser – long runway required for take-off.

WHITE-CHEEKED DUCKS

Red-crested Pochard (female) – much larger, long bill, long neck.

Smew (eclipse male) – small.

Common Scoter (female) – larger.

Ruddy Duck (eclipse male) – tiny, sloping forehead/long tail.

Ducks: Goldeneye, Harlequin and Long-tailed Ducks

Goldeneye – head-throwing display.

Goldeneye – steep but sloping forehead. Slimmer hindneck. Head more triangular.

Barrow's Goldeneye – steep 'cliff-face' of forehead. Ample hindneck. Head looks larger than Goldeneye.

Barrow's Goldeneye – larger than Goldeneye.

Goldeneye – highest part of crown in middle, so crown peaked.

Barrow's Goldeneye (*below*) – highest part of crown at forehead, so crown flatter.

Harlequin Duck (female) – high crown/rounded head, small bill. Smaller than Scoters. Long, sharp tail, often cocked.

Females

Barrow's Goldeneye – smaller bill.

Harlequin (female) – small, dark. High forehead like Goldeneye, but head more evenly rounded, 'fits on neck properly'.

Harlequin – bird of rapids, torrents, rough seas. In contrast to other ducks, commonly dives under water from perch or even in flight.

Common Scoter (female) – flatter crown, larger bill.

Long-tailed Duck – males unmistakable, long, pointed tail.

Goldeneye – head looks too large for neck.

Harlequin – similar dumpy shape to Goldeneye in flight, but flies low over water, head held up.

Long-tailed (female)

Winter male

Pintail

Goldeneye – often flies quite high, head held horizontally.

Summer male

Long-tailed – often in large groups, far out to sea.

Long-tailed – female small, short tail. High crown, small bill.

Ducks: Scoters

Common Scoter (male) – smaller than Velvet Scoter. Small bill, rounded head shape. Swims more buoyantly than Velvet Scoter.

Common Scoter – cocks tail while swimming. Velvet Scoter less so.

Common Scoter – very shy and quick to fly.

Common Scoter (female) – thinner neck.

Eider (eclipse male) – flatter crown, more sloping forehead, larger bill.

Velvet Scoter (female) – thick neck.

Velvet Scoter (male) – long-bodied. Larger bill gives large-headed appearance.

Scaup (female) – shorter-bodied, higher-backed than Scoters, rides higher in water.

Scaup (*below*) – dives with leap.

Velvet Scoter – when stretching and wing-flapping, holds head up.

SURF SCOTER
A third species of scoter, the Surf Scoter is a rare visitor to Europe.

Surf Scoter (male) – slightly larger than Common but smaller than Velvet Scoter.

Common Scoter – when stretching/wing-flapping, characteristically points head downwards.

Common Scoter (*left*) – when diving usually leaps up, enters water with wings closed.

Velvet Scoter – when diving sinks down without leap, enters water with wings open (as Eider).

Velvet Scoter (male, American race)

Surf Scoter – flattish crown, swollen bill gives Eider-like head shape.
Common Scoter – rounded crown.

Surf Scoter – dives with slight leap, usually with wings half-open.

Surf Scoter (female) – when wing-flapping/stretching, holds neck up, as Velvet Scoter.

Mixed flock of *Common and Velvet* (with white wing-bar) *Scoters*.

Raptors: Types

A step to identifying birds of prey is to narrow down possibilities by assigning birds to a particular broad category. These pages should help; however, not all species are so easily assigned – some of the more puzzling species are illustrated overleaf.

Vultures often congregate in groups. (Eagles only do this on migration, at certain favoured areas.) Vultures keep 'student hours', starting the day very late as they wait for thermals to form.

VULTURES
Generally huge with massively broad wings and obvious 'fingers'. Tails noticeably short. Eagles often large, but heads protrude more obviously, tails longer.

EAGLES
Range of sizes, most large, usually much larger than Buzzards. 'Eagle-like' characteristics include long, broad wings with obvious 'fingers', protruding head. Most have long, parallel-edged wings.

LAMMERGEIER
Distinctive bird, unlikely to be confused with anything else. Huge, long wings and long, wedge-shaped tail.

WHITE-TAILED SEA EAGLE
Huge, almost vulture-sized eagle, short, wedge-shaped tail, enormous, protruding head.

OSPREY (*right*)
Distinctive: very long/narrow wings characteristically held angled in flight, giving bowed appearance. Often gives impression of large gull.

Imperial Eagle

Bonelli's Eagle

Although hard to define, eagles typically have 'majestic' mien, probably combination of large size, rather slow but powerful movements, long, protruding head and large bill.

FALCONS

All have very pointed wings, their most important characteristic. Many comparatively small, with comparatively long tail. In flight, move with flappy, fast wing-beats.

KITES

Large, distinctive birds of prey with long, narrow wings and tail. In flight they hold wings slightly arched downwards, carpal joints projecting distinctively forwards. Both head and long tail held in slight droop; body rises/falls a little as wings beat (also in smaller harriers, but unusual in birds of prey).

Tail expertly twisted in flight, allowing for impressive manoeuvrability. Wings long, broad, more sharply pointed than Buzzard's, tails much longer.

Hawks are secretive birds, spending much time hidden in woodland.

HAWKS

Compact birds of prey, rather broad, almost rounded wings, long tail. Wings shorter/ blunter than most birds of prey, and consequently tail longer than wing-width.

HARRIERS

Large, almost Buzzard-sized, much larger than Kestrel. Wings longer than Buzzard's, parallel-edged. Tails much longer.

Distinctive, with long, pointed wings and long tail. When flying, hold wings up in distinctive V. Almost always seen flying slowly at low level over open country. Don't soar very often. Owl-shaped faces (forward-pointing eyes).

Buzzards often seen perched on roadside poles (in contrast to vultures, most eagles, hawks).

BUZZARDS

Often soar high; sometimes several will do so at a time.

Medium-sized birds of prey. Smaller than eagles or vultures, but much larger than Sparrowhawk or Kestrel. Plump-bodied, long, broad wings, shorter than eagles. Wings slightly fingered at tip, blunt rather than pointed. Fingers not nearly so obvious as on eagles or vultures.

Raptors: Types

EGYPTIAN VULTURE, BOOTED EAGLE (PALE), BUZZARD (PALE), OSPREY, SHORT-TOED EAGLE

Short-toed Eagle – long but very broad wings held slightly bowed in flight. Distinctively broad head/longish tail.

Booted Eagle (pale) – broader wing than Buzzard, especially the 'hand', which has fewer 'fingers'. Has longer, squarer tail. Far smaller than Egyptian Vulture.

Egyptian Vulture – larger, with pointed head, long pointed wings, wedge-shaped tail.

Buzzard (pale)

GOLDEN EAGLE AND BUZZARD

Golden Eagle – in flight, elegant but very stable. Can fly on straight path.

Osprey – wings make obvious kink when glides. Narrower wings than superficially similar Short-toed Eagle.

Lesser Spotted Eagle – heavier than Booted Eagle, with shorter tail.

SMALL EAGLES AND BUZZARDS

Booted Eagle – when soaring, wings slightly bowed.

Buzzard – when soaring, wings clearly raised.

Buzzard – rocks to and fro according to vagaries of wind.

Lesser Spotted Eagle – larger than Buzzard, but similarly small head/neck. When soaring/gliding, wings clearly bowed.

Booted Eagle (dark phase) – broader wings than Buzzard, more prominent fingers/more parallel-edged outline. More square-ended tail.

BLACK KITE, MARSH HARRIER AND
BOOTED EAGLE (DARK PHASE)

Black Kite – smaller head than Booted Eagle. In forward glide wings project at carpal joints, wings arch down (both in contrast to Marsh Harrier). 'Fingers' more obvious than on Marsh Harrier.

Booted Eagle – more solid/muscular than Black Kite or Marsh Harrier, wings held level in soaring/gliding. Shorter, more sharply square-ended tail than Marsh Harrier.

Bonelli's Eagle – larger than Honey Buzzard but similar in shape, with small head/long tail. More evenly parallel wings, tail squarer ended.

Osprey

Buzzard

Marsh Harrier – in forward glide wings raised in shallow (but obvious) V. Rounded end to tail; useful distinguishing feature when bird flies high over.

Short-toed Eagle – wings long and broad, long, square-ended tail with sharp corners. In active flight progresses with deep, powerful wing-beats. Longer tail than Buzzard, square cut at end, with sharp corners. Tail as long as wings are broad.

Honey Buzzard – obviously protruding head. When actively flying, wing-beats are characteristically loose.

Honey Buzzard – slightly larger than Buzzard or Booted Eagle.

Booted Eagle (*left*) – in forward flight moves with power and grace characteristic of eagle, with deep wing-beats keeping a straight course, interspersed with longer glides than Buzzard.

SMALL EAGLES
AND BUZZARDS

Raptors: Types GOSHAWK, BUZZARD, HONEY BUZZARD, GYR FALCON

Goshawk – longer tail than Buzzard, more protruding head. Plumper body than Buzzard or Honey Buzzard, especially at rear.

Goshawk – broad arm, pointed hand. Wing-tips more pointed than on Buzzard/Honey Buzzard, less so than Gyr Falcon. Latter lacks Goshawk's bulge to the secondaries.

Goshawk

Buzzard

Honey Buzzard

Sparrowhawk – blunt-ended wings.

KESTREL, MERLIN AND SPARROWHAWK

Sparrowhawk – powerful wing-beats, typical flap-flap-glide flight style.

Kestrel – when soaring, looks quite Sparrowhawk-like, but wings look narrow at base and more pointed. Tail usually spread more.

Gyr Falcon – Goshawk's size and bulk, but longer/more pointed wings.

Sparrowhawk – short neck, compact.

Kestrel – pointed wing-tips.

Levant Sparrowhawk

Kestrel – usual flight flappy and not very powerful-looking, with fewer glides. Hovers; Merlin and Sparrowhawk do not.

Kestrel – will make surprise strike at birds near ground level, like Sparrowhawk (not common hunting method, but frequent in some individuals).

Goshawk (juvenile) – heavier at the rear than Sparrowhawk or Kestrel.

Male

Female

Merlin – wings broad-based but very pointed, in complete contrast to Sparrowhawk. Tail shorter than Sparrowhawk or Kestrel.

Raptors: Perched profiles

Sparrowhawk – in comparison to Goshawk has slender rear body/thin legs.

Short-toed Eagle – very distinctive, with large, rounded, owl-like head. Quite often seen perching on telegraph poles/trees.

Saker – often perches on poles/pylons (as Lanner). Long wings.

Goshawk – thicker rear end. More powerful talons/larger bill. Thicker, less spindly legs than Sparrowhawk. Sometimes perches on treetops.

Rough-legged Buzzard – in contrast to other Buzzards, has feathered legs.

Long-legged Buzzard – as name implies, has longer legs than Common Buzzard. Also has rather longer body in profile.

Lanner

Buzzard – often seen perched.

Merlin – perches in open. Small but tapered, small head and long wings/tail.

Peregrine – perches on cliffs/buildings, not poles/pylons. Shorter wings than Lanner or Saker.

Lesser Spotted Eagle

Marsh Harrier – slimmer body than Buzzard.

Spotted Eagle – thicker, more shaggy thighs than Lesser Spotted Eagle. Fuller nape, larger head/bill.

Raptors: Feeding techniques

HOVERING

Hovering is a little like 'running on the spot'. Birds remain at the same point in the air, moving neither forwards nor backwards, held aloft by beats of wings. Specialised hunting technique; not many birds hover, terns and kingfishers being notable exceptions. Among birds of prey, only species shown here are likely to be seen hovering.

Common Kestrel – best known/most common hovering bird. Hovering is most important feeding technique. Small raptor that hovers with rapid, very flappy wing-beats. Usually hovers above fields/pasture, often by roadside verges. Often hovers at dusk, even by moonlight.

Lesser Kestrel (not illustrated) – very similar to Common Kestrel. But usually in flocks, not alone; tends to hover for shorter periods. 'Impatiently' breaks out of hover to circle round and start again; hovers with fewer beats.

Adult male

Red-footed Falcon – often hovers over prey, drops beside it/runs to catch it on ground. Hovers with deeper wing-beats than Kestrel. Usually seen in flocks.

Eleonora's Falcon – often seen hovering over sea, mainly in autumn. In autumn at dusk or dawn many individuals from colony hover or soar over sea at various heights, in wait for migrant birds.

Female – final plunge after hovering.

Juvenile

Black-winged Kite – similar wing-beats and technique to Kestrel, but wings are much broader, especially at base.

QUARTERING

Levant Sparrowhawk
Rather than using ambush technique of Sparrowhawk or Goshawk, flies at moderate height above ground and dives down to prey on ground.

HOVERING

Short-toed Eagle – very large; only eagle that hovers. Diagnostic. Hovers about 15–30m up, may make way down stepwise, often adjusts close to ground before making final lunge. Has unusual diet of snakes.

Osprey – diagnostically, hovers above lakes before plunging in, wings half-folded, to catch fish near surface. Often begins hovering very high, moving down in series of short steps.

Rough-legged Buzzard (and *Long-legged Buzzard*) – hover far more frequently/ persistently than Common Buzzard.

Final lunge on snake.

Common Buzzard – large, clumsy hoverer. Often 'hangs in the wind', with little or no flapping, rather than hovering. Usually seen on windy day when other feeding techniques do not work so well.

QUARTERING

The aerial version of searching for a golf ball: birds move slowly forwards low over ground, head down in search of prey hidden in grass.

Hen Harrier – flies over more open habitats. Often pursues birds it has flushed in rapid chase. In breeding season, follows regular course.

HARRIERS

Quartering is favoured by long-winged harriers.

Montagu's Harrier (not illustrated) – patrols over very open areas, with little vegetation. Often very low down. Tends to follow regular course.

Marsh Harrier – flies low over marshes/fields, 2–6m up, then suddenly plunges upon prey, sometimes almost turning over in process. Often flies along edges, where prey can be easily surprised. Quartering seems to follow no regular pattern.

A number of large species fly low over ground in order to catch prey by surprise.

Raptors: Feeding techniques

SCAVENGING

The art of eating meat from already dead animals. Can include human refuse and scraps.

Black Vulture – forages at lower height than Griffon Vulture, in smaller parties or alone.

Griffon Vulture – members of a colony space out over countryside, in sight of each other, each soaring over allotted searching area for carrion. All come down when some is sighted.

Lammergeier (*left*) – specialises in eating bones; waits until other vultures have finished at a carcass. Also drops bones from height to break open nutritious marrow; employs same method on live tortoises.

Egyptian Vulture (*above right*) – enthusiastically encompasses all forms of scraps/refuse in its scavenging and is also partial to human excrement. Often found at rubbish tips.

Black Kite – far bolder/more adventurous scavenger than Red Kite. Takes food from town squares/rubbish dumps, even straight from people. Also cleans up road kills from tarmac and verge.

Red Kite – eats carrion/offal; less dependent on rubbish tips/human settlements than Black Kite. Also takes far more live prey.

Booted Eagle – characteristically plunges to earth in spectacular dive, often from great height, for mammals or small birds.

SOAR AND PLUNGE

Many species spend much time aloft, soaring/watching ground below. When prey sighted, they plunge to earth.

Golden Eagle – often plunges from height on to larger prey items, e.g. hares or young deer.

PERCH AND POUNCE

Birds of prey of all sizes carry out this method of attack. Prey is sighted from a stationary point, before being pounced on from above.

Imperial Eagles – often sit upon haystacks/trees before pouncing on favourite food (susliks, hamsters, gerbils). *Spanish Imperial Eagles* use same method to catch rabbits.

SURPRISE ATTACK

Sparrowhawk – bursts upon unsuspecting small birds on fast, low approach, often using bushes/ other objects to shield it from prey at last moment.

Goshawk – similar methods to Sparrowhawk; also takes mammals, which the smaller bird does not catch.

Merlin – often creeps up on prey by adopting short periods of undulating flight, fooling small birds into thinking it is harmless species e.g. thrush.

STOOPING

The *Peregrine*, in particular, is famous for this devastating method of catching and killing bird prey. Rising to considerable height above target, it uses its momentum/remarkable aerial skill to dive down upon prey and strike in mid air; impact usually breaks victim's neck.

SWEEPING FOR INSECTS

A number of species catch large flying insects in mid air, often transferring them from talons to bill while aloft. These include Lesser Kestrel, Hobby (as here) and Red-footed Falcon.

Gyr Falcon – does not stoop on its prey like Peregrine, instead catching birds or mammals on or near ground.

UNUSUAL TECHNIQUES

Honey Buzzard (not illustrated) – digs out larvae of wasps (main summer diet) on ground.

Bonelli's Eagle – often sits in tree/ambushes birds that have just taken off.

Osprey – plunges into water to grab fish.

EXHAUSTION FLIGHT

White-tailed Eagle – catches water birds that have persistently dived to escape, but are exhausted.
Merlin – locks on to flying bird like guided missile.

Raptors: Kites

In flight kites hold wings slightly arched downwards, with carpal joints projecting distinctively forwards. Head/long tail held in slight droop; body rises/falls a little as wings beat. Tail twists in flight. Both species show great expertise in the air.

Black Kite – smaller head.

Red Kite – head larger, paler.

Red – narrower wings overall. 'Hand' longer/narrower, with only 5 'fingers' clearly visible.

Red – wing-beats noticeably deeper/looser, as befits larger bird.

Black – shorter wings with broader tip, 6 'fingers' visible on 'hand'.

Red – resident all year in Europe.

Black – only seen in summer. More closely associated with water than Red Kite.

Black – less impressive, more flappy flight.

Red – slightly larger than Black.

Black – looks darker.

Red – tail long/deeply forked. When soaring, this is still clear.

Black – shorter tail, less of a fork. Fork almost disappears soaring.

Red – body slender.

Black – body slightly stockier.

Black-winged Kite – very distinctive, unlikely to be confused with anything else, except perhaps distant gull.

Black-winged – short, square-ended tail, owl-like head. Mainly found in plains with scattered trees.

Raptors: Vultures

Lammergeier (sub-adult)

Lammergeier (adult, *left*) – unique, cross-like shape. Narrow, pointed wings/long, wedge-shaped tail.

Black Vulture – of these two huge vultures, Black slightly larger, head looks more obvious in flight. Largely black.

Griffon Vulture – two-toned.

Egyptian Vulture – small; pointed head.

Griffon – when seen from below, secondaries bulge noticeably, giving wings S-shaped curve.

Egyptian (*right*) – shares wedge-shaped tail of Lammergeier, but far smaller, stockier, shorter wings.

Black (*above*) – wings evenly broad, giving parallel 'barn door' shape. Secondaries also slightly more pointed than Griffon's, conferring more jagged edge to hind-wing (very subtle difference).

Lammergeier (*below*) – rare bird of inaccessible mountain areas. Cruises in slow motion.

Black – when soaring (and gliding), holds wings flat.

Egyptian

Griffon – when soaring, holds wings in shallow V. When gliding wings flatten out.

Griffon – when coming in to land, legs dangle down. *Black* – when coming in to land, holds legs up until last moment; often raises tail.

Black – seen in ones or twos, often over wooded areas (single nest in tree).

Egyptian – smallest.

Lammergeier

Black – larger than Griffon.

Griffon

Griffon – in flocks/colonies, mainly mountains (colonial on cliffs).

Raptors: Large Eagles

Golden – 'ultimate eagle', very large bird, long, broad wings/very deeply cut 'fingers'. When gliding slowly, wings often held up, as when soaring.

Adult

Golden – tail about as long as width of wing.

At higher speeds wings may be held flat/arched slightly downwards.

Golden Eagle – only eagle that soars with wings held up at slight but noticeable angle.

Golden – bird of wild mountains, also remote forests and marshes.
Imperial Eagle – avoids highest mountains, more a bird of plains/steppes.

Adult

Spotted Eagles – smaller than Golden or Imperial (Lesser Spotted not much larger than Buzzard (see p62)). Shorter wings, head protrudes less. More compact-looking.

Spotted Eagles – tail proportionally shorter than that of Golden.

Adult

Imperial – tail shorter/narrower than wing width, with sharp squared-off corners.

(Eastern) Imperial Eagle (juvenile)

Spotted Eagles – soar with flat (typically Spotted, *right*) or slightly bowed (typically Lesser Spotted, *above*) wings.

Spotted Eagles – parallel-edged wings.

Adult

Imperial – soars with flat wings (occasionally lifts wings in V for moment).

Imperial – very slightly smaller and darker than Golden. Head/neck can also be slightly more obvious. **Spanish Imperial Eagle** slightly heavier, especially about head/neck.

Adult

Imperial – most have parallel-edged wings.

Spanish Imperial (juvenile)

Imperial – at higher speeds 'arm' raised and 'hand' slightly lowered, but still looks largely flat.

Juvenile

Steppe Eagle – extreme Eastern Europe only, in summer. Open, dry habitats. Heavy flight, slower wing-beats than Spotted Eagles. When gliding wings slightly bowed, but not as much as in Spotted.

Lesser Spotted Eagle – commoner than Spotted. Often found on open plains, which Spotted avoids, also found in wetlands. Migrates south in Aug/Sept, and all leave Europe.

Spotted – rare, mainly associated with wetlands, breeding in nearby forests. Migrates south in Sept/Oct; few winter in Europe.

Spotted – deeply bowed wings with sharp bend at carpal joints can suggest heron (no such impression on Lesser Spotted).

Spotted Eagles – fly with faster/shallower wing-beats than larger eagles, Lesser Spotted slightly the faster.

Lesser Spotted (juvenile)

Spotted – larger than Lesser Spotted (*right*), but exceedingly similar in shape and flight characteristics.

Juvenile

Sparrowhawk mobbing *Lesser Spotted.*

Lesser Spotted (adult)

Lesser Spotted (*above*) – outer wing ('hand') less ample/ blunter, with less obvious 'fingers'. Lighter flight than Spotted.

Adult

Spotted – more undercarriage. Heavier than *Lesser Spotted* when gliding.

Spotted (*right*) – 'fingers' look more deeply notched. Broader wings make tail appear proportionally shorter. Heavy, clumsier flight.

Adult

Steppe Eagle – longer wings and more protuding head than Spotted. Size of Imperial but shorter tail with rounded end.

White-tailed Eagle – huge, very hefty eagle with characteristic shape. In contrast to others, short, wedge-shaped tail; head/massive bill project much further in front of wings.

Juvenile

Osprey – flies with wings held forward at carpal joints and arched down – bent in two dimensions.

White-tailed – glides/soars with wings mainly flat, although 'hand' may droop slightly.

Adult

Juvenile

Osprey – summer visitor to lakes/sea coasts, mainly Northern Europe.

White-tailed – long, very broad, parallel-edged wings with obvious 'fingers'.

White-tailed – water, mainly sea-cliffs, large lakes. Generally rare, widely distributed.

Raptors: Small Eagles

Short-toed and *Booted Eagles* – summer visitors to Europe, mountain/ hilly country- side with scattered woods.

Short-toed (adult) – distinctive when gliding. Carpal joints held well forwards, almost up to head, but long flight feathers still give straight rear edge to wings.

Short-toed – glides on slightly arched wings, soars on flatter wings. (Also hovers, see p67.)

Short-toed – long tail, about equal to width of wing. Often twists it, like a Kite.

Bonelli's Eagle – glides on flat wings. Doesn't soar very often.

Short-toed (juvenile) – quite large, characteristically pale underside. Long wings like typical eagle, but so broad and rounded as to give impression of outsize Buzzard.

Bonelli's (sub-adult) – relatively small head compared to Booted and especially Short- toed.

Bonelli's (adult) – slightly smaller than Short-toed, much larger than Booted.

Bonelli's – long, broad wings with very squared-off edge, but still obvious 'fingers'.

Bonelli's – when gliding, distinctive shape, carpal joints held forwards/straight rear edge (like Short-toed) but with small, well-protruding head.

Bonelli's – slightly smaller than Short-toed, much larger than Booted.

Booted – when soaring, wings slightly bowed; increases gliding.

Bonelli's – long tail, equal to width of wings.

Booted – small eagle, no larger than Buzzard. Two main colour morphs: dark and pale, in ratio of 1:2 (dark here).

Booted (pale) – in contrast to Short-toed and Bonelli's, has parallel-edged wings.

Booted – tail about equal to width of wings.

Raptors: Harriers

Marsh Harrier – largest harrier. Looks much the heaviest, broader/more bulky appearance, almost approaching Buzzard. Usually seen flying over reed-beds. Present in Europe in winter.

Hen Harrier – lighter in build than Marsh, longer tail. Flight has lighter feel, but not so light as Montagu's/Pallid Harriers. Often over moorland, northern bogs/open country. All year in Europe.

FEMALES

Pallid Harrier – closest to Montagu's in build, flight very slightly less unstable-looking, wings raised in shallower V.

Hen – wing-tip made up from 5 primaries, so looks comparatively blunt. Overall, has broader 'arm' and 'hand' than other smaller Harriers. Overhead, may recall hawk.

Hen – tail longer than Marsh.

Marsh – shortest tail.

Marsh – broadest wings of four species, wing-tips relatively rounded.

Montagu's Harrier – common over large expanses of farmland/plains, also heathland. Summer visitor, Apr–Sept.

Pallid – similar habitat to Montagu's, also summer visitor. Eastern in distribution.

JUVENILES

Montagu's and *Pallid* – tail still longer, much longer than breadth of wings.

Pallid

Montagu's and *Pallid* – wing-tip made up from 4 primaries (5th is short), so wing-tip more pointed. Overhead, more likely to recall falcon, not hawk.

Montagu's

Marsh

Pallid (male) – sharpest wing-tip.

MALES

Hen – will sometimes glide on flat wings.

Hen – male 'sky-dancing'.

Pallid – in contrast to very similar Montagu's, will glide on flat wings.

Hen – when flying, has quicker wing-beats than Marsh, with shorter glides.

Montagu's (male) – longer wings than Pallid. Always glides on wings raised in V.

Marsh

Marsh *Hen*

Montagu's

Pallid

Montagu's – wings-tips reach to tail-tip when perched. *Hen* – shorter wings.

Montagu's

Pallid

Hen

Raptors: Buzzards

Common Buzzard – by far the commonest species, found throughout Europe all year round. Rough-legged Buzzard is northern species; Long-legged Buzzard breeds in far south-east. Honey Buzzard widespread/often common, summer visitor only.

Common – often fans tail when soaring. When not fanned, tail straight-edged with sharp corners.

Common – often seen on posts/roadside poles, on ground in open.

Honey Buzzard – slightly larger than Common, longer wings/tail. Wings clearly bulge in middle, so 'pinched-in' effect where they join body near tail.

Honey – often shows notch in tail (other Buzzards don't).

Honey (juvenile)

Honey – tail as long as wing width.

Common – tail definitely shorter than width of wing.

Honey (female)

Common (pale)

Honey – rarely seen perched or on open ground (stays deep in forest).

Common – beginning stoop.

Honey – has unique display routine. Flies in U-curve and, at top, lifts wings above head and shakes them.

Rough-legged Buzzard – hovering.

Honey (male)

Common – calls a lot. Rest much less vocal.

Common (pale)

Golden Eagle

Long-legged Buzzard – larger/bulkier than rest, longer wings. Long wings, long tail, more protruding head/serene power give unmistakable eagle-like impression.

Common Buzzard

Rough-legged – noticeably slower wing-beats than Common, with easier, more fluid movement.

Rough-legged Buzzard – larger than Common, with obviously longer wings, slightly longer tail. At times this long-winged, long-tailed buzzard can look like harrier.

Honey Buzzard – slower/more fluid wing-beats than Common, with emphasis on upstroke. Head/neck protrude distinctively, recalling Cuckoo or even Woodpigeon.

Common and *Rough-legged* – when soaring, hold wings in V. In Long-legged the V is sometimes more pronounced.

Honey (female)

Honey – usually holds tail closed; bulges very slightly in middle, blunt corners. Tendency to twist/turn tail in flight, unlike others. When soaring, holds wings flat or even slightly bowed. Wings often twisted when soaring.

Rough-legged – when gliding, carpal joints pressed slightly further forward than Buzzard. Seen straight on, 'arm' slightly raised and 'hand' held flat.

Honey (male)

Long-legged – wings look straighter, carpal joints less projecting, wing-tip less swept back than Common or Rough-legged.

Rough-legged – hovering.

Common – when gliding, wings flat. Faster, stiffer wing-beats.

Long-legged – even slower/more powerful wing-beats than Rough-legged; nothing like stiff wing-beats of Common or 'Steppe'.

'Steppe' Buzzard – eastern race of Common Buzzard, similar in plumage to Long-legged.

Raptors: Hawks

Goshawk – much more robust than Sparrowhawk, broader breast/hip-heavy look.

Male

Goshawk – steady on flight-path, longer glides/slower, shallower flaps. Although flapping flight may recall crow, always looks much bigger.

Goshawk – bulge at secondaries giving S-shaped edge to wings.

Sparrowhawk (*below*) – smaller than Goshawk, wing-beats quicker, looks lighter. Flight-path less smooth than more powerful Goshawk. Always clearly smaller than crow.

Goshawk – thicker neck than Sparrowhawk/more protruding head.

Sparrowhawk – shorter neck than Goshawk.

Female

Female

Sparrowhawk – 'arm' of wing shorter than Goshawk's, but 'hand' comparatively longer.

Levant Sparrow-hawk (*right*) – mainly forests/woodland away from people, confined to lowlands.

Female

Sparrowhawk – common. Mainly woodland bird, but often found near human habitation, including gardens.

Male

Goshawk – tail shorter, more rounded than Sparrowhawk's.

Levant Sparrowhawk – wings thinner/more pointed than Sparrowhawk, 4 'fingers' in wing-tip, straighter trailing edge.

Sparrowhawk – broader wing-tip with 5 'fingers'; secondaries bulge.

Sparrowhawk – smaller/slimmer than Goshawk, considerably less bulk at base of tail.

Juvenile

Juvenile

Levant Sparrowhawk – tail shorter/more rounded than Sparrowhawk's.

Male

Male **Sparrowhawk** ambushing Greenfinch.

Levant Sparrowhawk – very similar to Sparrowhawk, but more lightly built.

Juvenile Levant Sparrow-hawk

Levant Sparrowhawk – iris colour of adult brown.

Sparrowhawk – iris yellow.

Levant Sparrowhawk – more rapid wing-beats than Sparrow-hawk, longer glides.

Female

Female

Male

Levant Sparrowhawk – in contrast to others, migrates in flocks, only visits Europe for summer.

Male *Goshawk* 'mantling' over Magpie kill.

Raptors: Larger Falcons

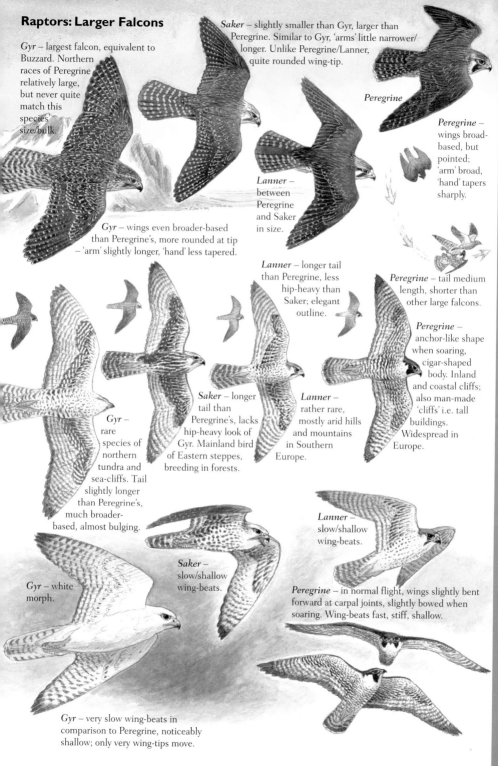

Gyr – largest falcon, equivalent to Buzzard. Northern races of Peregrine relatively large, but never quite match this species' size/bulk.

Saker – slightly smaller than Gyr, larger than Peregrine. Similar to Gyr, 'arms' little narrower/longer. Unlike Peregrine/Lanner, quite rounded wing-tip.

Peregrine

Peregrine – wings broad-based, but pointed; 'arm' broad, 'hand' tapers sharply.

Gyr – wings even broader-based than Peregrine's, more rounded at tip – 'arm' slightly longer, 'hand' less tapered.

Lanner – between Peregrine and Saker in size.

Lanner – longer tail than Peregrine, less hip-heavy than Saker; elegant outline.

Peregrine – tail medium length, shorter than other large falcons.

Peregrine – anchor-like shape when soaring, cigar-shaped body. Inland and coastal cliffs; also man-made 'cliffs' i.e. tall buildings. Widespread in Europe.

Gyr – rare species of northern tundra and sea-cliffs. Tail slightly longer than Peregrine's, much broader-based, almost bulging.

Saker – longer tail than Peregrine's, lacks hip-heavy look of Gyr. Mainland bird of Eastern steppes, breeding in forests.

Lanner – rather rare, mostly arid hills and mountains in Southern Europe.

Lanner – slow/shallow wing-beats.

Saker – slow/shallow wing-beats.

Gyr – white morph.

Peregrine – in normal flight, wings slightly bent forward at carpal joints, slightly bowed when soaring. Wing-beats fast, stiff, shallow.

Gyr – very slow wing-beats in comparison to Peregrine, noticeably shallow; only very wing-tips move.

Raptors: Smaller Falcons

Kestrel – very common bird of prey, seen beside roads/in towns and cities all over Europe. Resident.

Male

Kestrel – dark claws.

Lesser Kestrel – scarce/local, in Southern Europe in towns/on cliffs. Summer visitor only.

Male

Lesser Kestrel – white claws.

Kestrel – long wings/tail. In comparison to most other falcons, wings look narrow at base.

Female

Female

Lesser Kestrel – very difficult to tell from Kestrel on shape alone, but fractionally slimmer bird, slightly narrower/more pointed wings that (unlike Kestrel) almost reach tail-tip on perched bird.

Kestrel – narrow-based wings held fairly straight out in normal flight.

Female

Lesser Kestrel – tail slightly shorter/thinner than Kestrel; some birds have slightly longer central tail feathers, giving tail tapered look (diagnostic when present).

Male

Red-footed Falcon – unlike Hobby, often perches on overhead wires, will perform short sallies downwards.

Hobby – not colonial; well-spaced pairs, often using Carrion Crow nests. Scythe-like shape, narrow, sharply pointed, swept-back wings. At long distance, looks just like large, slow-motion Swift.

Hobby

Red-footed Falcon – wings usually held swept-back. Broader-based than Hobby, less pointed.

Eleonora's Falcon – comes in colour phases, pale and dark, in ratio 3:1, often seen together.

Eleonora's – dark.

Eleonora's – light.

Female

Male

Merlin – nests in well-spaced pairs on northern moorland.

Eleonora's Falcon – colonial, living near sea/breeding on offshore islands/cliffs.

Kestrel – very 'flappy', mechanical wing-beats, rather lacking in power: *not* 'dashing'.

Lesser Kestrel – always breed in colonies, members hunt together. *Kestrel* – usually (not always) hunts, nests alone.

Female

Male

Kestrel – long, slightly rounded tail.

Red-footed Falcon – like cross between Kestrel (long tail, regular hovering) and Hobby (swept-back wings, colour, sweeping flight-style).

Red-footed Falcon – like Lesser Kestrel a colonial species, breeding in old Rook's nests in trees.

Hobby – smaller and in every way thinner than Peregrine, with much narrower/ more pointed wings.

Juvenile

Hobby – short, square-cut tail.

Hobby and *Red-footed Falcon* – dashing/dynamic in flight, long sweeps high in sky on swept-back wings.

Red-footed Falcon – 1st-summer male.

Red-footed Falcon – longer tail than Hobby, shorter tail than Eleonora's Falcon. Smaller than Eleonora's Falcon.

Juvenile

Eleonora's – light.

Eleonora's Falcon – large/tapered, much longer tail than Peregrine or Hobby, longer wings than Hobby.

Eleonora's Falcon – like Hobby, but often flies with more 'relaxed', less forced wing-beats. At other times dashing/dramatic.

Male

Merlin – far smaller/more compact than Hobby, broad-based wings.

Sparrowhawk – blunt-ended wings.

Female

Eleonora's Falcon – dark.

(*Merlin* juvenile – similar in plumage to Hobby, far more compact. Far stiffer, less fluid wing-beats, only tips move.)

Male

Merlin – small/compact.

Merlin – typically faster, flicking wing-beats than others, short glides.

Peregrine – juvenile.

Merlin – broad-based but pointed wings, rather front-heavy silhouette, suggests miniature Peregrine.

Merlin – does not sweep around sky, but fast and direct at ground level: power/agility in miniature.

Gamebirds: Habitats

Where a gamebird lives offers an excellent clue to identity, since some species have mutually exclusive requirements.

Red Grouse – treeless heather moorland, Britain only. Feeds almost exclusively on heather.

Willow Grouse – boreal zone, mainly birch forests, especially boggy areas; also willow scrub. In winter moves down into more sheltered, forested terrain, where eats willow and birch catkins.

Ptarmigan – more extreme habitats than Willow Grouse, including Arctic tundra/barren mountaintops. Drawn to cold, windy, open places, usually with rocks/low vegetation. Avoids sheltered, scrubby places, even in winter.

Black Grouse – mixture of scattered groups of low trees (especially birch and conifers) intermingled with open habitats e.g. moor, heath or bog.

Capercaillie – mainly mature coniferous (pine) forests, with trees well-spaced/ plenty of shrubby, berry-bearing understorey. Needs plenty of cover. In winter, eats pine shoots and needles.

Hazel Grouse – extensive undisturbed closed forests, favouring mixed stands of conifers/broad-leaved trees with copious understorey, especially where damp, overgrown gulleys. Often found feeding in birches, alders and hazels.

Golden Pheasant – found mainly in young (15–30 years old) dense plantations of conifers (pine, larch), either with dense understorey or none at all (Britain).

Lady Amherst's Pheasant – woodland with very thick understorey of bramble, rhododendrons (Britain).

Quail (*below*) – in large open agricultural fields with grass or crop less than 1m tall, without bushes/trees. Mainly summer visitor, the only one on these pages.

Common Pheasant – in farming areas with open fields interspersed with copses or scrub. In mountainous areas confined to wooded valleys.

Reeves' Pheasant – forests of oak, ash, hornbeam with thick understorey (France, Germany, Czech Republic).

Red-legged Partridge – mainly drier areas than Grey Partridge, well-drained fields, heathland, sandy areas. Also in less open, more bushy places than Grey. Mainly found at low levels, but reaches 2,000m in France (where Rock Partridge overlaps).

Grey Partridge – open farmland and pasture, hedgerows for nesting/shelter and earth for dust-bathing. Prefers more lush areas than other partridges, avoids deserts, rocky places and (generally) high mountains.

Rock Partridge – usually high mountain regions, between tree-line/snow-line (especially 1,000–2,000m). Particularly drawn to south-facing slopes with rocks, grass and low bushes.

Chukar – more arid places than other partridges, including semi-desert. Often in high mountains; much at home in rocky places with low bushes; also descends to cultivated lowlands.

Barbary Partridge – wide variety of habitats, only found in Sardinia and Gibraltar. Often on similar rocky, scrubby mountain slopes to Rock Partridge and Chukar.

Gamebirds: Grouse

Willow Grouse and Ptarmigan are rotund, short-tailed grouse with rather small heads. Red Grouse is a form of Willow Grouse found only in Britain.

Red Grouse – reddish coloured all over, including winter.

Willow/Red Grouse – slightly larger, stubbier bill than Ptarmigan's.

Black Grouse – males display at 'lek', usually close together, in clearing or bog, on ground in more open areas than Capercaillie. May display any time of year, especially spring/autumn.

Willow/Red Grouse – shy, usually makes off quickly at approach of danger.

Ptarmigan – gentle, dove-like head.

Black (male) – far smaller/less bulky than Capercaillie with longer tail and much smaller head.

Black (female)

Ptarmigan – often very tame, allowing close approach.

Ptarmigan – in spring, summer (*above, top*) and autumn (*above, bottom*) more coldly coloured than Willow Grouse.

Hazel Grouse – small, partridge-sized grouse, long tail. Upright stance, short crest.

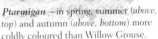

Capercaillie – males display together in 'lek', producing communal show although performers can be well-spaced. Begins at dawn in trees, later on forest floor. Displays in spring.

Capercaillie – male (*above, left*) is huge, turkey-sized bird, unlikely to be confused with anything else.

Hazel – often in trees, can walk along branches.

Capercaillie (female) – similar to, but much larger than, female Black Grouse. (Also larger than male Black Grouse.)

Hazel – males display on their own, mainly on forest floor, beating wings or making short jumps.

Capercaillie – individual wing-beats discernible during 'bursts'. Impressive, very noisy take-off with loud wing-flaps, soon becomes silent.

Capercaillie – flies off through trees, turning with unexpected agility this way and that to avoid trunks. In flight, shows more rounded tail than female Grouse.

Willow/Red Grouse (*above*) – when flushed, makes off low with explosion of wing-beats, continues on course with alternating glides/bursts of flaps.

Black Grouse – less crashing take-off than Capercaillie, quieter wing-beats.

Black – tends to make long flights over valleys.

Black – often goes off flying on higher track than Willow/Red Grouse.

Willow Grouse – smaller than Black, shorter tail, without slight notch. Neck sticks out a bit less.

Hazel Grouse – makes off with whirring wing-beats, twists through trees, quickly lands.

Willow Grouse or *Ptarmigan* – in display, flies towards edge of territory, rises high, glides for short distance and flutters down.

Grouse feed mostly on ground; but especially Dec–Mar, several species take to trees.

Black – droppings half length of finger, compact.

Capercaillie – males often perch in treetops (unlike other grouse).

Black – at home in trees, even on thin branches where can perform ungainly gymnastics, hanging/hopping.

Capercaillie – droppings distinctive: as long as human finger, curved; in winter made up of pine needles.

Red Grouse – doesn't turn white in winter.

Willow (*above left*) – in winter will take to trees to feed on willow/birch buds. *Ptarmigan* (*above right*) only rarely does this.

Gamebirds: Partridges

ALECTORIS PARTRIDGES:
Red-legged, Rock, Barbary and Chukar

Grey Partridge – almost throughout Europe (missing in most of Iberia).

Red-legged Partridge – often digs for food. *Grey* – picks for food, doesn't usually dig.

Red-legged – darkest Alectoris. Often perches on posts, trees, even roofs!

Grey – stays on ground.

Barbary – Sardinia and Gibraltar only.

Red-legged – mainly, not exclusively, lowlands. Commonest, most adaptable, least shy of the four. In Britain, France and South-west Europe.

Chukar (right) – extreme South-east Europe (South-east Greece, Crete, Cyprus). Shier, more secretive than Rock or others. Unlike Rock, has second peak of calling mid-morning.

Rock – mainly in high mountains of Central Europe (Alps, Italy, Balkans). Largest Alectoris (only just), also greyest. Main calling period is just after dawn.

Barbary – pinkest Alectoris, slightly more rounded head.

Partridge (young) – blunt-ended tail. *Pheasant* (chick) – longer tail with sharp tip.

Black Francolin – flies with power more reminiscent of Pheasant than partridges, less of a burst away.

Common Pheasant (female) – long tail.

Black Francolin – only found in one area in Cyprus, where local, very shy/very furtive. Rather plump, but upright.

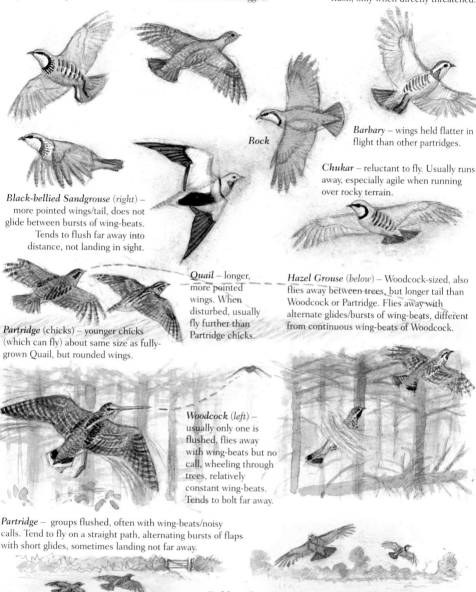

Red-legged Partridge – heavier in flight than Grey.

Grey Partridge – lighter flight/faster take-off than Red-legged.

Barbary – least inclined of all to flush, only when directly threatened.

Rock

Barbary – wings held flatter in flight than other partridges.

Chukar – reluctant to fly. Usually runs away, especially agile when running over rocky terrain.

Black-bellied Sandgrouse (*right*) – more pointed wings/tail, does not glide between bursts of wing-beats. Tends to flush far away into distance, not landing in sight.

Quail – longer, more pointed wings. When disturbed, usually fly further than Partridge chicks.

Hazel Grouse (*below*) – Woodcock-sized, also flies away between trees, but longer tail than Woodcock or Partridge. Flies away with alternate glides/bursts of wing-beats, different from continuous wing-beats of Woodcock.

Partridge (chicks) – younger chicks (which can fly) about same size as fully-grown Quail, but rounded wings.

Woodcock (*left*) – usually only one is flushed, flies away with wing-beats but no call, wheeling through trees, relatively constant wing-beats. Tends to bolt far away.

Partridge – groups flushed, often with wing-beats/noisy calls. Tend to fly on a straight path, alternating bursts of flaps with short glides, sometimes landing not far away.

Red-legged – flocks often split up when flushed.

Grey – flocks stay together when flushed.

Grey – inclined to squat, only flushing at last minute, not going far.

Red-legged – runs away rather than squats; faster than Grey.

Red-legged – larger and more heavily built than Grey.

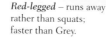

Gamebirds: Pheasants

Common Pheasant – flocks in
winter often restricted to one sex.

All Pheasants feed with much scratching,
which Partridges do not do.

Common (male) –
unmistakable, although
greatly variable in plumage.

Golden Pheasant (female) – bill/
legs brownish-yellow.

Golden – less gregarious than others,
'groups' numbering only 1–3, even in winter.
Often seen fleeing into cover at a run.
Hardly ever flies, but takes off with less
wing-noise than Common.

Golden (female, *above*) – small, slim,
delicate, more domed crown than
female Pheasant, longer tail.

Golden
(male) –
much smaller
than Common.

Lady Amherst's Pheasant
(female) – very similar
to Golden, but
slightly longer
tail. Note bill/legs
are grey.

Lady Amherst's (male, *above*) – larger
than Golden.

Reeves' Pheasant (female) – larger than Golden or
Lady Amherst's. Similar size to Common, but
longer tail.

Reeves', Lady Amherst's Pheasant –
flocks in winter, often of 6 or more birds.

Three invisible birds? Quail, Corncrake and Buttonquail

Small Buttonquail – very small, no bigger than Skylark – far smaller than Corncrake. Short, blunt, curiously angled wing in flight. When it lands, holds very characteristic posture for just a moment – body upright, wings slightly open. (Others don't do this.)

Corncrake – chunky; recalls small/slim Partridge, but legs dangle down and longer wings beat more slowly.

Skylark – similar size to Quail, but flight fluttery, without flurry of fast wing-beats. Long tail.

Small Buttonquail – flies off with obvious wing-noise (others don't).

Corncrake – flies off with prominently dangling legs, distinguishing it from others on this page.

Quail – size similar to Small Buttonquail, but shows long, narrow, pointed wings in flight, giving completely different shape.

Corncrake – sometimes pokes above grass; long legs, 'blunt pencil' bill.

Corncrake – widespread in middle latitudes of Europe, not Mediterranean or far north; summer visitor to damp meadows/ fields with damp patches.

Quail – shorter legs than Corncrake; tiny bill, patterned face.

Small Buttonquail – rotund; not much tail; pale eye.

Small Buttonquail – southern Spain only; very rare; present all year in low, dry vegetation on warm soils, particularly heaths of dwarf palm and asphodel. Quail also found in this habitat.

Quail – widespread in Europe in summer, except Scandinavia; in crops/fields with wide open spaces.

Quail – when flushed, often flies quite a way, in contrast to others on this page.

Rails: Finding Rails

Most rails live in dense waterside vegetation and are very shy/secretive. With thin, small bodies (generally pigeon-sized or less) to help them slip through the plant stems, and cryptic colouration to go with habits/habitats, they typically provide a challenge to see at all, let alone identify. But Moorhens and Coots are the exception. Coots swim around highly visibly on open water like ducks; Moorhens are tremendously amphibious, one moment swimming, the next creeping along the margins.

Coot

Moorhen

The key to seeing the more elusive rails is to find a place where open mud abuts thick vegetation, and keep scanning along the edge.

Water Rail

Spotted Crake

Rails often show themselves when they move between blocks of vegetation (sometimes swimming): watch gaps carefully.

Water Rail

Look also in places where fallen-over stems of reeds/other plants form platforms (especially good for Little Crake, but here a Spotted).

Rails also favour ditches, so watch along both edges.

Little Crake

Rails tend to ply a regular beat, so keep looking where they have appeared before.

In cold winter weather, rails are often much easier to see because favoured feeding spots are frozen over.

Watch suitable habitat at dawn and dusk.

Water Rail

Keep quiet and still. Hides in nature reserves are often good, comfortable places to sit and look for rails.

9

Rails: Moorhen and Coots

Coot – broad frontal shield, rounded on top. Crown flatter/nape more rounded than Crested Coot's.

Crested Coot– head different shape to Coot's. Crown peaked, giving triangular shape (enhanced by tiny red knobs present in breeding season).

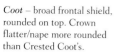

COOT **CRESTED COOT**

Crested Coot

Moorhen

Crested Coot

Coot

Moorhen's nest more hidden in vegetation than Coot's.

Coot – frontal shield/bill 'cut in two' by wedge of feathering pointing outwards towards nostril (not in Crested).

Crested Coot – frontal shield slightly narrower, 'cut off' at top by the red knobs.

Crested Coot – subtle bluish tinge to bill.

Moorhen – angular on water, long tail sticking up/head pointing forwards. Normally only one or two seen at a time.

Moorhen – considerable jerking of head as swims, 'like cyclist peddling up hill'. *Does not dive.*

Coot – subtle creamy tinge to bill.

Coot – more rounded than Moorhen, especially to 'stern'. In contrast to Moorhen, forms flocks floating on water.

Coot – nod of head as swims. *Repeatedly dives* when feeding, in contrast to Moorhen.

Moorhen – green legs with long, slender toes. Obvious long tail sticks up and is constantly flicked.

Moorhen (juvenile) – same shape as adult, but red-and-yellow shield not fully developed.

Coot – bluish legs with lobed toes. Tail shorter, back much more rounded.

Coot (juvenile) – no white shield, still with rounded appearance of adult.

Rails: Smaller Rails

Moorhen – flies readily, fast, slightly floppy action and heavily trailing legs.

Water Rail – similar to Moorhen, but weaker-looking. More willing to take flight than smaller crakes.

Moorhen (juvenile) – larger/plumper than Water Rail.

Water Rail – quite catholic in requirements, favouring both reed-beds and sedge bogs, also other types of aquatic vegetation.

Water Rail – at all times and ages, can be distinguished from the other rails by its *long bill*.

Spotted Crake – breeds mainly in sedge bogs/wet rushy meadows, not normally in reed-beds. Requires combination of very shallow freshwater with considerable growth of dense plant cover, so usually found at heart of extensive wetlands.

Water Rail – smaller than Moorhen; body looks laterally flattened when seen from in front or behind.

Spotted Crake – larger, plumper than Little or Baillon's Crake. Rather oval shape.

Spotted Crake – slightly smaller than Water Rail. Short, heavy bill. Looks compact at front.

Baillon's Crake – drawn mostly to wetlands with combination of sedges/relatively shallow water.

Sexes of Little Crake differ markedly, whereas male/female Baillon's Crakes very similar.

Little Crake – differs from Baillon's Crake or Spotted Crake in breeding in large reed-beds above relatively deep water, especially where bulrush and reedmace grow alongside reeds. Bird of deep-water at heart of swamps.

Baillon's Crake – tiny ball-shaped bird.

Little Crake – small/slim.

Baillon's Crake – short primary projection; primaries 'bunched'.

Little Crake – primaries project further, less bunched than Baillon's Crake. Primary projection especially obvious when tail lifted up. More aquatic bird than other small rails/crakes, swimming far more often, perhaps more regularly seen running over floating leaves. Especially favours platforms of fallen reeds on deep water.

Baillon's Crake – marginally smaller than Little Crake (House Sparrow size), despite latter's name. Tends to look a little darker than Little Crake.

Note: On migration all crakes/rails can be found in similar habitats, including quite small patches of wetland. In winter, Water Rail stretches habitat to take in riversides and saltmarshes.

Little Bittern – flies with trailing legs, not much larger than Moorhen. Slower in actions on ground.

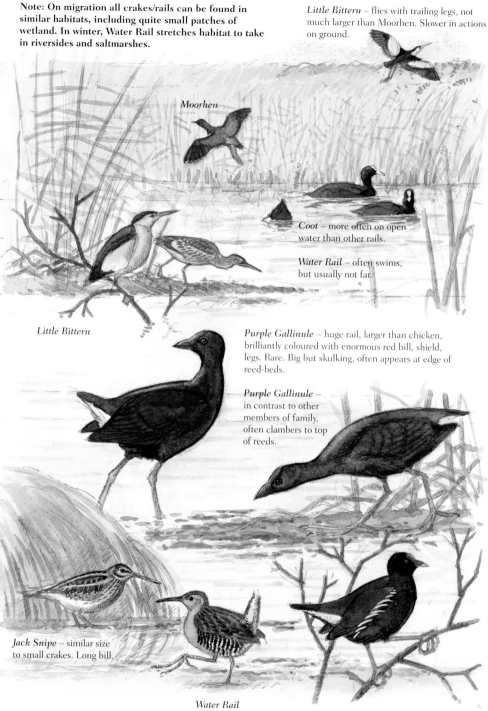

Moorhen

Coot – more often on open water than other rails.

Water Rail – often swims, but usually not far.

Little Bittern

Purple Gallinule – huge rail, larger than chicken, brilliantly coloured with enormous red bill, shield, legs. Rare. Big but skulking, often appears at edge of reed-beds.

Purple Gallinule – in contrast to other members of family, often clambers to top of reeds.

Jack Snipe – similar size to small crakes. Long bill.

Water Rail

Moorhen – far more able than Coot to climb around vegetation; regularly climb trees.

Cranes and Bustards

Demoiselle Crane – tendency to dangle legs in flight can be a useful character. Flight lighter than Common Crane, but still very slow wing-beats, wings flat, neck outstretched.

Demoiselle Crane – shorter/thinner neck gives slightly different outline. Note more rounded head. Tail tends to look shorter/secondaries may bulge a little.

Common Crane – long neck, very slow wing-beats, wings flat, neck held outstretched.

Demoiselle Crane – breeds in upland steppes. Very rare in Europe (breeds Crimea). Passes through Cyprus on migration (Aug).

Demoiselle Crane – slighter, shorter, sharper-looking bill, more rounded crown, shorter, thinner neck than Common Crane.

Common Crane – breeds in marshy areas, including bogs, mainly in north. Winters on lakes/plains.

Common Crane – thick-based, dagger-like bill, flattish crown, relatively thick neck.

Common Crane – very large/tall. 'Bulge' at tertials, in manner of Ostrich.

Demoiselle Crane – slightly smaller, not obviously so in life. No bulge at tertials; these sweep neatly over the tail, like dinner jacket.

Demoiselle Crane – more fluent gait that Common Crane, runs more easily.

Common Crane – remarkable dancing display, performed by pairs together.

Grey Heron – easily told from cranes by retracted neck, bowed wings/faster wing-beats.

White Stork – similar flight style to cranes, slow wing-beats, outstretched neck, but less elongated, shorter neck/shorter legs.

Great Bustard – similar flight style to cranes, neck outstretched, slow wing-beats, but looks very heavy-bodied, like enormous bird of prey. Much white on wings.

Female

Male

Little Bustard – takes off with loud sound of wing-beats. Fairly long wings, bowed, with wing-beats not lifted far above horizontal; much white shows.

Red-legged Partridge – wings broad/blunt. Short neck/tail. Explosion of wing-beats, then glides/flaps before landing.

Pin-tailed Sandgrouse – long, pointed wings, long tail, very fast wing-beats. Small.

Stone Curlew – wings narrow, long/pointed, arched down. Wing-beats slow/deliberate, no sound at lift-off.

Little Bustard – far smaller than Great Bustard, not much larger than duck.

Female

Little Bustard – male displays to female, turning/showing black-and-white neck, also leaping into air while flapping wings. Wings make whistling sound.

Male

Great Bustard – lives on broad, open plains, including cultivated areas. Usually in modest numbers, even in winter. Huge, stately, heavy-bodied, heavy-legged.

Little Bustard – similar habitat requirements to Great Bustard, but tolerates more intensive cultivation. Often in large flocks in winter.

Male

Great Bustard – male much larger than female, but even female dwarfs Little Bustard.

Great Bustard – male displays to female. Appears to turn itself inside out, looking 'like a foam bath'.

Waders: Families of Waders

Avocets and **Stilts**
2 species. Elegant, long-legged waders that nest in saltwater habitats in colonies. Bills specialised.

Stilt

Avocet

Oystercatchers
1 species. Heavily built black-and-white wader. Thick, straight bill.

Stone Curlew
1 species. Strange, large-eyed, large-headed 'wader' of arid habitats. Semi-nocturnal. Very thick knee-joints. Cryptically coloured.

Pratincoles
2 species. Aerial 'waders' with long wings, feeding on flying insects in swallow-like flight. Very short, curved bills. Colonial.

Godwits – large, tall. Long, slightly uptilted bills.

Plovers (*above*) – 8 species. Waders with short bills, relying on sight for finding food. Use obvious 'stop-run-peck' feeding technique. Unable to perch on tree or bushes because lack hind toe.

SANDPIPERS AND ALLIES
Godwits, Curlews, Woodcock, Snipes, Shanks, Phalaropes, Turnstone and Sandpipers

28 species. Large, diverse family. Most have hind toe, so better at perching than plovers. Most feed by touch, not sight, so tend to have proportionally longer bills than plovers. They don't use plovers' stop-run-peck technique.

Curlews – large, tall. Long, downcurved bills.

Woodcock and **Snipes** – round-bodied waders with long, straight bills. Feed by probing. Cryptically coloured and secretive, hard to see.

'Shanks' and **Freshwater Sandpipers** – small or medium-sized, longish bills/legs. Often chase visible prey. Often by freshwater.

Small Sandpipers – small, quite short legs. Bill-tips highly sensitive. Touch-feeders, fairly continuous action. Nest in Arctic or sub-Arctic, highly migratory.

Turnstone – squat, short-legged wader, rocky shores. Stout, short bill turns items over.

Phalaropes – aquatic waders that swim, float like corks, often spinning round and round. Winter in open ocean.

Waders: Who wades?

Despite their name, many 'waders' are reluctant to wade at all. Some avoid getting their feet wet, some just paddle, some wade properly, a few will take the plunge and swim.

Little Stint – will feed in very shallow water.

Dunlin – mainly shallows.

Curlew Sandpiper – wades more deeply than Dunlin.

Ringed Plover – will get feet wet, but not enthusiastic.

Green Sandpiper – shallows.

Knot – shallows.

Note: *Snipe* also wades in shallow water.

DEEPER WADERS AND SWIMMERS

Deep waders: up to the belly   **Regular swimmers**   **Confirmed swimmers**

Black-winged Stilt – long legs enable it to wade in deeper water than others.

Godwits – often submerge head when feeding.

Avocet (not Black-winged Stilt).

Ruff – will submerge head when feeding.

Greenshank

Spotted Redshank (Redshank only rarely).

Redshank

Phalaropes

Note: *Whimbrel* wades to moderate depths, *Curlew* up to belly.

Purple Sandpiper (swims in wave wash over rocks).

NON-WADING 'WADERS'

Plovers prefer to keep feet dry. Grey Plover, however, often feeds along creeks and sometimes wades, in contrast to other larger plovers.

Note: *Woodcock* also avoids wading.

Dotterel

Golden Plover

Pratincoles

Stone Curlew

Waders: Arctic breeding waders

EXTREME ARCTIC

Sanderling – coastal tundra on flat ground, Greenland only.

Knot – moist tundra.

Bar-tailed Godwit – swampy Arctic lowland tundra, sometimes near trees. Much further north than Black-tailed Godwit.

Purple Sandpiper – Arctic coasts, also high mountain plateaux.

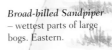

Grey Phalarope – marshy tundra, Iceland only, very rare. Always coastal. Prefers pools with muddy edges, not with emergent vegetation.

Broad-billed Sandpiper – wettest parts of large bogs. Eastern.

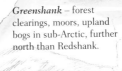

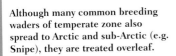

Greenshank – forest clearings, moors, upland bogs in sub-Arctic, further north than Redshank.

Red-necked Phalarope – freshwater marshes/bogs, often far inland and at high altitude. Often on pools with emergent vegetation.

Although many common breeding waders of temperate zone also spread to Arctic and sub-Arctic (e.g. Snipe), they are treated overleaf.

Dotterel – Arctic/coastal tundra, mountain plateaux. Needs low vegetation on flat, dry, well-drained soil.

Golden Plover – drier parts of coastal tundra, mountainsides, temperate moorland.

Grey Plover – damp tundra in lowland high Arctic, usually wetter places than Golden Plover. Breeds at much lower density than Golden Plover.

Little Stint – coastal, drier tundra of High Arctic – less extreme Arctic than Sanderling, but further north than Temminck's Stint.

Turnstone – bare, rocky, stony coasts (sometimes adjacent meadows).

Terek Sandpiper – lowland rivers, lakeshores in tundra. Eastern.

Spotted Redshank – lightly wooded tundra, further north than Greenshank.

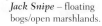

Whimbrel – low Arctic moorland/tundra. More northerly than Curlew.

Temminck's Stint – sheltered lakesides/by rivers, sometimes near human habitation, often far inland. Less Arctic than Little Stint.

Jack Snipe – floating bogs/open marshlands.

Green Sandpiper – damp woodland areas, even forests. Places eggs in old nests of other birds, usually thrushes, in trees.

Wood Sandpiper – marshes with scrub, open parts of northern forests. Usually nests on ground.

Great Snipe – moist areas on mountainsides/wooded tundra. Found further south than Jack Snipe. Eastern.

Waders: Temperate and Continental breeding Waders

UPLAND BOGS –
Curlew (right), Snipe (above).

Most waders inhabit a number of different types of countryside for breeding. The ones shown here are typical examples.

UPLAND MOORLAND –
Golden Plover (left), Dunlin (right), Curlew (far left).

WOODLAND – *Woodcock.*

BOGS NEAR WOODLAND – *Great Snipe.*

UPPER REACHES OF RIVERS – *Common Sandpiper.*

AGRICULTURAL FIELDS –
Lapwing (in flight), Oystercatcher.

BARE, ARID AREAS (including heathland, fallow fields) –
Stone Curlew.

FRESHWATER MARSHES – *Marsh Sandpiper* (left),
Snipe (centre), *Redshank* (right).

SANDY BEACHES – *Kentish Plover.*

RIVERINE AND LAKE-SIDE SHINGLE – *Ringed Plover*
(left), *Little Ringed Plover* (bottom right), *Oystercatcher*
(background).

COASTAL SHINGLE – *Oystercatcher* (left and
flying), *Ringed Plover* (bottom). (Little Ringed Plover
doesn't nest on coastal shingle.)

Redshank

Pratincoles

Curlew

Black-tailed Godwit

Ruff

**FRESHWATER MARSHES,
FIELDS AND MEADOWS**

SALTPANS AND LAGOONS –
Avocet, Black-winged Stilt, Spur-winged Plover (far right).

Waders: Feeding techniques on a winter estuary

Sanderling – braves surf and wet sand at shore, dashing between breaking waves, picking up surface-living invertebrates. Usually in small, tight-knit groups.

THREE SIZES OF TOUCH-FEEDING WADERS:
Bar-tailed Godwit,
Knot and *Dunlin*

Knot – often immerses bill and moves forward, making furrow – technique known as ploughing. Continuous action, not stop-start. In very dense flocks.

Bar-tailed Godwit – deep prober, using stitching action (continuous series of probes) as well as surface-picking. In well-spaced flocks.

Dunlin – probes to moderate depth, sometimes stitching, other times not. In tight flocks. Continuous feeding action.

Grey Plover – spreads well out over muddy creeks and saltmarsh, some individuals actually holding territory. Uses plovers' stop-run-peck feeding system using sight (*see* Ringed Plover), but performs it much more slowly. The heavy bill can crush crabs etc.

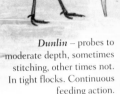

Redshank – very common wader, feeds over mud by picking and probing; also wades. Usually in parties, quite well-dispersed. Feeds by continuous walking, never stop-run-peck.

Oystercatcher – often feeds over rocky shores, in small, dispersed parties, taking shellfish.

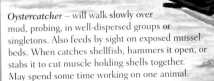

Oystercatcher – will walk slowly over mud, probing, in well-dispersed groups or singletons. Also feeds by sight on exposed mussel-beds. When catches shellfish, hammers it open, or stabs it to cut muscle holding shells together. May spend some time working on one animal.

Purple Sandpiper – on rocky shores only, right by breaking waves and surf. Runs over rocks and seaweed, picking by sight. Small flocks, often with Turnstones. Takes some plant material, unusual for wader.

Curlew – walks sedately, mostly probing. Birds space well out. Takes deep-dwelling worms, but also surface-living creatures such as crabs. Mostly in saltmarsh and soft mud around creeks.

Ringed Plover – on sandy or shingly shores. Feeds by sight, as bill is too short for probing. Shows typical plover stop-run-peck action: remains stationary while watching for movements, runs to and pecks at prey detected.

Turnstone – forages over rocky, seaweed-covered shores in small flocks. Turns items over with strong, short bill, catches whatever is revealed. Feeds by sight. Moves busily but quite slowly.

Snipe – upper reaches of estuaries, saltmarshes. Champion prober, feeds singly or in small, well-dispersed groups. Uses touch only. Often stays put and inserts bill around it, making semicircle of holes. Regular insertions of bill, one after another, are called 'stitching'.

Golden Plover

Lapwing – often on upper reaches of estuaries. Feeds with plover's stop-run-peck action. Sociable, but spreads out. May be joined by Golden Plover.

Waders: At the roost

Godwits – in lines or Vs.

Knots

Entering the roost:
Oystercatchers – enter in tight flocks.

Grey Plovers – in small, loose groups, in irregular lines.

Knots – in large groups.
Small Waders – in large, quick-flying groups.
Curlews – in loose, ragged lines.

Some waders perform pre-roost aerial manoeuvres:
Knots – in vast, amoeba-like swirls, often oval shape. Move more slowly than large flocks of smaller waders.
Godwits and Curlews – twist and tumble.
Dunlins – wheel around rapidly, with frequent changes in direction.
Others, including Sanderlings and Redshanks, don't perform.

Godwits (Bar-tailed) – tend to be found at edge of roost, often with feet in water.

Dunlins

Grey Plovers

Redshanks

At the roost:
Knots – pack tightly.
Dunlins, Ringed Plovers and Sanderlings – quite tightly, often running round feet of larger species.
Redshanks and Grey Plovers – quite tightly.
Curlews, Oystercatchers and Godwits – more dispersed.

Redshanks – prefer to stick with their own kind at the roost.

Knots

Oystercatcher

Dunlin

Ringed Plover

Sanderling

Ringed Plover

On estuary, waders roost/rest according to tides. High tides cover feeding areas, so makes sense for them to rest/preen at this time. Many roost on islands and other areas above high water.

Phalaropes – roost in large flocks, swimming in water, often in deep ocean.

Turnstones (*right*) and *Purple Sandpipers* – often roost on jetties, beakwaters and groynes.

Turnstones – generally pick last areas to be covered, and first areas to be uncovered, by high tide.

Sanderlings – often form tight, single-species roosting groups on sand-bars or other upper-shore sites.

Curlews – if possible, roost with own kind, in saltmarshes or fields.

Lapwings (*centre*) and *Golden Plovers* – roost on inland fields, often together. Fairly loosely packed.

Many species typically roost by day and feed by night, including *Woodcock*, *Snipe*, *Jack Snipe* and *Lapwing*.

Waders: Large or distinctive waders

Phalaropes swim on water, with amazing buoyancy, like corks. Often found out to sea. Exceptionally tame. Often in flocks. Feed by 'spinning' in circles.

Red-necked – rapid, twisting flight low over water like swallow.

Grey – more powerful flight on longer wings, like small wader.

Non-breeding

Breeding

Breeding

Grey – bulkier than Red-necked, larger headed. Thicker bill seems blunt-tipped. More confident actions. Sometimes seen in autumn 'wrecks' when some forced inland by gales.

Red-necked – smaller, slighter than Grey. Spins slightly faster. Needle-like bill, much thinner than Grey. Almost never seen in autumn.

Turnstone – dumpy, quite small wader with waddling walk – legs look too short for it. Tame.

Breeding

Non-breeding

Turnstone – flies in tight, well-disciplined groups.

Turnstone – feeds by turning over stones, sometimes in impromptu teams to overturn large objects. Busy, preoccupied action. Small groups.

Oystercatcher – flies in small groups, ragged lines. Fast wing-beats, about as quick as duck. Very direct flight.

Oystercatcher – robust wader with sedate walk. Feeds alone or in small, well-scattered groups, on rocks/sandy shores. Very noisy.

Avocet – elegant wader, only one with strongly uptilted bill. Walks briskly. Swims, wades, upends. Picks from water with head well down, or 'scythes' – sweeps bill from side to side. Sociable, often hunts in packs. Wary.

Avocet – breeds in large colonies on bare surfaces.

Avocet – sleeping birds often 'lost' among flocks of small gulls or Shelducks.

Avocet – powerful flight, often in dense flocks.

Black-winged Stilt – breeds in looser colonies, more amongst vegetation than Avocet.

Black-winged Stilt – looser flocks than Avocet. Glides more. 'Flicking' wing action.

Black-winged Stilt – tall and elegant, but has straight bill. Graceful, steady walk on spidery legs. Consummate wader, but doesn't swim. Picks rapidly from water, and will probe. Tends not to scythe. Sociable. More approachable than Avocet.

Collared Pratincole – erratic, swooping flight.

Stone Curlew – stiff wing-beats in flight, wings bowed.

Pratincoles – mostly seen flying gracefully, like terns or swallows, feeding on flying insects.

Black-winged Pratincole (right) – less erratic, lazier flight. Longer primaries, shorter-looking tail.

Black-winged Pratincole – wings definitely longer than tail. Longer legs than Collared. Slightly bulkier overall. Breeds among taller vegetation than Collared, adds more lining to its nest. Eastern.

Stone Curlew – large-headed; huge, staring eyes. Looks hunched. Stands still/squats with bent legs. Runs forwards characteristically with head down. Short bill; true Curlew has long, curved bill. Feeds by stop-run-peck method; especially fond of moths. Semi-nocturnal/summer visitor.

Collared Pratincole – wings as long as tail when perched. Shorter legs than Black-winged. Breeds on bare ground.

Waders: Large Plovers

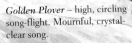

Golden Plover – high, circling song-flight. Mournful, crystal-clear song.

Golden – large flocks in flight form ovals, or V-shapes. Wings narrow and pointed, flight direct/fast. Very wary – tightly packed flocks circle repeatedly before landing.

Golden – mostly on inland pastureland in winter, often with Lapwing. More upright than Lapwing. Often paddles foot, but doesn't wade. Thinner bill than Grey.

Grey Plover – powerful flier, usually in small flocks of 10–20. Much more approachable than Golden. Slower wing-beats than Golden Plover.

Dotterel – flight fast/direct, but plump body obvious.

Grey – non-breeding.

Dotterel – often displays on ground. Absurdly tame.

Grey – mostly on estuaries and seashores in winter. Bulky plover with a powerful, heavy bill, noticeably large head and eyes. Habit of looking hunched and miserable. Not foot-paddler.

Grey – breeding plumage.

Dotterel – on mountains and hills inland, migrates to north Africa for winter. Slightly smaller than Golden Plover, more compact and chubby-looking, with proportionally larger head.

Lapwing – often in flocks with Golden Plover on ground, but separate in flight. Wings broad/rounded, diagnostic. Slow, floppy flight. Flocks often large/fairly dense.

Lapwing – at distance, flocks 'twinkle', with birds intermittently showing white underside and dark upperside.

Spur-winged Plover – fairly wary, but sluggish.

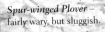

Spur-winged – longer legs than Lapwing, and smaller.

Lapwing – often in huge flocks on farmland. Distinctive. As all on this page, uses stop-run-peck feeding method. Paddles foot. Often feeds by moonlight.

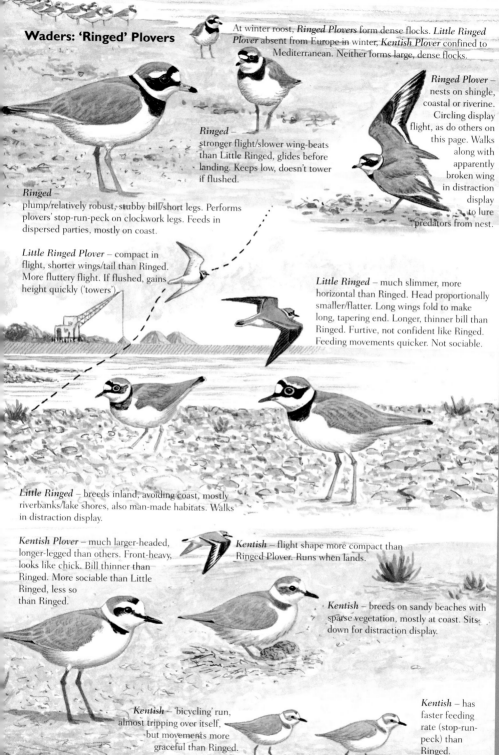

Waders: 'Ringed' Plovers

At winter roost, *Ringed Plovers* form dense flocks. *Little Ringed Plover* absent from Europe in winter, *Kentish Plover* confined to Mediterranean. Neither forms large, dense flocks.

Ringed –
stronger flight/slower wing-beats than Little Ringed, glides before landing. Keeps low, doesn't tower if flushed.

Ringed Plover – nests on shingle, coastal or riverine. Circling display flight, as do others on this page. Walks along with apparently broken wing in distraction display to lure predators from nest.

Ringed –
plump/relatively robust, stubby bill/short legs. Performs plovers' stop-run-peck on clockwork legs. Feeds in dispersed parties, mostly on coast.

Little Ringed Plover – compact in flight, shorter wings/tail than Ringed. More fluttery flight. If flushed, gains height quickly ('towers').

Little Ringed – much slimmer, more horizontal than Ringed. Head proportionally smaller/flatter. Long wings fold to make long, tapering end. Longer, thinner bill than Ringed. Furtive, not confident like Ringed. Feeding movements quicker. Not sociable.

Little Ringed – breeds inland, avoiding coast, mostly riverbanks/lake shores, also man-made habitats. Walks in distraction display.

Kentish Plover – much larger-headed, longer-legged than others. Front-heavy, looks like chick. Bill thinner than Ringed. More sociable than Little Ringed, less so than Ringed.

Kentish – flight shape more compact than Ringed Plover. Runs when lands.

Kentish – breeds on sandy beaches with sparse vegetation, mostly at coast. Sits down for distraction display.

Kentish – 'bicycling' run, almost tripping over itself, but movements more graceful than Ringed.

Kentish – has faster feeding rate (stop-run-peck) than Ringed.

Waders: 'Shanks'

Spotted Redshank – great flier, with manoeuvrability.

Spotted Redshank – slightly larger than Redshank, more elegant, longer neck. Bill much longer, thinner, with slightly (often noticeably) drooped tip. Also has longer legs.

Spotted Redshank – all birds on this page given to wading in deep freshwater, but Spotted Redshank is most inclined to swim and upend, often in groups.

Redshank – more compact than Spotted, shorter legs and bill. Stockier, often giving not very elegant impression. Noisier than others on this page, often hysterical.

Redshank – often lifts wings when landing, Greenshank doesn't.

Redshank – probes, picks from surface while walking. Wades too. Only swims occasionally. Often feeds in dispersed flocks.

Redshank – only one here that is common estuary bird. Others prefer freshwater.

All have aerial song-flight, with switchback pattern. Greenshank may rise to 300m, others much lower.

Greenshank – probes, picks, often makes sudden lunge after mobile prey such as fish. Feeds alone. Can wade deeper than Redshank.

Greenshank – tall, elegant, quite stout, slightly upcurved bill. Lanky, larger than Redshanks. Quite noisy.

Marsh Sandpiper – dainty walk, picks from surface of water. Usually feeds alone.

Marsh Sandpiper – especially rapid take-off.

Marsh Sandpiper – half the size of Greenshank, needle-thin bill. Legs are so long they can give impression of Black-winged Stilt. Very slim.

Waders: Freshwater Sandpipers

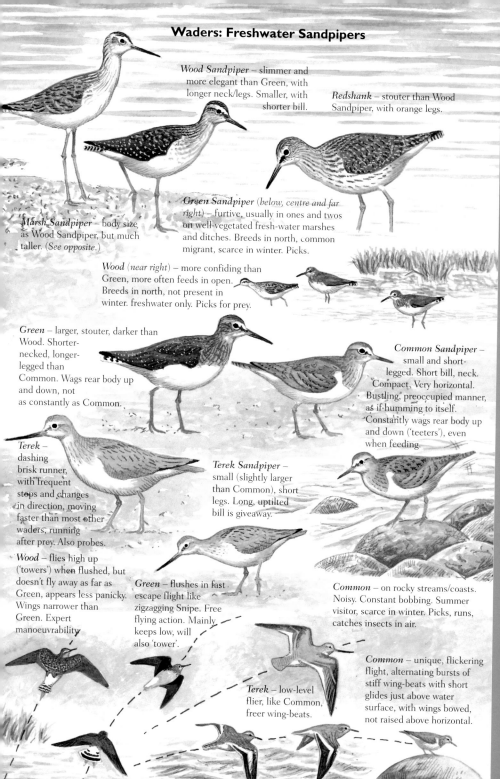

Wood Sandpiper – slimmer and more elegant than Green, with longer neck/legs. Smaller, with shorter bill.

Redshank – stouter than Wood Sandpiper, with orange legs.

Marsh Sandpiper – body size as Wood Sandpiper, but much taller. (*See opposite.*)

Green Sandpiper (*below, centre and far right*) – furtive, usually in ones and twos on well-vegetated fresh-water marshes and ditches. Breeds in north, common migrant, scarce in winter. Picks.

Wood (*near right*) – more confiding than Green, more often feeds in open. Breeds in north, not present in winter. freshwater only. Picks for prey.

Green – larger, stouter, darker than Wood. Shorter-necked, longer-legged than Common. Wags rear body up and down, not as constantly as Common.

Common Sandpiper – small and short-legged. Short bill, neck. Compact. Very horizontal. Bustling, preoccupied manner, as if humming to itself. Constantly wags rear body up and down ('teeters'), even when feeding.

Terek – dashing brisk runner, with frequent stops and changes in direction, moving faster than most other waders, running after prey. Also probes.

Terek Sandpiper – small (slightly larger than Common), short legs. Long, uptilted bill is giveaway.

Wood – flies high up ('towers') when flushed, but doesn't fly away as far as Green, appears less panicky. Wings narrower than Green. Expert manoeuvrability.

Green – flushes in fast escape flight like zigzagging Snipe. Free flying action. Mainly keeps low, will also 'tower'.

Common – on rocky streams/coasts. Noisy. Constant bobbing. Summer visitor, scarce in winter. Picks, runs, catches insects in air.

Terek – low-level flier, like Common, freer wing-beats.

Common – unique, flickering flight, alternating bursts of stiff wing-beats with short glides just above water surface, with wings bowed, not raised above horizontal.

Waders: Smaller Sandpipers (including Ruff)

Purple Sandpiper – feeds over rocky shore at water's edge, dodging waves. Stocky, plump, larger than Dunlin, shorter legs. Round-shouldered. Bill slightly downcurved, quite long. Uniquely, tail sticks out beyond wing-tips. In parties. Feeds mainly by picking over seaweed – often hard to see. Not seen on intertidal mud.

Grey Plover – shorter bill than Knot or Redshank, larger eye, longer legs, upright stance, very different stop-start feeding action.

Knot – almost as big as Redshank, but much shorter legs. Bill shorter, sturdier than Dunlin's. Feeds over intertidal mud, often in tighter flocks than Dunlin. Distinctive, head-down 'creeping' feeding action. Picks, probes, ploughs.

Knot

Dunlin – smaller/slimmer than Knot, thinner bill.

Redshank – longer legs than Knot (and red!), plus longer, straighter bill.

Ruff – distinctive shallow wing-beats and glide in to land.

Dunlin – abundant prototype wader. Bill slightly decurved, especially drooping at tip; unfortunately of variable length (different races). Hunched look, head down. On intertidal mud/in pools. Often wades. Picks/probes with steady, non-stop action, also 'stitches'. Sociable, often in big flocks.

Ruff – weird, small-headed, lumpy wader of variable size (from Redshank [males] to Dunlin [females]) – seemingly designed by committee. Walks like pigeon, steady walk with slow pecks and few languid probes. Downcurved bill. Moves with hunched back and tail raised. Not at intertidal mud, mostly freshwater. Usually in small dispersed parties.

Ruff

Dunlin

Dunlin – variable bill length.

Little Stint

Little Stint – madly energetic, almost exhausting to watch. Tiny, short-legged, diagnostically short bill, which is straight, unlike that of Dunlin and Curlew Sandpiper. Usually picks from surface.

Curlew Sandpiper – noticeably fatter/longer necked than similar Dunlin, longer, more evenly curved 'Curlew' bill. Longer legs make it more elegant, allow it to wade deeper than others, except Ruff. Often with Dunlins and stints. Probes/picks. Small groups in west, often larger in east.

Curlew Sandpiper

Sanderling

Knot

Knot

Dunlin

Knot – long-winged profile is contrast to plump profile when walking.

Sanderling – larger/rounder bodied than Dunlin, shorter, straighter bill. Dashes along beaches, in/out of surf, as if powered by clockwork. No hind toe. Not often on mud. Fast action suggests Little Stint, but latter are smaller, with thinner bill. Picks from surface. In small flocks, up to 30.

Little Stint – displays with slow wing-beats and glides in flight.

Little Stint

Broad-billed Sandpiper – quite tame, crouches first before flying off.

Broad-billed Sandpiper – slightly smaller than Dunlin, longer, thicker bill, kinked at tip. Also shorter legs. Holds head further in front of body than others, looks front-heavy. Characteristic slow feeding action with deliberate vertical probes, especially unlike stints. Mainly in small numbers, often with stints. Prefers freshwater.

ESCAPE FLIGHTS

Temminck's Stint – birds rocket away, towering, in complete contrast to Little Stint.

Dunlin, Knot, Ruff and *Curlew Sandpiper* – wary, but fly away low.

Temminck's Stint – remarkable hovering display. Long wings/tail make it look horizontal. Markedly Common Sandpiper-like (*see* p111). Alone or in pairs, unlike sociable Little Stint. On sheltered pools, not coastal. Far more deliberate feeding than energetic Little Stint.

Purple Sandpiper, Sanderling – quite tame, allow fairly close approach and don't flush far.

Little Stint – also tame. In flocks of small waders, Little Stints often the first to return after they have been flushed.

Little Stint

Dunlin, Knot, Sanderling and *Purple Sandpiper* – winter in large numbers in Europe.
Ruff and *Little Stint* – winter in small numbers in Europe.
Broad-billed Sandpiper and *Temminck's Stint* – all leave Europe for winter.
Curlew Sandpiper – passage migrant only in Europe.

Temminck's Stint (*left*) – shorter legs than Little Stint, crouched posture/creeping feeding action.

Waders: Curlews and Godwits

Whimbrel – more erect posture than Curlew when standing.

Whimbrel – more often seen on rocky beaches than Curlew. Only bird on this page that tends to leave Europe in winter.

Whimbrel – unlike Curlew, does not need to run to take off. Much faster wing-beats than Curlew, almost like duck, with lighter action.

Whimbrel – smaller than Curlew (compare main picture below). Less sedate; moves around more, may run. Bill straight, kink at tip.

Whimbrel – more of surface feeder than Curlew, picking more. When probes, probes less deeply. Less inclined to wade.

Curlew – runs to take off. Slow, powerful wing-beats, almost like large gull.

Curlew – probes deeply in mud and seaweed, also picks from the surface. Often wades.

Females have longer bills.

Curlew – largest wader. Tall, stately, walks slowly over mud. Evenly-downcurved bill of variable length.

Curlew and *Whimbrel* – circling song-flights, the Whimbrel's much higher in the sky.

Black-tailed Godwit – erect and leggy – note distance between 'knee' and belly. Graceful walk, upright. Bill straight, neck held up.

Godwits – have 'switchback' display-flights.

Godwits – good fliers, with powerful, flickering wings.

Black-tailed Godwit – less on intertidal mud, more on upper reaches. Enters deep water, frequently submerging head – more so than Bar-tailed.

Breeding plumage

Bar-tailed Godwit – much more agile in flight than Black-tailed.

Bar-tailed Godwit – often feeds on intertidal mud, usually in tight flocks, probing with 'stitching' action. Wades, immerses less than Black-tailed.

Bar-tailed Godwit – much shorter legs, especially 'knee' to belly. Legs look too short for it, gait is somewhat awkward. Bill usually more curved than Black-tailed Godwit's (upwards).

Waders: Woodcock and Snipe

Snipe – display is high circling on rapid wing-beats. Makes bleating sound.

Jack Snipe – high switchback display-flights over Arctic tundra. Sounds like galloping horses.

Snipe – probes with long bill into muddy ground. Sewing machine-like, deep probing in semi-circle. Wades in water.

Great Snipe – several display together on ground, posturing.

Woodcock – in display flies in wide circle over treetops, irregular flickering wing-beats. Makes croak/loud squeak. Broad, rounded wings.

Jack Snipe – picks on mud surface. Rocks up and down as if on springs (as Woodcock). Much smaller than Snipe, shorter bill. Much harder to see, very furtive. Often crouches motionless.

Great Snipe – probes deeply in muddy ground, also found in drier places e.g. short turf. Slightly larger/plumper than Snipe, with proportionally shorter bill.

Woodcock – deep probes with long bill on woodland floor, mostly at night. Up and down rocking motion of rotund body.

Snipe – often feed in small groups. Others feed solitarily.

Snipe – flushes at about 10–15m, calling like squelch of kiss. Zigzags wildly away in panicky fashion, often towering high and landing some distance away.

Great Snipe – flushes at some distance (about 5m), without any mad zigzags of Snipe, silently. Gives lethargic impression, flops down suddenly at short distance.

Woodcock – flushes when observer is few metres away, silently but for swish of wing-beats. Twists away through trees.

Jack Snipe – flushes when observer very close, only metre or so away, silently. No hint of wild zigzagging. Goes short distance, then flops down suddenly.

Skuas

Long-tailed Skua – most adults light-coloured. Long tail-streamers, longer than width of wings. Long, narrow-based and pointed wings.

Arctic Skua (light phase) – much narrower base to wings than Pomarine, similar pointed 'hand'. Distance from behind wings to the tip of tail is slightly greater than width of wings.

Great Skua – broad arm, short 'hand', sometimes with almost rounded tip.

Great – all have much the same plumage. Very short tail, no obvious projection.

Arctic – flight lighter than that of Pomarine, less steady or determined, far more dashing. Usually migrates alone, tending to fly lower over sea than Pomarine.

Pomarine – almost all adults light-coloured. Tail projections spoon-shaped.

Herring gull (1st winter) – similar size to Great Skua, but less bulky. Wings longer, narrower-based, less pointed.

Pomarine (light phase) – broad 'arm', pointed 'hand'.

Artic – both light and dark phases common. Tail projections pointed.

Great – powerful, purposeful flight on steady course, shallow, consistent wing-beats. Looks menacing.

Arctic (dark phase) – about size of Kittiwake, therefore smaller/much less bulky than Pomarine, with slimmer tail.

Great – about size of Herring Gull. Big, heavy skua, chunky body, broad tail.

Pomarine (dark phase) – about size of Lesser Black-backed Gull. Larger/more bulky than Arctic, slighter than Great, longer tail. At distance may recall Great Skua; Arctic never does. Flight steady/measured, shallow wing-beats (recalls flight of Herring Gull). Glides less than Arctic, does not shear waves in manner of shearwater, which Arctic sometimes does. On migration (especially spring) often in small flocks, flying quite high over sea.

Long-tailed – about size of Black-headed Gull. Slim, slender, delicate, long tail.

Herring gull

Great Skua – only skua to chase Gannets, plus wide variety of other birds. Sneaks up low over sea, chases powerful, agile, aggressive. Often eats birds, especially Puffins.

Arctic Skua (juvenile) – chases auks, terns, smaller gulls. Twists/turns in impressive pursuit-flight, with exciting accelerations on flexed-back wings. Pursuits often sustained and terrier-like.

Arctic

Pomarine (juvenile, below) – chases larger species, including gulls/large shearwaters. Chases shorter than those of Arctic, with less twisting/turning. Often end violently, with death of victim.

Long-tailed Skua – chases terns mainly. Far less menacing than other skuas.

Sandwich Tern

Long-tailed (juvenile) – flight noticeably light/buoyant, almost like tern's. Body often rises/falls slightly with each wing-beat. Flaps more continuously than other skuas, and, on breeding grounds at least, is well able to hover. In strong winds, hugs waves and rocks from one side to the other. Often grabs food from water surface in mid-flight.

Great Shearwater

Arctic – in strong winds, often resorts to 'shearwatering', flapping then gliding low over sea.

Long-tailed – rounder head gives gentle expression, bill short/thick. Very slim body, but quite broad-chested, more so than Arctic.

Great Skuas attacking Kittiwake.

Great – larger head with longer bill than Pomarine. Barrel-shaped body, powerful head and neck, deep chest.

Arctic (dark phase) – longer, finer bill than Pomarine, less rounded head. Slimmer body than Great or Pomarine, flatter chest.

Pomarine – in common with Great Skua, often feeds on carrion (Arctic and Long-tailed seldom do.)

Pomarine (light phase) – head large, rounded. Powerful bill. Heavy, broad-bodied, barrel-chested.

Gulls: Types of Gull

Large *gulls* frequently soar very high on thermals and can look like birds of prey; but wings much thinner.

Herring Gull – large gulls. Masters of riding currents, soaring effortlessly even in strong winds. Can hold position in air.

Bird of prey (*Buzzard*).

Great Black-backed Gull – large gulls have powerful flight, with slow, deep wing-beats.

Large gulls often fly in close formation.

Gulls flying to roost often take up V-formation.

Great Skua (see pp116–17).

Black-headed Gull – smaller gulls fly with faster wing-beats, more agile in twisting/turning.

Common Gull – medium-sized gull, less predatory than larger gulls, but highly adaptable, taking live food, scraps, scavenging.

Black-headed – smaller gull. In flight the wings of small gulls bend back at 'elbow'. Black-headed take wide variety of foodstuffs, even insects.

Great Black-backed (several plumages) – larger gulls are heavy-bodied brutes, often catching live food, including other seabirds.

Little Gull – smallest gull, specialising in snatching flying insects at water surface.

Slender-billed Gull – tapered gull with long bill.

Black-headed – ubiquitous small gull.

Mediterranean Gull – smallish gull with blob-tipped bill.

Kittiwake – coastal, elegant.

Glaucous Gull – northern form of Great Black-backed.

Herring – abundant, coastal.

Little – smallest gull.

Audouin's Gull – rare.

Great Black-backed – dwarfs smaller gulls. Huge, dangerous bill.

Lesser Black-backed Gull – long winged and elegant.

Yellow-legged Gull – closely related to Herring.

Iceland – far northern gull, long-winged but heavy.

Ring-billed Gull – rare, larger relative of Common.

Common – friendly-faced.

Gulls: Herring and Yellow-legged Gulls

Herring Gull – North Atlantic, mainly breeding on coasts.

Yellow-legged Gull – Mediterranean/Eastern Europe. On western coasts, mainly cliffs and at sea. In east, by lakes and marshes.

Yellow-legged – larger than Herring, but slimmer, with longer legs, larger red spot on bill.

Yellow-legged Gulls always seem to look immaculate.

Yellow-legged – red or dark orange orbital ring, making pale iris more obvious.

Herring – yellow/pale orange orbital ring. Yellow/orange gape.

Herring – pink legs.

Yellow-legged – yellow legs.

Lesser Black-backed Gull – yellow legs but darker back. Slim with tapered rear end.

Lesser Black-backed

'Caspian Gull' of Eastern Europe – looks 'nosy', has longer bill with less sharp angle on lower mandible.

Herring (Western Europe)

Herring – 1st winter.

Yellow-legged – 1st winter.

Yellow-legged – wings generally longer/ narrower than those of Herring Gulls of Western Europe.

Gulls: Yellow-legged and Audouin's Gulls

Audouin's (juvenile) – short tail looks narrow.

Audouin's – very much a 'sea-gull', confined to Mediterranean/Atlantic coasts, often far out at sea. Very graceful flier.

Audouin's Gull – longer, narrower wings than Yellow-legged. Broad inner wing ('arm') but pointed wing-tips.

Yellow-legged Gull – broader, less pointed wings.

Audouin's – shorter bill, stubby-ended. Always looks dark in adults. Tends to look drooped.

Yellow-legged (juvenile) – plumper/longer-tailed than Audouin's.

Yellow-legged compact head.

Audouin's – wings slightly arched in flight, not in Yellow-legged.

Yellow-legged – yellow (adult) or flesh-coloured (immature) legs.

Audouin's – glides more than Yellow-legged, for longer. Gliding/wheeling can be reminiscent of Gannet.

Audouin's (3rd winter) – sloping forehead.

Yellow-legged – longer bill than Audouin's. Looks pale in adults.

Yellow-legged – bulkier than Audouin's, more ample rear end.

Audouin's – typically snatches fish from water surface.

Audouin's – compare how far feathering goes down bill.

Audouin's – dark eye/gently sloping forehead gives mild expression.

Yellow-legged – pale eye/ rounder forehead.

Audouin's (1st winter) – plunge-dives; other larger gulls don't.

Audouin's – black legs.

Audouin's – long-legged look. Daintier walk than Yellow-legged. Slightly smaller than Yellow-legged, more elegant/'refined'. Narrow wings give pointed rear end.

Gulls: Black-backed Gulls

Great Black-backed Gull – slow, lumbering flight action.

Lesser Black-backed – slender wings, elegant outline, long 'hand' to wing, pointed tip.

Lesser Black-backed Gull – smooth flying action, easy wing-beats.

Lesser Black-backed – always looks like gull.

Great Black-backed Gull – can look like heron.

Heron

Great Black-backed – long but broad wings, proportionately shorter 'hand', rounded tip.

Great Black-backed – 3rd winter.

Huge *Great Black-backed Gull* takes off with some effort.

Great Black-backed – body very bulky, with thick neck/deep chest. Long legs/horizontal stance.
Lesser Black-backed – much less bulky, slimmer, more elegant. Shortish legs and sloping stance.

Lesser Black-backed – much thinner bill with little angle.

Great Black-backed – massive, intimidating bill. Prominent angle on lower mandible ('gonydeal angle').

Great Black-backed – 2nd winter.

Lesser Black-backed

Great Black-backed – legs pink in all stages.

1st winter

Lesser Black-backed – legs of adults yellow (difference can be hard to see).

Great Black-backed – abrupt rear end.

Herring Gull – shape similar to Great Black-backed, size to Lesser.

Great Black-backed – usually about 25% larger than Lesser Black-backed.

Gulls: Glaucous and Iceland Gulls

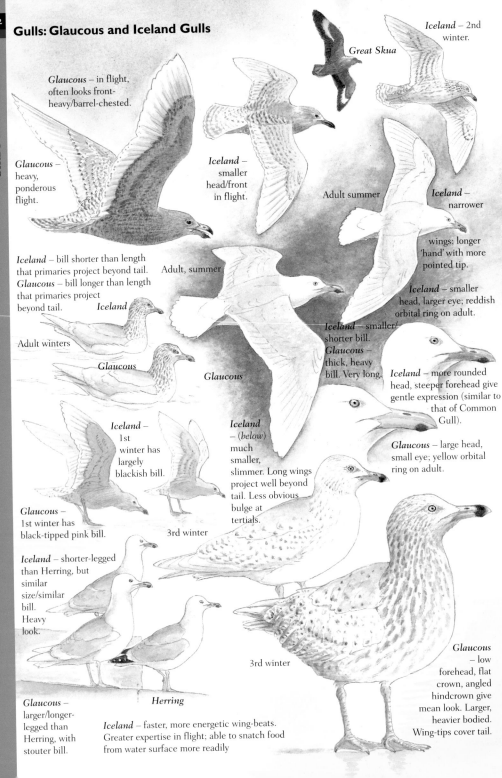

Iceland – 2nd winter.

Great Skua

Glaucous – in flight, often looks front-heavy/barrel-chested.

Glaucous – heavy, ponderous flight.

Iceland – smaller head/front in flight.

Adult summer

Iceland – narrower wings; longer 'hand' with more pointed tip.

Iceland – bill shorter than length that primaries project beyond tail.
Glaucous – bill longer than length that primaries project beyond tail.

Adult, summer

Iceland – smaller head, larger eye; reddish orbital ring on adult.

Iceland

Adult winters

Glaucous

Glaucous

Iceland – smaller/shorter bill.
Glaucous – thick, heavy bill. Very long.

Iceland – more rounded head, steeper forehead give gentle expression (similar to that of Common Gull).

Glaucous – large head, small eye; yellow orbital ring on adult.

Iceland – 1st winter has largely blackish bill.

Iceland – (below) much smaller, slimmer. Long wings project well beyond tail. Less obvious bulge at tertials.

Glaucous – 1st winter has black-tipped pink bill.

3rd winter

Iceland – shorter-legged than Herring, but similar size/similar bill. Heavy look.

3rd winter

Glaucous – larger/longer-legged than Herring, with stouter bill.

Herring

Iceland – faster, more energetic wing-beats. Greater expertise in flight; able to snatch food from water surface more readily

Glaucous – low forehead, flat crown, angled hindcrown give mean look. Larger, heavier bodied. Wing-tips cover tail.

Gulls: Common, Herring and Ring-billed Gulls

Herring Gull – large, heavily built gull, often with waddling footsteps. Pink legs. Fierce-looking thick bill. Yellow with red spot. Usually flatter head, giving slight frown. Pale yellow iris gives mean expression. Much larger than Common or Ring-billed.

Common Gull – small, elegant gull with dainty, free-moving footsteps. Yellowish/greyish legs.

Ring-billed Gull

Common – Upright head, long wings/body in elegant silhouette. Feeds more readily inland, especially on agricultural/playing fields. Short, slim bill, coloured yellow/greenish yellow. Round head. Doe-eyed, gentle expression.

Adult winters

Herring – larger bill. Pale eye.

Common – small bill. Dark eye.

Ring-billed – thicker bill than Common; parallel edges give it a curious look of always being slightly open. Pale eye.

Herring

Common

2nd winter

Herring – broad/heavy in flight.

Common – narrower wings than Herring, but with ample 'hand'. Fluent flier with deep fast wing-beats.

Herring – slower wing-beats than Common. Much more prone to soar and to hold arched wings to ride wind.

Ring-billed – broader-based wings than Common in flight.

1st winter

Ring-billed – stands more upright than Common, longer legs. Vigorous strutting walk, distinctively mobile.

Ring-billed – often has rather flat-backed look, especially on water.

Gulls: Mediterranean, Black-headed and Common Gulls

Black-headed Gull (*right*) – small, with red legs and bill. *Common Gull* (*below*) – larger and plumper than Black-headed, darker grey back, yellow/grey legs.

Adult winter

Common – more fluent flight and sweeping wing-beats than Black-headed.

Common – more ample, 'healthier-looking' wings.

Black-headed – slim body, very pointed, rather thin wings. Quick, at times flickering, wing-beats.

Common – larger-headed, shorter-necked. Shorter, blunter bill.

Black-headed – small head, long neck. Long, thin bill.

Common – flatter profile.

Black-headed – distinctly uptilted wing-tips on water.

1st winter

1st winter

Mediterranean Gull – distinctly broad/short wings compared to others.

1st winter

2nd winter

Mediterranean – confident, strutting walk on long legs. Black-headed – shorter legs, more tiptoeing walk.

Mediterranean – broad white wings may give similar appearance to Little Egret.

1st winter

Adult winter

Mediterranean – thicker bill.

Adult summer

Common

2nd winter

Mediterranean – slow, stiff, often shallow wing-beats; glides more than Common or Black-headed.

Common – full, smooth wing-beats.

Black-headed – small, slim, round-headed. Long, sharp bill.

Mediterranean – slightly larger, chunkier body than Black-headed, more angular head. Shorter, thicker bill very different. Distinct 'blob-tipped' look, visible even at distance.

Black-headed – deep, fast wing-beats.

Gulls: Kittiwake and Common, Little and Black-headed Gulls

Common Gull – frequent inland.

Kittiwake – confined to sea, very rare inland (usually after storms).

Common – 1st winter.

Common – slower wing-beats, more flexible than Kittiwake.

Common – broader/longer wings than Kittiwake. Yellow/greyish legs, depending on age/season.

Kittiwake – narrow wings, characteristically uniform in width. Black legs at all seasons/ages.

1st winter

Adult winter

Common Gull (*right*) – very horizontal stance. *Kittiwake* (*far right*) – distinctly 'sitting back on tail' stance (short legs), wing-tips often cross over tail (not in Common Gull).

Adult summer

Adults of both **Kittiwake** (*top, right*) and **Common Gull** (*top, left*) have characteristically gentle expressions.

Black-headed Gull

Little

Little Gull – neckless, short-legged.

Black-headed – pointed in outline, long-necked.

Black-headed

Little

Adult summer

Adult summer

Little

Little – feeds by snatching items from surface of water 'on the run'. **Black-headed** does this less continuously/expertly.

Black-headed (juvenile)

Little – distinctly short, rounded wings, blunt-ended.

Adult winter

Kittiwake – much larger, longer wings.

Little – tiny body, short wings.

Little – 1st winter Little Gulls have more pointed wings than adults.

Black-headed – adult winter (*above, in air*); adult summer (*above, on water*) – pointed wings.

Little – buoyant on water.

Little – agile, unpredictable flight-path, prone to jinking turns. Black-headed less agile, more predictable.

Gulls: Black-headed and Slender-billed Gulls

Black-headed Gull – iris dark. Eye centrally placed. Rounded forehead.

Slender-billed Gull – iris white. Eye appears to lie slightly to rear of head. More sloping forehead than Black-headed; feathering extends further on to base of bill. Name is misnomer. Bill longer than Black-headed, and, if anything, thicker.

Black-headed – very common, widespread. Often found inland.

Slender-billed – scarce/local. Mainly Mediterranean region, typically sticking to coast. Flocks often keep aloof from other gulls, sticking together.

Adult summer

1st winter

1st winter

Slender-billed – will spin around in water like Phalarope (not seen in Black-headed).

Slender-billed – very characteristic even appearance to front/rear. With neck stretched forwards, front/rear rise up at similar angle.

Slender-billed – sometimes swimming legs can be seen above water line (not in Black-headed).

Slender-billed – longer legs, giving bird front-heavy appearance. 'Anaemic' leg colour of 1st years.

Mediterranean Gull – much thicker bill, blob-like tip. Rounded forehead. 'Black eye' on head.

Black-headed – first-years have orange-yellow legs.

1st winter

1st winter

1st winter

1st winter

Slender-billed – commonly wades along water's edge, picking food from surf.

Slender-billed – obvious long-winged, hump-backed profile in flight. Like elongated Black-headed Gull with slower wing-beats.

Black-headed – pointed wings, quick flaps.

Mediterranean – short, broad, blunt wings.

Adult summer

1st winter

Slender-billed – longer wing than *Black-headed*, especially broader 'arm' (inner wing).

Black-headed

Slender-billed – tail long, rounded. Shorter in Black-headed.

Black-headed

Slender-billed – regularly plunge-dives into water like tern, much more often than Black-headed.

Gulls: Rare Gulls

Ross's Gull – High Arctic species of pack-ice. Feeds in delicate manner, snatching items from sea. Adult in summer unmistakable.

Ivory Gull – High Arctic species. Feeds around pack-ice on corpses of seals/whales, excrement of polar bears/other Arctic mammals. In flight, heavy-bodied with broad-based wings, sharply pointed. Strong/elegant action.

Ross's – very small gull, slightly larger than Little Gull, but shorter bill/distinctly plump breast.

Ross's – long tail/sharply pointed wings.

Ivory – juvenile

Ross's

Adult summer

Ivory (right) – on ground pigeon-like and plump. Very short black legs.

1st winter

Adult winter

Common Gull – similar size to Ivory.

Ivory – diagnostic bill colour.

Ivory (adult)

Ivory – 1st winter

Adult summer

Ross's

Ross's (adult summer)

Black-headed Gull

Sabine's Gull – another Arctic species, seen regularly in North Atlantic in autumn.

Sabine's (juvenile)

Ross's

Adult winter

Yellow-legged – shorter legs than Great Black-headed, often has waddling run.

Great Black-headed Gull – flat forecrown accentuates huge bill.

Sabine's (right) – distinctive bill pattern. Sunken head.

First Winter

Black-headed (adult winter)

Adult

Great Black-headed – bulging tertials. Slightly larger than Yellow-legged, but slimmer, noticeably long legs and quick run.

Adult

Sabine's – long, thin, pointed wings. Smaller than Black-headed. Keeps hood until October

Great Black-headed – breeds in European Russia, on steppes. Looks like huge hooded gull.

Great Black-headed – very long/slim wings, more bowed than other large gulls.

Yellow-legged – much smaller than Great Black-headed.

BIRDS BY BEHAVIOUR

Gulls: Breeding sites

Herring Gull – small to large colonies. Near clifftop.
Yellow-legged Gull – usually small colonies, always away from other gulls. Nests often close to/under bushes.

CLIFFS

Great Black-backed Gull – singly or small colonies. Inaccessible pinnacles. Fiercely predatory on fellow seabirds (eats Puffins, shearwaters etc.). Nest is large pile of seaweed etc.

Glaucous Gull – in far north. Usually singly, some loose colonies. Steep coastal cliffs. Often on pinnacle. Substantial nest.

Kittiwake (*below right*) – usually vast colonies on steep sea-cliffs. Commutes in group to bathe in freshwater nearby.

Lesser Black-backed Gull – on flat grassy areas on top of cliffs. Not singly; always in colonies, often large. Tends to avoid cliffs occupied by Herring Gulls.

Common Gull – grassy slopes.

ISLANDS Yellow-legged

Audouin's Gull – almost always on low rocky islands. Usually small, fairly scattered colonies of up to 20, also singly. Keeps away from colonies of other gulls.

Kittiwake – on cliffs.

Common – small rocky stacks.

MOORLAND

Black-headed Gull – lowland moors only.

Lesser Black-backed

Common – often nests far from water, more so than other gulls. Often near moorland lakes. On ground in vegetation. Well-dispersed nests. Usually small colonies.

SAND DUNES

Lesser Black-backed Gull – dunes. Flat, grassy areas. Often mixed colonies with Herring Gulls.

Herring Gull – sand dunes.

LAGOONS

Black-headed Gull

Mediterranean Gull

Slender-billed Gull – saline/freshwater lagoons. Small colonies in Western Europe, larger colonies in Eastern Europe. Densely packed/clumped. On ground in open, often on mud. Often among Gull-billed or Caspian Terns.

MARSHES

Black-headed – large, dense colonies, some inland, often on lake islands. Nest usually low vegetation.

Common Gull – nest often raised, e.g. on tree or boulder. Nests further apart than for Black-headed. Colonial.

BUILDINGS

Herring and locally *Lesser Black-backed Gull* on high roofs.

Great Black-headed Gull – steppe lakes. Small colonies, rarely mixing with other gulls.

Gulls: Gulls at sea

AN ATLANTIC COASTLINE IN AUTUMN

Kittiwake – wings often held straight out to look very parallel-edged.

Gannet

Black-headed Gull – pointed wing-tips. Buoyant flight.

Sabine's Gull – smaller than Kittiwake, lighter flight. Wings rise/fall well above/below body, in contrast to Kittiwake.

Sabine's – often dives into water to feed, in contrast to Kittiwake. Rare. Autumn.

Kittiwake – light/buoyant flight. Broader wings than Sabine's.

Little Gull – often flies in lines. Adults have rounded wing-tips. Tends to migrate in flocks.

Little – agile flight, fast, deep wing-beats, constant changes of direction, dips/turns, rather hesitant. Fluttering flight.

Ross's – very small gull, slightly larger than Little, shorter bill/distinctly plump breast.

Ross's Gull – longer tail than Little. Longer/more sharply-pointed wings than Little.

Common Gull – slower wing-beats than Kittiwake.

Kittiwake – fast wing-beats. Outer wing angled back in calm conditions.

Kittiwake – common around coasts any time of year.

Sabine's – in strong wind, shears, but less expertise than Kittiwake. Often dips down very low over water.

Sabine's – usually flies low over sea. Deep wing-beats, very like tern.

Black-headed – faster wing-beats into strong wind, wings close to body.

Herring Gull – strong flight; powerful, slow wing-beats. Sails/soars more than smaller gulls. Often in groups.

Common – in strong wind narrow wings sharply angled back, deep wing-beats. Outer wing looks long. Blunter ended than Black-headed.

Kittiwake – deeper wing-beats in strong wind. Much shearing, recalling shearwater.

Herring – flies powerfully into strong wind, deep wing-beats on usually steady course. Less manoeuvrable than small gulls, but sails effortlessly.

Gulls: Gulls vs Terns

Gulls – often glide and soar, wings motionless, for long periods.
Terns – keep flapping. Rarely glide for more than a few seconds.

Gulls – buoyant, effortless flight; slow, shallow wing-beats.

Terns – graceful, light flight, heavy wing-beats.

Terns – slender; narrow, pointed wings bent sharply backwards; usually strongly-forked, long tail.

Terns – frequently hover on the spot. *Gulls* don't.

Gulls – well-built, rotund; long wings, short square-ended tail.

Most *sea-terns* plunge-dive to catch fish, often from a hover. *Gulls* only occasionally plunge into water, looking inelegant.

TERN-LIKE GULLS

GULL-LIKE TERNS

Smaller gulls, such as *Black-headed Gull* (right of three), have quite narrow, pointed wings. Some have light, darting, jinking flight – beware *Little Gull* (centre), *Kittiwake* (left).

Gulls obtain much food from the ground, at rubbish dumps, fields etc. *Terns* avoid such places – catch most food while flying over water.

Caspian Tern (*left*) and *Gull-billed Tern* (*right*) fly heavily, show larger heads and thicker necks than other terns.

Gulls habitually swim on sea, *Terns* almost never do.

Terns do perch and walk, but don't walk far, preferring to fly.

Gulls are comfortable on land; run about a lot (longer legs than terns).

Gulls present throughout year in Europe. Terns only Mar–Oct.

Gulls have thick bills, often with angled-up lower mandible.

Terns thinner/more angular. Many have black caps.

Terns have long, sharp bills.

Terns: The flight of Terns

Sandwich Tern – distinctive 'head-down' patrol, long, flat crown. Looks very white. Regular, quite deep wing-beats. Wings obviously angled back.

Roseate Tern – faster, shallower wing-beats than Common or Arctic, like Little Tern.

Stiff-winged, equal emphasis on both strokes.

Arctic Tern – diagnostic. 'Step-hover', i.e. pauses between hovers, before final plunge from low height.

Roseate – brief whirring hover, then powerful angled dive, giving impression of simply 'flying into water', good splash/longer immersion than Common or Arctic.

Sandwich – short hover, sudden vertical dive, good splash.

Common Tern – usually good hover/confident vertical dive.

Little – often dives at very edge of water, in shallows, only from 3–6m above water. Makes good splash. Hovers quite long, sometimes 'step-hovers'. Regularly repeats several dives in quick succession.

Little Tern – characteristic flight, very rapid wing-beats, almost like wader in level flight. Butterfly-like. Very light/hyperactive.

Common (immature)

Arctic (adult non-breeding)

Sandwich

Arctic (immature)

Over freshwater, **Common Tern** often flies down to dip from surface and plunge-dive.

Whiskered Tern, Black Tern and **White-winged Black Tern** – occasionally do weak dives, but typically only dip down to take food from water.

Black (non-breeding)

Black Tern – light, buoyant, highly erratic flight. Often hovers over freshwater. Deeper/faster wing-beats than White-winged Black Tern.

White-winged Black – shallower wing-beats than Black give it less buoyant, slower flight. Hovers less.

White-winged Black (juvenile)

Gull-billed Tern – very white. Leisurely, languid flight. Shallow, stiff wing-beats, wings straighter out than other terns. Doesn't normally plunge-dive.

Gull-billed (adult)

Gull-billed (non-breeding)

Caspian Tern – huge tern, slow, strong wing-beats. Spectacular plunge-dives.

Caspian

Groups of **Common** and **Arctic Terns** work area of sea thoroughly. **Roseate Terns** (*see* p132) range more widely, longer distances between dives, individuals more scattered.

'*Marsh Terns*' (Black, White-winged Black or Whiskered) – often migrate over sea. Smaller/lighter than Common Terns, agile flight, more jinks from side to side. Never hover/dive, but pick from surface.

Whiskered (non-breeding)

White-winged Black (non-breeding)

Gull-billed – most likely species to be seen far from water, over grassy fields and even trees.

Black (immature)

Whiskered (juvenile)

Gull-billed (immature)

Whiskered Tern – steady flight at 5–10m over water, on long patrols. Less agile, jerky flight than Black or White-winged Black Terns. Doesn't hover.

Fishing *Sandwich Tern* often flies above sea at 10m or more, *Roseate Tern* at similar height (8–15m), **Common** and **Arctic Terns** 3–8m. *Sandwich Terns* often fish further out from shore.

Terns: 'Commic' and related Terns

Arctic Tern – from below, all primaries look translucent.

Common Tern – faster downstroke than Arctic, slower upstroke – upstroke slightly easier to see. *Arctic Tern* – faster upward 'snap' than Common, slower downstroke. More delicate, bouncy, flickering flight than Common.

Arctic Tern – narrowest wings of the three larger terns, perceptibly narrower than Common Tern's, give the impression of being placed slightly ahead of centre. Tail longer than that of Common.

Roseate Tern – looks white from below.

Common – from below, only the inner primaries, at bend of wing, look translucent.

Roseate – narrow wings look fairly centrally placed on body. Tail extremely long in adults.

Arctic – in comparison to Common, body rises and falls more with each wing-beat.

Common – broadest wings of the three, which look centrally placed. Tail shorter than Roseate or Arctic.

Little Tern – tiny, half the size of the others. Very narrow wings/short tail.

Common – inner wing ('arm') proportionally longer than Arctic, outer wing ('hand') shorter.

Arctic – 'arm' very short, allowing for long 'hand', which looks much more pointed, very slightly curved back.

Roseate – looks very white at all times, with long tail trailing behind, often ruffling in winds/often folded into spike.

Roseate – longest legs.

Roseate Tern – slightly smaller than Common, long-bodied/short-winged. Very long tail streamers.

Juveniles

Juvenile

Little Tern

Juvenile

Common Tern – longer legs, shorter tail, than Arctic.

Arctic Tern – tail streamers project well beyond wing-tip.

Arctic – head more rounded; bill shorter, blood-red.

Common – long, flattish head/bill. Bill usually red with black tip.

Little – bill yellow with black tip.

Roseate – flat head/very long bill. Bill all dark, or reddish at base.

Arctic – rounder head than Common, slimmer body/more elegant, streamlined look. Shorter legs than Common or Roseate, appears squat/legless.

Common – flatter head, more angular look than Arctic.

Roseate – coasts only; on beaches, usually on islands, often under tall vegetation.

Arctic – on coasts except in far north (small lakes on tundra). On islands etc., without vegetation (legs are too short for grass!).

Common – common breeder inland as well as coasts, on lakes, reservoirs etc. On shingle beaches, islands etc., often with a little vegetation.

ARRIVALS AND DEPARTURES

Arrival dates: *Common Tern* – Apr; *Little Tern* – Apr; *Arctic Tern* – late Apr; *Roseate Tern* – mid-May.

Roseate Tern – often leaves Europe as early as Aug.

Common Tern – often begins its moult July/Aug after breeding season. *Arctic Tern* begins moult much later, after it has left Europe.

Little – like Common, also inland as well as coasts, on large lakes/rivers. Colonies are more scattered than those of three larger species.

Terns: Caspian, Gull-billed and Sandwich Terns

Gull-billed Tern – broad-based wings, outer wing looks short; short, stout neck.

Sandwich Tern – looks very white. Front-heavy tern, wings set further back than on Common Tern, short tail.

Gull-billed – white-looking tern. Broad-based wings look forward set; short tail.

Caspian Tern – huge.

Sandwich – long, narrow wings. Looks slimmer than Gull-billed.

Common Tern

Sandwich – often arrives earlier than other terns in spring (Mar in Britain). A few even winter in Mediterranean.

Caspian – huge size (compare with Common). Distinctively large head/short tail.

Sandwich – flat head, with crest in breeding season. Long black bill with yellow tip 'dipped in paint'.

Gull-billed – rounded head, thick neck, no crest. Longer legs than Sandwich, looks more gull-like. Short, thick black bill.

Caspian – huge head, suggestion of a crest. Enormous, carrot-like red bill.

Caspian (juvenile/1st winter)

Sandwich (1st winter)   *Gull-billed* (1st winter)

Gull-billed – often near coast, also marshes/lakes well inland. In colonies, often on sand. Feeds on insects.

Caspian – mainly on sea, will migrate overland. Breeds in small colonies/singly on remote islands. Feeds on fish.

Sandwich – confined to sea, rare inland. Breeds in colonies on sandy/shingle islands/beaches. Feeds on fish.

Terns: Marsh Terns

White-winged Black – slightly blunter wings than Black.

White-winged Black Tern – slightly broader wings than Black.

Black Tern – narrowest wings.

Whiskered Tern – broadest wings of the three.

White-winged Black – non-breeding.

Black – tail-notch.

White-winged Black – shallow, barely visible tail-notch.

Black – non-breeding.

Whiskered – slightly larger/sturdier than other marsh terns.

Whiskered – tail-notch.

White-winged Black – alights on water/wades more frequently than Black.

Black Tern – hovers more readily than White-winged Black or Whiskered.

Whiskered – non-breeding.

Black – breeding.

White-winged Black – breeding.

Black – long, sharp black bill.

Whiskered – breeding.

Whiskered – largest marsh tern; long legs/thick red bill.

Black and *Whiskered Terns* arrive Apr, breeding on marshes with floating vegetation. *White-winged Black Tern* arrives in May, often found on smaller pools than Black, in more transitional habitats such as floodlands. More easterly.

White-winged Black (top of three) – shorter bill/round head gives appealing expression.

Auks

Razorbill – wings set centrally. Front-heavy profile. Faster wing-beats than Guillemot.

Guillemot – wings set ahead of centre. Pointed profile.

Puffin – wings set far back. Fatter, more compact than Razorbill or Guillemot, very large head.

Razorbill – bill inclined upwards in flight. Straighter back than Guillemot, holds head/tail higher. Long tail cloaks feet, giving pointed end.

Guillemot – bill held straight out in flight; 'hunch-backed'. Feet project beyond tail, giving stubby end.

Brünnich's Guillemot – bill inclined downwards in flight. Slightly longer wings than Guillemot, more hunch-backed.

Black Guillemot – pot-bellied. Very fast wing-beats, very low over water. Pointed tail can be slightly raised.

Little Auk – tiny size and fast wing-beats make flocks look like Starlings or waders. Long, narrow wings.

Red-throated Diver – non-breeding.

Black Guillemot – sits high on water. Pot-bellied, thick neck, small head. Singly/small parties. Least sociable.

Black Guillemot – breeding.

Non-breeding

Guillemot

Razorbill – long tail distinctly cocked.

Puffin – high on water like cork. Much smaller than Guillemot/ Razorbill.

Guillemot – long-bodied. Non-breeding.

Little Auk – tiny auk, only Starling-sized, half size of Puffin. Often floats very low in water, with wings drooped in.

Non-breeding

Guillemot – tail rounded and not very obvious.

Little Auk – non-breeding.

Razorbill – smaller than Guillemot. Non-breeding.

Non-breeding

Brünnich's Guillemot (not illustrated) – thicker bill/neck than Guillemot. More stocky build/slightly larger than Guillemot. Shorter tail than Razorbill, often cocked.

Razorbill – distinctive blade-like bill, thick neck. Bill always looks much thicker than Guillemot's or Brünnich's Guillemot's.

Puffin – huge bill. Outer sheath shed in winter (*right*), but still very broad then.

Guillemot – sharp, pointed bill.

Brünnich's Guillemot – thicker bill than Guillemot. Upward angle to tip of lower mandible (gonydeal angle). Thicker neck, steeper forehead.

Little Auk – hardly any bill at all!

Puffin – grassy slopes on clifftops, in burrows that it often makes itself.

Razorbill – broad ledges, scattered.

Guillemot – birds meeting at nest-site clash bills in 'mutual fencing' display, and perform 'sky-pointing'.
Brünnich's Guillemot – does not perform these displays.

Guillemot – remarkably densely packed narrow cliff-ledges.

Brünnich's Guillemot – narrower steeper ledges than Guillemot, not on flat surfaces. Birds more spaced, little body contact. Arctic only.

Razorbill – departure from breeding cliff: spreads wings and tail, makes irregular wing-beats to glide down to sea.
Guillemot – departure from breeding cliff: plummets down.

Little Auk – High Arctic only. Nests in various crevices/scree slopes. Colonies enormous.

Black Guillemot – among boulders near water, often at bottom of cliffs.

Black Guillemot – sharp, pointed bill.

Sandgrouse

Sandgrouse flock – often flies higher than other birds, almost out of sight. Commuting flocks visit water sources early morning. Essentially birds of arid places/deserts.

Pigeon flock – short, thick tails. Broader, less-pointed wings than sandgrouse. Often loosely packed.

Golden Plover flock – more obvious heads, short tails.

Slimmer than sandgrouse. Glide.

Pin-tailed Sandgrouse – strictly lowland bird, living in sandy places, e.g. dried-out watercourses. Avoids places with too much grass or rock.

Black-bellied Sandgrouse – mainly bird of steppes/plains. Ascends to much higher elevations than lowland Pin-tailed. Tolerates wild and undisturbed stony/grassy habitat.

Pin-tailed – smaller/slimmer than Black-bellied.

Pin-tailed – birds arriving at water often land in shallows and swim (not seen in Black-bellied).

Black-bellied

Black-bellied – small groups (max 25). Arrives at watering places 15 minutes later than Pin-tailed (3 hours after dawn).

Sandgrouse – often run along ground surprisingly fast, heads up above vegetation.

Pin-tailed

Pin-tailed

Pin-tailed

Black-bellied

Black-bellied – large, sturdy, broad-winged. Fast wing-beats, but slower than Pin-tailed.

Pin-tailed – often huge groups, especially at water. Thousands may gather excitedly, performing aerial manoeuvres similar to Starlings. This behaviour not seen in Black-bellied.

Cuckoos

Cuckoo – medium-sized; small head. Pointed wings.

Great Spotted Cuckoo – larger, with crest. Wings broader/less pointed than Cuckoo's. More tail-heavy, especially when landing.

Cuckoo

Cuckoo – female of brown type.

IDENTIFYING CUCKOOS
Medium-sized, with pointed wings and long tail. Wing-beats fast; wings don't appear to be raised above horizontal. Almost always keep low in flight. Usually alone or (Great Spotted) in pairs. Do not form flocks.

Kestrel (female) – broader head.

Nightjar – broader head, nocturnal.

Cuckoo (juvenile)

Cuckoo – often mobbed by small birds. Wide range of small hosts (here, shown right, Reed Warbler).

Jay – short tail.

Magpie – shorter wings.

Great Spotted Cuckoo – more prone to feeding on ground than Cuckoo. Raises tail while hopping. Both eat large insects, including hairy caterpillars.

Great Spotted Cuckoo – often detected by clamour of Magpies, its favourite hosts, or Jays/various crows. In contrast to Cuckoo, host often raises chick alongside own brood.

Great Spotted Cuckoo – cackling sounds, at times almost like gobbling of turkey. Unlike Cuckoo, has display-flight, in which it ascends silently from a tree, and glides down.

Cuckoo – often sings from wire or treetop, and in level flight.

Pigeon-like birds

Kestrel

Collared Doves

Carrion Crows

Cuckoo

Pigeons – compact birds, plump body/small head. Tail fairly long.

Collared Doves

Sparrowhawk – not often seen perched in open, but assumes much more upright posture than Pigeon/Cuckoo. Head much larger/legs much longer. Doesn't sit on wires.

Carrion Crow – large head/bill. Being of similar size, Crows/Pigeons can be easily confused in silhouette, but Crows have larger head, heavier bill, longer legs.

Roller – quite pigeon-like in silhouette, but larger head/more prominent bill.

Cuckoo – characteristic posture with wings drooped/tail held up.

Kestrel – large head/characteristic hunched, 'fed up' posture. Slim, compact, more upright than Pigeon/Cuckoo. In contrast to Sparrowhawk, often perches on wires.

Cuckoo – slim, long body. Less 'chesty' than Pigeon, longer wings/tail.

Nightjar – uniquely, usually sits along branch. Huge head, minute bill.

Pigeons – medium-sized birds with pointed, slightly swept-back wings/long tails.

Pigeons – fly with regular wing-beats, or (Doves, *right*) 'flicking' action. Take off with clattering of wings and, when landing, often raise tail up slowly before lowering it. Flight is fast and usually on straight course.

Sparrowhawk – flies with distinctive 'flap-flap-glide' style, few full wing-beats followed by glide. Impression of greater power/momentum than Kestrel, Cuckoo or Pigeon.

Kestrel – very flappy/stiff, shallow wing-beats, wings definitely rise well above horizontal, unlike Cuckoo. Wings much longer/more pointed than Pigeon's.

Cuckoo – medium-sized with narrow, sharply pointed wings, long, pointed tail, longer than Pigeon.

Jackdaw – shape/size very similar to Pigeon, but larger head/broader wings, with 'fingers' showing slightly. Wings beat at same rate as Pigeon, so flight very similar. Jackdaw will often glide/soar; Pigeons don't.

Cuckoo – regular wing-beats; wings seem to be beaten only below horizontal. Head/bill seem to be held upwards; veers slightly as if uncertain of where to go.

Carrion Crow – larger/broader-winged than Pigeon/Jackdaw; 'fingers' obvious.

Nightjar – quite similar in silhouette to Kestrel or Cuckoo, but has rather large head/different manner of flight.

Carrion Crow – very lazy flight with slow, deliberate wing-beats. Regularly soars/glides.

Jay – of Pigeon size but with very distinctive fluttering wing-beats with unstable feel, swoops and undulations as it lands.

Pigeons and Doves

Stock Dove – usually in pairs/small parties. Will feed in flocks in winter, often with Woodpigeons. Very shy, flies off when people approach.

Woodpigeon – big/portly, with 'beer gut'. Waddling walk. Eyes lemon yellow.

Longer tail than other grey pigeons/doves.

Woodpigeon, Feral Pigeon and *Collared Dove* – when living in company with humans can be absurdly tame.

Stock Dove – compact, with delicate mien of dove. Black eyes. When walking, tail points towards ground.

Feral Pigeon – compact/slightly plumper than Stock Dove, slightly more horizontal stance. Red eyes. Often in tight parties of medium size. Typically each party holds birds with different plumage patterns (diagnostic of Feral Pigeon).

Turtle Dove – very shy. Difficult to see at all. Often visible on wires, but only at a distance.

Collared Dove – pale, long-tailed. Fond of walking. Flocks in winter, usually near grain silos.

Collared Dove – in towns/gardens, thriving in patchwork of habitats made by people. Nests in trees/bushes, usually placing structure close to trunk.

Turtle Dove – alone among our pigeons, exclusively summer visitor, only seen Apr–Sept.

Woodpigeon – almost anywhere, but particularly farmland. Builds stick nest, often at end of branch.

Rock Dove – coastal cliffs, breeding in caves. Also in mountains.

Stock Dove – wooded areas with mature trees, especially oaks. Nests in holes in trees.

Turtle Dove – in open country, dense hedgerows/open woods with good undergrowth. Nests in large bush.

Feral Pigeon – towns/cities, nesting on ledges, bridges; many-plumaged domesticated form of Rock Dove (same species).

Stock Dove – in display glides around treetops, often in wide circle, starting with soft wing-claps and holding wings up at shallow angle.

Feral Pigeon/Rock Dove – similar flight to Woodpigeon, but faster wing-beats. Wings angle back. Constant wing-flaps.

Feral Pigeon – in display makes short glides away from nesting ledges, clapping wings as it begins, then holding them up in V shape.

Stock Dove – far more compact than Woodpigeon, shorter tail/'stubby' wings. Wing-beats often come in bursts, giving 'flickering' effect.

Woodpigeon – in display, without veering left/right, flies steeply upwards, claps wings loudly, then glides downwards with wings/tail spread.

Woodpigeon – powerful flight on straight course, with constant wing-beats that do not give 'flickering' effect. Slower/'looser' wing-beats than other pigeons, and longer tail.

Collared Dove – slim/long-tailed in flight. Wing-beats come in erratic bursts, giving 'flickering' effect.

Collared Dove – in display flies up from elevated perch, often a rooftop aerial, then glides downwards with wings/tail spread, often in a spiral. Sometimes makes soft wing-claps during ascent.

Turtle Dove – display closely resembles that of Collared Dove, but is more given to wing-clapping on ascent.

Turtle Dove – migrates in small flocks, low down.

Turtle Dove – similar to Collared Dove in flight, but looks shorter-tailed. On longer flights will often pitch from side to side, which is very characteristic. Spreads tail up on landing to show 'necklace of white pearls'.

Collared Dove – only pigeon/dove with a special call made upon landing, a 'kree-ar' sounding like a party trumpet.

Owls: Large Owls

Snowy Owl – huge/very distinctive, whitish body, feathered feet. Usually perches on ground, with horizontal posture. Tends to sit on lookout rock, blending in with surroundings.

Snowy – eyes yellow. Expression can be a little dopey.

Eagle Owl – Europe's largest owl, much larger than Buzzard. Huge/barrel-shaped, large head/short tail. Only large owl with ear-tufts (completely dwarfs superficially similar Long-eared Owl).

Male

Female

Snowy – watches from ground/ elevated rock, then flies on to prey, which may be 700m away. Mainly lemmings/voles. May also catch birds after aerial chase.

Eagle Owl – ear-tufts indicate emotional state. Raised when bird excited.

Great Grey Owl – huge (length of Eagle Owl) with enormous rounded head, very long wings/ longish tail, much slimmer than Eagle Owl. Eyes yellow, expression 'grand'. Facial disc has pattern like growth rings on tree trunk

Eagle Owl – seen from side, face doesn't look flat as on most owls. Eyes orange, giving cat-like expression.

Great Grey – feeds mainly on voles. Perches 1–4m above ground, on post/bush, drops on to prey. Can detect voles under snow, trick also perfected by other northern owls.

Eagle Owl – probably hunts mostly by dropping from perch. Feeds on variety of prey, including birds.

Ural Owl – eyes small/black, bill yellow. Expression variously described as blank, peaceful or 'nun-like'.

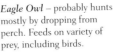

Ural – only slightly smaller than Great Grey, smaller, more rounded head, shorter wings/longer tail. Takes small mammals/birds by dropping from perch on to prey below.

Ural – much resembles Tawny Owl, but washed-out version, half as large again.

Great Grey Owl – flight so slow as to recall Heron, with characteristic long glides. Longer wings but shorter tail than Ural Owl.

Eagle Owl – wings broad/rounded. Flies with unexpectedly fast, shallow wing-beats, interspersed with straight glides on arched wings. Gives impression of power/stability. When disturbed during day, sometimes soars high into the sky. May look like Buzzard.

Ural Owl – wings broad/tail noticeably long/wedge-shaped. Flight Buzzard-like, with flaps/steady, sustained glides.

Snowy Owl – huge, with round face/horizontal posture. Flight powerful/ direct. Most pointed wings of any owl, with long 'hand'. Flight with rapid, deep wing-beats, often very agile.

Barn Owl – far smaller, with heart-shaped face/upright, long-legged posture. Flight delicate/wavering.

Snowy – found on Arctic tundra, breeding on ground, usually on raised hummock – needs good view all around. Movements dictated by food, so is unpredictable in appearance and does not breed every year.

Great Grey – seen from side, face flat. Shape said to resemble ship's funnel.

Great Grey – breeds in mature, dense forests of pine/fir, far into Arctic, hunting in glades/ adjoining moorland. Mainly resident. Lays eggs in old raptor's nest, typically that of Goshawk.

Ural – breeds mainly in open forests with tall trees, glades, usually moist areas/open water (wetter/more open places than Great Grey). In north, mainly among conifer forests, but also in Central and Southern Europe in montane deciduous forests, especially beech. Resident. Nest in tree-hole, tree stump, old raptor's nest.

Eagle Owl – wilderness areas throughout Europe, including mountains, rocky valleys, large forests, especially coniferous. Resident/needs huge territory. Nest usually on cliff-ledge.

Owls: Smaller Owls

Little Owl – fairly small, squat, long-legged owl, with broad, rounded head. Proportionally smaller head than Tengmalm's, shorter tail. Yellow eyes, 'frowning'/scowling expression. Easy owl to see. Often perches during day in open (e.g. on fence post); commonly flies from one perch to next. When excited, bobs up and down.

Little – typical hunting method of sitting on perch and dropping on to prey below, but also hunts on ground, running and hopping along seeking beetles/ earthworms.

Little – quite a catholic diet, including small mammals, birds, frogs and insects.

Scops Owl – yellow eyes, milder expression than other small owls.

Pygmy Owl – very small, equivalent in size to Hawfinch/ Starling; by far the smallest owl. Has proportionally smaller/rounder head than Tengmalm's. Often perches in treetop in broad daylight. Jerks tail up and down/from side to side.

Pygmy – yellow eyes, rather 'stern' expression.

Hawk Owl – head shape/pattern resembles Tengmalm's, but much larger bird, with longer tail.

Tengmalm's Owl – yellow eyes, unmistakable 'astonished' expression.

Scops – very small, thrush-sized owl, smaller/much slimmer than Little Owl. Head proportionally large. Horn-like ear-tufts can be difficult to see, but give head more squared-off look than Little Owl. Mostly hunts by perch and pounce, also sometimes catches moths in its feet in flight. Mainly feeds on insects (hence summer visitor to Europe).

Tengmalm's – feeds by waiting on perch, on average 1.7m above ground, before pouncing on to prey on the ground. Can feed in clearings or within dense forest, mainly on small mammals. Fairly small owl, noticeably large, squared-off head. Longer tail than Little Owl.

Tengmalm's – most young of smaller owls resemble adults, but Tengmalm's young are very different, sooty-brown.

Tengmalm's – tends to hide in thick canopy of spruce tree during day; difficult to see.

Little Owl – typical of open areas with scattered mature trees, also rocky places. Avoids forests, requires short turf/soil for feeding. Nest is hole in tree, wall, rocky outcrop, building.

Scops Owl – owl of open woodland, relies on clumps of trees mixed with open areas. Often in farmland, gardens, towns, but not attracted to rocky places like Little Owl is. Nest in hole in building or tree. Mainly summer migrant, Feb–Oct.

Scops – very difficult to see. Doesn't perch readily in open during day, hides away in shaded spot.

Scops – when discovered by day, changes posture, becomes taller/thinner, with more obvious ear tufts/squinting eyes.

Little – rounded wings, flies with bursts of wing-beats/glides, producing bounding action, always low over ground.

Scops – longer wings than other small owls. Flight action completely different to Little Owl, with hardly any undulation, if at all.

Tengmalm's Owl – rounded wings. Flight resembles Tawny, not Little Owl, with bursts of quick wing-beats interspersed with straight glides.

Pygmy Owl – more pointed wings, narrow tail. Flight very distinctive, bounding up/down like Woodpecker's, often quite high up. Flight changes to fast/direct when chasing prey.

Pygmy – sometimes feeds by waiting on perch/pouncing on to mammals on ground. Ambushes birds in air, striking from below. Often hunts at bird tables. Feeds on small mammals and birds up to, or greater than, own size.

Pygmy – in tall forests, especially of fir, preferably with access to clearings, moorland, water. Mainly resident. Also in mountain regions in Central Europe. Nest in hole, usually Great Spotted Woodpecker's.

Tengmalm's – in dense forests, especially spruce, without too much open ground. Perfectly able to hunt both within dense growth and in clearings. Mainly resident. Also found in mountain regions south to Pyrénées. Nests in a hole, usually old one made by Black Woodpecker.

Owls: Medium-sized Owls

Tawny Owl – roosts in hole or along branch near trunk, often high above ground, especially where there is cover.

Tawny – size of Crow. Bulky owl, large, rounded head, short tail, broad wings. Black eyes, 'wise' or 'kindly' expression. Commonest owl in cities/gardens, requiring large trees (with holes) to thrive. Also found in woods/parks. Needs plenty of lookout posts/clearings. Nest in hole in tree.

Short-eared – about size of Tawny, more lengthy/less compact, very long wings. 'Ears' seldom visible. Smaller head than Long-eared or Tawny. Posture usually horizontal.

Long-eared Owl – smaller than Tawny, slimmer-looking, much longer wings. 'Ears' are not always apparent; when bird relaxed are barely visible. Has larger head than Short-eared. Posture usually upright. Orange eyes, cat-like expression. Needs areas where open spaces abut woodland/forest, including copses in farmland. Lays eggs in old Crow's nest in tree.

Short-eared Owl – yellow eyes, glaring expression.

Long-eared – roosts in thick trees, usually just 2–4m above ground. In winter, several may roost together.

Short-eared – open country species, avoiding trees. Most at home in moorland/bogs. Nest on ground.

Hawk Owl – yellow eyes, 'demented' expression.

Hawk Owl – smaller than Tawny or Long-/Short-eared Owls, with distinctive shape. Much the longest tail of any owl, and most pointed wings. Large, flat-crowned head.

Barn Owl – small black eyes, soft expression.

Barn – size of Tawny, but ghostly-white. Very slim body, large rounded head with heart-shaped face, very long legs. Posture very upright. In farmland/pasture areas, also marshes. Nest usually in building (or tree-hole).

Hawk Owl – on forest edge, open forest/mountains, where trees begin to peter out. Often by burnt areas, large clearings/bogs. Unpredictable in appearance, almost absent in some years, depending on food. Nests usually in a tree-hole, on top of stump, or abandoned nest of raptor.

Tawny Owl – flies straight, direct/fast, strong, quick wing-beats interspersed with long glides, wings slightly bowed. Often flies higher than other owls. Flight action lacks flapping, tilting, wavering style of Long-eared, Short-eared and Barn Owls.

Tawny – wings broad and rounded.

Tawny – main feeding method is to wait on perch/dive down on to prey. Bird stays on each perch for few minutes before moving on to next lookout.

Long-eared Owl – wings broad/long. Slightly shorter/more rounded than Short-eared.

Long-eared – flight slow/leisurely, not purposeful as Tawny. Bird not following straight course but continually banking from side to side. Body rises and falls slightly with each flap.

Tawny and *Barn Owls* are resident. *Long-eared* and *Short-eared Owls* evacuate northern parts of range in winter. Small parties of both species may be seen in open, even flying over sea.

Short-eared – roosts on ground, often in groups.

Short-eared Owl – wings narrower/longer than Long-eared, although hard to see. Usually held further forward, which can be readily apparent.

Short-eared – flight similar to Long-eared, slow/leisurely with frequent turns/glides, obvious 'rowing' action. Flight more unstable-looking than Long-eared, with more wavering. In contrast to Long-eared, often momentarily holds wings in shallow V.

Hawk Owl – wings very pointed.

Hawk Owl – main feeding method is similar to Tawny. Can also hover before striking.

Sparrowhawk – smaller head obvious.

Sparrowhawk – slimmer, with smaller head. Doesn't often perch conspicuously on treetop.

Hawk Owl – flight usually hawk-like, bursts of quick wing-beats interspersed with glides on straight course. Flight far more swift/agile than other owls when required.

Hawk Owl – size/long tail gives hawk-like shape, especially at distance. Habitually perches in open on treetop.

Barn Owl – flight similar to Long-/Short-eared Owls, slow, buoyant, wavering action, changes of height, side-slips, glides, hovers. Legs often dangle (diagnostic – unlike other owls). Wings longer than Tawny.

Owls: Day or night?

CREPUSCULAR OWLS

These species are most active in hours of twilight, around dusk/at dawn, so are easier to see than truly nocturnal owls.

Tawny Owl (occasionally hunts by day when young in the nest).

Great Grey Owl (sometimes hunts throughout day).

Barn Owl

Owls sometimes discovered at daytime roosts by small birds, which gang together to harass/scold them.

Ural Owl

DIURNAL OWL

Mainly active during the day.

Scops Owl

Hawk Owl

Short-eared Owl

Long-eared Owl

Snowy Owl

STRICTLY NOCTURNAL OWLS

These species are only active at night, hunting between dusk and dawn. By day remain concealed at roost site.

Tengmalm's Owl

Pygmy Owl

Eagle Owl

Little Owl (but often moves around by day).

Nightjars

General notes: active at night, usually late dusk to dawn. Occasionally flushed from ground by day. Usually seen flying in twilight.

Nightjar – deep wing-beats, jinks, turns, spells of hovering. Glide with wings held in V. Long, pointed wings, long tail. Catch flying insects, like nocturnal swallow. Usually fly low in darkness.

Cuckoo – similar size, but shallow wing-beats, only obvious below body-line. Doesn't jink/hover.

Large head with tiny bill.

Nest and roost on the ground.

Often perch *along*, not across branches, particularly at end of dead branch.

European Nightjar – sandy habitats, including heathland, especially with pine trees.

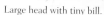

Red-necked Nightjar (below) – slightly larger than Nightjar, with proportionally larger head. Tail looks slightly longer. Tendency to feed on ground more often than Nightjar.

Red-necked Nightjar – often among stone-pines, but similar sandy habitats to Nightjar.

Red-necked Nightjar – larger size/longer tail than Nightjar. Flight said to be more powerful, with more swooping/fewer twists and turns.

European Nightjar – flight full of twists, turns, hovers.

Aerial birds

Bee-eater – often flies very high.

Bee-eater – flight like House Martin's, quick, fluttering wing-beats followed by glide. Often seems to stall.

Bee-eater – long pointed wings/very long tail, with pin-like projections.

Hobby – famous for resembling Swift when far off; similarity is striking. Very much giant slow-motion Swift, with slower movements, giving more of a sensation of power. Tail unforked.

Swift – manner of flight includes a long sweep and strange flutters that make it look as though each wing is beaten out of sync with other. Wing-beats often look a little stiff.

Swift – shape is like sickle. Wings long/pointed/narrow. See how narrow wings are where join body.

Greenfinch – song-flight in spring/summer has distinctly Swallow-like style. Flies in wide sweep with fluent wing-beats, but soon lands on tree/aerial.

Swallows and *Martins* often perch on wires. If bird can be seen to land, it's not a Swift!

Starling – often take to the skies to catch aerial insects on summer days. Fluttering flight can recall Swallow or Martin, but triangular wings are distinctive.

Martin – shape more compact than Swift or Swallow. Wings broad-based/stubby, tail shorter. Fly in small arcs, not sweeps, with distinctly fluttering wing-beats; flight lacking power of Swift.

Swallow – manner of flight includes Swift-like sweeps, but usually just above ground, much lower than Swifts normally fly (except in cloudy/damp weather). Flight far more fluent than Swift, with deeper wing-beats.

Swallow – shape is long/streamlined. Wings much broader than Swift, and less pointed. Wings broad where meet body.

Swifts

Alpine Swift – especially in mountains, but also some lowland towns.

Alpine – usually flies higher than others. Can cover vast distances (up to 1000km a day), at great range of heights.

Pallid Swift – also in mountains in Italy, Switzerland and Bulgaria.

Common Swift – flickering flight with incredibly fast wing-beats, some glides.

Pallid – slightly slower wing-beats than Common Swift, more glides.

Common – angular, slim.

Alpine – powerful and dynamic. Noticeably slower, deeper wing-beats than others, individually discernible.

Pallid – blunter wing-tips surprisingly obvious. Blunter tail with shallower fork. Broader head/neck. Looks heavier.

Common – breed far inland, often towns/urban settings. To breed, often select high buildings e.g. church towers.

Pallid – strongly associated with coast. Often replace Common Swift in coastal Mediterranean, in towns and sea-cliffs.

Alpine – 1½ x size of Common Swift.

Common Swift – short visit, May–Aug.
Pallid Swift – much longer, Apr–Nov.
Alpine Swift – Apr–Sept.

Common and *Pallid Swifts* indulge in crazy, screaming chases around buildings. *Alpine Swifts* avoid air-space with too many obstructions – fly higher.

White-rumped Swift

White-rumped – is rare breeder in some Spanish mountains. Arrives late in May, takes over Red-rumped Swallow nests. Long, forked tail, can be closed to make spike. Often with Swallows and Martins.

Colourful birds

Kingfisher – fast flight over river for long distances. Slow-flowing rivers.

Kingfisher – often hovers.

Dipper – similar fast flight. Darker. Fast-flowing rivers, with rapids.

Kingfisher – dives into river or lake with splash.

Kingfisher – very small, plump. Large head, dagger-like bill, short tail. Perches over river, head inclined down. Bobs head to judge distance. Tail bobs as if attached to head by string.

Hoopoe – crest can be raised, looks amazing!

Hoopoe – in country with plenty of bushes/trees mixed with open turf for feeding. Quite small, size of large thrush. Feeds on ground, probing with bill. Easily overlooked.

Hoopoe – flies like giant moth, with unsteady wing-beats, usually very low.

Jay – larger, no crest.

Bee-eater – long tail with central spike. Often perches on wires.

Roller – size of small crow. Large head, very thick bill.

Bee-eater – needs riverbanks/sandy banks for nesting, so usually found near rivers. Breeds in colonies. Sociable, in flocks, usually seen flying.

Roller – lives in dry open country in hot climates, needs large trees for nesting. Summer visitor. Scarce in west, commoner in east.

Roller – flight slow but strong, slightly clipped wing-beats. Spectacular 'rolling' flight display, with swoops, twists, turns.

Roller – perches prominently e.g. on wire/telegraph pole/dead tree. Flies down to seize food; returns to perch.

Rose-ringed Parakeet – very short, hooked bill.

Small, highly mobile bird with pointed wings/long tail. Loud screeching accompanies every move. Highly sociable, roosting in huge groups/foraging in small groups.

In parks/gardens. Introduced to some parts of Europe, including Britain.

Woodpeckers: Black and Green Woodpeckers and Wryneck

All these species feed mainly on ants; all are seen on ground more often than other woodpeckers.

Black Woodpecker – feeds on ground and at rotten tree stumps.

Black – crow-sized. Flight not up and down, but on straight, unsteady course, head held up. Similar to Jay. 1–2 bursts of wings to keep bird up. More woodpecker-like on landing.

Black – characteristic thin-necked look. Holds head right back away from trunk. Hacks at branches/stumps.

Green – large head, thin neck, long bill. Doesn't hack, only taps at wood.

Green Woodpecker – smaller than Black. Characteristic up-and-down, bounding flight, usually on course just above ground. Each upward sweep is powered by 3 or 4 rapid wing-beats, on downward sweep wings are closed. Sweeps upwards when landing.

Wryneck – small, heavy-tailed, spiky billed. Can cling to trees like other woodpeckers, but more often perches across branch, like perching bird. Weak tapping at most.

Green – feeds mostly on ground, digging out anthills.

Wryneck – weak, hesitant, slightly undulating flight. Often with long glides. Tends to slip away, low down.

Wryneck – in sunny patches on ground. Feeds with tail held up. Also hides away in bushes.

Grey-headed Woodpecker – shorter bill, longer tail, smaller than Green. Neck thicker, so head looks sunken into body. Bill shorter and more slender. Doesn't hack, only taps. Regularly feeds on ground, less often in open than Green. More inclined to feed in trees than Green, very elusive.

Grey-headed – flight-path up and down like Green, but flight lighter, less of an effort than Green's.

Woodpeckers: Black-and-white Woodpeckers

Woodlark – similar shape to Lesser Spotted, but shorter tail, more rounded wings.

Great Spotted Woodpecker – more powerful flight than Lesser Spotted, shallower undulations. Longer bill obvious. Starling-sized. Medium-sized, with long, sharp bill.

Great Spotted – more prone to active excavation for food than Syrian; feeds on wood-boring insects. Syrian tends more towards probing with tongue.

Lesser Spotted Woodpecker – flies with deep undulations, like small, short-tailed bird. Sparrow-sized. Flutters between perches in trees.

Lesser Spotted – tiny. Rounded head, short bill. Plump.

White-backed Woodpecker – 10% larger than Great Spotted. Long, powerful bill. Longer necked.

Lesser Spotted – eats mainly insects year round, on trunks, branches, twigs, leaves. In winter searches among rotten wood. Taps gently, doesn't hack.

Middle Spotted Woodpecker – very restless canopy species, constantly moving position. Only spotted woodpecker that will sit crosswise on branches. Slightly smaller than Great Spotted. Small bill/rounded head. Faded appearance to head pattern.

Syrian Woodpecker – similar build to Great Spotted.

Three-toed Woodpecker – 10% smaller than Great Spotted. Large-headed and sharp-billed.

White-backed Woodpecker – feeds on trunks of dead trees, also at base and on fallen trees. Tame/fearless. Pecks deeply into dead/rotting trees, often making craters. Feeds on wood-boring beetles.

Three-toed (far right) – mainly on spruce. Sluggish/often very tame, allowing remarkably close approach. May feed for long time at one spot. Feeds on dead wood, pecking delicately, not hacking heavily, mainly on insects.

Lesser Spotted and *Middle Spotted Woodpeckers* regularly associate with moving flocks of tits and other small birds.

Lesser Spotted – movement less jerky than other woodpeckers, smoother. Constantly flits between branches. Restless and agile, often upside down. Shy.

Lesser Spotted – often roams around in winter, appearing in unlikely places such as hedgerows and even reed-beds.

Middle Spotted – feeds only on insects. Gleans bark/foliage, often acrobatically. Does very little hacking, bill is too weak. Will tap on dead/rotting trees.

Great Spotted Woodpecker – usually works surface of tree bark, not hacking deep.

Syrian Woodpecker – slightly more mobile than Great Spotted. If drops food, will fly down after it, unlike Great Spotted.

Syrian – perhaps most likely of spotted woodpeckers to be seen on ground. Only species that takes much plant material in breeding season.

Syrian and *Great Spotted Woodpeckers* both are shy, but common. In Eastern and Central Europe, where both occur, Great Spotted takes uplands (often in conifers), Syrian the lowlands.

Woodpeckers and their trees

Middle Spotted Woodpecker – in tall deciduous woods, especially oak/hornbeam; not conifer woods. Spends much time in canopy, more than Great Spotted, more often far out on branches. Works small-/medium-sized branches, not trunks. Does not bore for deeply buried food. Not on ground.

Black Woodpecker – in tall extensive forest with clearings. Most numerous in mature beechwoods/mixed woods. Makes rectangular holes (long in vertical axis) when searching for deeply buried insects. Feeds much on ground, spends hours hacking at rotten stumps, where makes large craters. Look out for bark debris on the floor below.

Male

Grey-headed Woodpecker – open deciduous forest beside rivers/lakes. Feeds less on ground than Green (more than most woodpeckers), more often on low trees. Often in cracks of walls/rock-faces.

Great Spotted Woodpecker – all types of forest, including dense stands. Mainly works trunks/larger branches. Not normally on ground. In Europe (not Britain) will bore holes in living wood to get sap, making 'rings' (see also Three-toed). Other woodpeckers rarely do this.

Grey-headed – works large trunks more often than Green. Often nests in large aspen.

Male

White-backed Woodpecker – in undisturbed forests with many dead/dying trees. Often by lakes/rivers. Prefers deciduous forests, including oak, beech, elm, aspen and birch.

Lesser Spotted Woodpecker – in open deciduous woods and scrub. Often near water. Not in conifers. Often seen higher in canopy than other woodpeckers. Often on thin twigs, far out from trunk. Not on ground.

White-backed – often feeds at base of thin trees or fallen trees, to 3m above ground. Makes large, conical holes into which it can almost disappear. This behaviour not typical of other species. Also makes diagnostic evenly worked bare patches on tree trunks.

Green Woodpecker – in large glades of mature, open, usually deciduous woodland. Also open country with scattered large trees. Most often seen feeding on ground. Makes conical holes in turf as probes in anthills (as does Grey-headed).

Black Woodpecker – can be found in large stands of tall, mature pines. Requires open ground on which to feed.

Grey-headed Woodpecker – can be found in mountain conifer woods and taiga, unlike the Green Woodpecker.

Male

Three-toed Woodpecker – most closely tied to coniferous forest, mainly spruce but also fir/larch. In taiga, often in swampy parts of forest with dead wood. In mountains, on steep slopes with mature spruce. Feeds mainly on lower trunks, especially on dead or dying spruces. Rarely on ground. Typically makes rings of holes in spruces to get sap, often several close together on trunk at different heights.

Syrian Woodpecker – prefers more open habitats than Great Spotted. Common in cultivated country and orchards, not often in forest. Feeds more often on ground than Great Spotted. Also feeds less in canopy, preferring thicker branches.

Male

Female

Wryneck – only in open woodland, usually deciduous. Along avenues of trees and in orchards. Usually feeds on ground, in dry sunny spots. Sits for long periods in same spot, also on branch or wall.

Great Spotted Woodpecker (not illustrated) – also often in pure conifer forests. Feeds on conifer seeds in winter; look for piles of cones on the ground below. Tends to feed on trunks, usually higher up than Three-toed.

Larks, Pipits and other small brown birds

SONG-FLIGHTS

Lark – song-flight is one sustained, hovering, gradual ascent, often followed by plummet to ground.

Crested Lark – several species, including the commonest (Sky Lark) have crests.

Lark – plump, often quite large. Bills stout to very thick.

Pipit – song-flight is more of an up-and-down performance. Rises quickly to top of ascent, rapidly ceases flapping and holds wings out/tail up as descends in 'parachuting' fashion.

Corn Bunting – song-flight simple, bird flies down from perch with legs dangling.

Larks – most have definite long-bodied, broad-beamed shape. Much heavier bodied than pipits, finches and other small birds.

Pipit – not one species has a crest.

Lark – most species of lark avoid perching on anything except ground, rocks or fence posts.

Pipit – slimmer than lark. Most pipits smaller than most larks. All species have slender bills.

Pipit – many species of pipit regularly perch in trees, bushes or wires.

Corn Bunting (above) – round-headed, thick bill, short tail. Hops, doesn't walk.

Larks and **Pipits** have long hind-claws (far right), adaptation to living on ground. Not seen in finches, sparrows etc., (right).

Lesser Short-toed Lark – very finch-like, but both larks have long hind-claws for terrestrial life and walking.

Linnet (female) – more compact than Short-toed Lark species, with long, strongly notched tail. Often perches in trees/bushes. Bill also smaller. Short hind-claw for perching – can be seen to hop with a close view.

Sky Lark (above) – often shows crest. Longer-bodied than sparrow, walks rather than hopping. Upper mandible curves slightly down.

Linnet – tight flocks wheel around in flight.
Short-toed Lark – same flock movement as Linnets. Short-toed Larks have jerky flight, often looking like Pipits.

Short-toed Lark – small/very finch-like, with conical bill.

Calandra Lark – upright stance.

Crested Lark – crouched stance.

Sky Lark – often crouches, shuffles around. (Note: Shore Lark has similar posture.)

Short-toed Lark – very small in comparison to other larks. Hesitant, jerky walk.

Dupont's Lark – upright stance, long neck/legs. Runs fast, body held horizontal.

Pipit – because of streaks, could be described as 'miniature thrushes', but really much smaller/thinner.

Song Thrush – feeds with stop-start action. Runs over grass, stops to watch/listen, pecks, runs on.

Starling (juvenile) – jaunty walk on long legs. Walking action sometimes recalls lark at distance.

Pipit – habitually wags/pumps tail when feeding/perched.

Lark – doesn't wag tail.

Sky Lark – fluttering low flight, long tail often spread. Flight low over ground on straight course, often with hovering.

Wagtail (1st winter) – long tail constantly wagged.

Pipit – dashes off with burst of calls, with weak, undulating flight. Often circles round, many changes of direction, as if undecided where to land.

Starling – similar size to Sky Lark, less fluttery flight, shorter tail.

Larks: Song-flights and habitats

Crested Lark – song-flight less frequent than in most other larks. Mainly sings from ground or perch. Song-flight starts from elevated perch, ascends into wind at sharp angle to at least 15m, often 30m, before singing; continues to rise until main song-flight at roughly constant height, with wide circles, drifting, gentle undulations, not much hovering. Descends at angle, doesn't plummet.

Wood Lark – lifts off from high perch, ascending in a spiral, singing; main song-flight up to 50–100m (lower if paired), circling, dipping, looping in roller-coaster style; descent usually gradual/ spiralling, still singing. In total covers much greater area than Sky Lark's song-flight.

Wood – in contrast to other larks, needs areas of scattered trees, including open woodland/heathland. Often perches on tops of trees/wires.

Crested – fields, arid areas, rural villages, cultivations. In north, has taste for the low-life: industrial estates, docks, railway sidings.

Thekla – song-flight infrequent, similar to Crested Lark's.

Thekla – very much an edge species, inhabiting areas where one habitat abuts another, e.g. where open ground lies next to rocky outcrop.

Short-toed Lark – ascends with fluttering flight to 8–15m, singing. Main song-flight bouncy, jerking up and down like a yo-yo, with fluttering wing-beats in sync with each song phrase; bird in spiral path, drifts and may ascend further to 50m. Descends with closed wings until near ground, may lift up again to repeat performance; final descent often slow, on spread wings.

Thekla – more inclined towards rocky areas than Crested. Also favours higher altitudes with barren landscape. At same time, is far more comfortable with bushy places than Crested, often using bush-tops as a perch.

Short-toed – breeds on dry fields, semi-desert, dry mudflats, other open, arid areas.

Lesser Short-toed Lark – similar to that of Short-toed but less obvious undulations, little yo-yo effect. Perhaps normally sings from lower down. Diagnostically, often changes speed of wing-beats in mid-flight (Short-toed never does this), sometimes fast, sometimes slow like Calandra Lark's.

Lesser Short-toed – in poorer/barer habitats than Short-toed, with less grass; often on saline soils.

Calandra – ascends to about 10m, singing; in main song-flight flies in circles, sometimes gradually rising; song-flight with very characteristic, stiff slow-motion wing-beats, emphasised on downstroke; circles around, drifts. Descent usually gentle.

Calandra – very much bird of steppes/grasslands.

Shore Lark – ascends from rock, steeply/silently at first; then sings while climbing stepwise, with brief pauses with wings closed, and main song-flight very high, up to 250m; descends with spectacular plummet, usually broken just above ground.

Shore – breeds in Arctic/Alpine habitats: mountains above tree-line, and tundra.

Dupont's – breeds on arid plains with sparse vegetation spread out into clumps/tufts. Vegetation often Artemisia, less than 50cm tall.

Sky Lark – usually ascends silently, climbing on fluttering wings to 10m before singing; main song-flight stabilises at 50–100m; hovering/circling; descends slowly in spirals and with song, then glides, but final few metres is silent drop.

Dupont's – ascends to height of 100–150m, almost out of sight, singing; main song-flight very protracted, up to 30 mins, wings slowly flapping; distinctive descent – plummets down but flutters at 2–3m before finally landing.

Sky – open agricultural field, grassland, meadows. Very common.

Larks: Crested, Thekla and Short-toed Larks

Crested – often digs for food.
Thekla – picks, doesn't dig down.

Crested – crest spiky.

Crested Lark – very flappy in flight, with some gliding.

Crested – plump-bellied, with hunched appearance.

Thekla – slightly 'goggle-eyed' look.

Crested – lower mandible of long bill straight; culmen curved. Overall effect is to make bill look pointed.

Thekla – when flushed, has habit of doubling back over observer (probably to remain inside territory).

Thekla – shorter bill than Crested. Both mandibles curved, making bill look blunter.

Thekla – crest looks 'more neatly cut', fan-like.

Lesser Short-toed Lark – bill very stubby and broad-based.

Thekla – marginally smaller than Crested, little less portly, making legs look longer.

Short-toed Lark – bill sharply pointed.

Thekla – often perches on bushes, which Crested seldom does.

Short-toed – tertials reach almost to wing-tips.

Lesser Short-toed – more rounded head than Short-toed which, together with short bill, gives quite distinct appearance.

Short-toed – small, finch-like, very washed-out, pale lark.

Short-toed

Lesser Short-toed – tertials end well before wing-tips, so 3 or more primary tips can be seen. Fractionally smaller than Short-toed. Streaky/greyish, like miniature Skylark.

Larks: Other Larks

Crested Lark – slightly larger than Sky, shorter tail/broader wings. Characteristically heavy-bellied. Crest always obvious, looks like tuft of wind-dried hair.

Sky – crest little more than bump. Bill short.

Calandra – obvious black under wing. Smoother, more decisive flight action than Sky, longer, broader wings.

Sky – medium-sized; plump, long-bodied, longer tail than others except Dupont's.

Calandra Lark – large, round-headed, uncrested lark with heavy bill. Shorter tail than Sky, broader wings.

Sky – makes off with low flight/fluttering wing-beats/hesitant progress. Wings slim for lark. More fluttery than other larks. Often hovers for an instant before landing; very characteristic.

Wood – very distinctive flight, a few flaps then wings held in, producing deep undulating course, like Lesser Spotted Woodpecker. Broad wings, short tail.

Wood Lark – often perches on trees/wires. Others don't.

Shore Lark – flight less hesitant than Sky, but smoother undulations low over ground. Habit of dipping down just out of sight. Often doubles back on observer. Shade smaller than Sky, looks darker. Slightly shorter bill/longer tail.

Wood – small lark with short tail, crest present but small/hard to see.

Dupont's – fast/very flappy flight, more so than other larks. Wings rather short/broad.

Dupont's – very shy/nervous, makes for tussock cover at great speed. Runs with body held horizontal. Incredibly elusive, best seen at dawn/dusk. About size of Sky, but very different shape, including long, downcurved bill. Longer legs than Sky or Crested, no hint of crest. Often stretches neck up, making it look long/slim.

Swallows and Martins

House Martin – flight more fluttery than Swallow, with slow air speeds. Turns/circles rather than jerks and flicks.

Often flies higher than others, among Swifts. Glides in gentle curves.

Crag Martin – flight with rapid sweeps like Swallow, but also long glides. Can be acrobatic and fast, with many twists and turns. Often high in sky.

Swift

House Martin – bull-headed, compact, with short, broad-based wings. Tail with moderate fork.

Crag Martin – often flies acrobatically back and forth across sunny cliff-faces, almost touching them.

Crag Martin – large, compact, heavy. Broader wings than Sand Martin. Tail barely forked.

Red-rumped Swallow – slightly bulkier than Swallow, shorter, more rounded wings held out like House Martin's. Tail streamers thicker/shorter than Swallow's. Slower wing-beats than Swallow, more shallow. Slower turns. Flight isn't 'dashing'. Patrols regular route.

Red-rumped Swallow – often flies higher than Swallow.

Swallow – long, pointed swept-back wings, long body. Tail strongly forked with wiry tail streamers (juvenile has shorter tail streamers than adult).

Swallow – doesn't glide much, then only briefly. *Red-rumped Swallow* – glides a lot, soars. *Swallow* – long sweeps with strong, fast 'rowing' action of wings. Rapid swerves, dashing effect.

Swallow – usually low, even at feet of grazing animals.

Sand Martin – small, slight. Long wings, short tail, shallow fork.

Crag Martin – much gliding. *Sand Martin* – little gliding.

Sand Martin – flight fluttering and weak, slower-paced than Swallow, more changes in direction. Wings often held in towards body. Usually flies low down.

Crag Martin – found on mountains and cliffs. Localised. Nest is half-cup of mud clinging to vertical cliff, often under overhang. Usually small colonies.

Red-rumped Swallow – mud nest attached to roof of cave or cavity, with entrance tunnel. Solitary, or loose colonies.

House Martin – mainly buildings, also cliffs. Species most likely to be seen in large, busy cities.

Red-rumped Swallow – mainly mountains/sea-cliffs, sometimes around bridges, buildings, ruins. Only in warm climate of Southern Europe.

House Martin – the Swallow/Martin most at home on the ground, where white feet are obvious. Closed mud nest attached to eaves of house, also on cliff-face. Colonies.

Red-rumped Swallow – more bull-necked than Swallow, stubbier bill.

Swallow

Swallow – mainly around farmland/small villages. Nest open cup on ledge, against vertical surface. Usually in building. Typically solitary nester.

Sand Martin – usually seen over water, near suitable sandbanks for nesting. Nest in tunnel in riverbank, sand pit, earthworks. Often large colonies.

Pipits: Song-flights and habitats

The *Pipits* are justifiably famous for their eye-catching aerial displays. Males take off from a perch at a steep angle, sing and return to earth. As they descend, they spread wings, lift tails and often dangle legs, spiralling downwards like paper aeroplanes.

Water Pipit – song-flight similar to Meadow Pipit's: ascends from ground at similar angle, rises to 10–30m, then circles across territory; descent slow and gliding.

Water – breeds on mountains in Continental Europe, in very open places, often near mountain streams.

Meadow Pipit – song-flight consists of a fluttering ascent from ground or low perch, often at shallower angle (say 40 degrees) than Tree Pipit. Often circles before returning to earth. Song begins immediately, as soon as bird begins to ascend.

Meadow – breeds in various types of open country, especially moorland. Also pastures. Widespread. Will perch in trees but never enters woods.

Rock Pipit – song-flight similar to Meadow Pipit, leaving from and returning to ground.

Meadow – in winter usually descends from upland moors, but otherwise found in similar places to those it uses for breeding.

Rock – breeds only along rocky coastlines of North-west Europe.

Rock – in winter, spreads out to a greater variety of coastal habitats than when breeding. A few also venture inland to reservoirs.

Red-throated Pipit – song-flight goes higher than Meadow Pipit's, lasts longer than Meadow and Tree Pipit's. Rises from ground or low perch, ascends, then often glides at same height for 50m before typical pipit parachute descent. Song usually begins during ascent, glide is silent, descent is accompanied by song.

Red-throated – breeds on mountains and grassy tundra (often among willow scrub) in the very far north of Europe.

Tree Pipit – breeds in open woodland, woodland glades, scrub, downland, heathland. Widespread. All other pipits avoid woodland.

Tree – rises from tree at about 60 deg to about 15m, then descends, often in spiralling fashion, down to another perch. Sings at peak of ascent/during descent. More confident performance than Meadow, usually rises higher.

Tawny Pipit – ascends steeply/silently from perch/ground, sometimes vertically, to 20–30m then, singing, describes long undulations over territory, each downward movement accompanied by one song-phrase; usually a gliding descent.

Water Pipit – many winter in a very different habitat to that used for breeding: lowland freshwater sites, including waterlogged fields and meadows, marshes and watercress beds.

Tawny – open, sandy places with little vegetation, including sand dunes. Southern/Central Europe.

Tree, Red-throated and *Tawny Pipit* – in winter, migrate to Africa.

Meadow Pipit

Pipits: Tree, Meadow and Red-throated

Meadow Pipit – slimmer bill than Tree Pipit's, not obviously pink. Mostly ground-dwelling, but does perch on wires, bushes, small trees, when long hind-claws can be obvious.

Red-throated Pipit – regularly feeds in the open, often in company with Meadow Pipits, especially on migration.

Meadow – customarily feeds out in the open, often in flocks.

Meadow – twitches tail, but lacks pumping action of Tree.

Meadow – rounder-headed than Tree, with round shoulders. Long hind-claw.

Meadow – distinctive shuffling creep, mouse-like.

Tree Pipit – slightly heavier/ longer bill, slightly angled upwards. Bill base is pink. When perched, often 'pumps' tail slowly up and down.

Tree – tends not to feed out in the open. Furtive and solitary.

Tree – slightly larger/ longer-bodied than Meadow. Looks more heavily built, with noticeably slimmer rear end.

Tree – often perches in trees.

Tree – relatively high-stepping 'confident' walk, smoother than others.

Tree – normal flight is relatively strong/decisive, with long undulations.

Red-throated – short bill with yellow base. Long hind-claw.

Red-throated – similar to Meadow Pipit, but plumper-looking, with broader back/deeper belly.

Tree – when flushed, makes purposefully for perch in a tree, often flying quite far. Does not panic.

Meadow – normal flight jerky, fluttery, weak, hesitant, with skipping action.

Red-throated – shorter tail than either Meadow or, especially, Tree Pipit.

Red-throated – mostly on ground; rarely perches.

Meadow – when flushed, rises in panicky fashion, calling hysterically, often uncertain where to land, changing direction constantly.

Red-throated – when escaping, tends to fly decisively far away. Flight quicker/stronger than Meadow's, similar to Tree Pipit's.

Red-throated – gait similar to Meadow Pipit's.

Pipits: Water, Rock, Tawny and Richard's

Rock Pipit – tame, allowing close approach. When flushed, tends to fly away low/not very far.

Rock/Water Pipits – dark red-brown or black legs.

Rock/Water – strong, almost swooping flight, with more obvious tail/broader wings than Meadow.

Rock – usually seen feeding over rocks and seaweed.

Meadow Pipit – crouches.

Rock – larger/bulkier than Meadow Pipit, with longer legs and bill. Upright posture.

Water (summer) – has a very upright posture, giving rise to some similarity to a wagtail or even a Wheatear. More liable to perch on bushes or trees than either Rock or Meadow Pipit.

Water – very shy, hard to approach. When flushed it flies up high, then far and away (often behind observer).

Water – on floodlands/marshes; not as stout as Rock.

Richard's Pipit – heavy, bounding flight. If alarmed, flies off considerable distance.
Tawny Pipit – less undulating flight than Richard's.

Tawny (adult) – large, wagtail-like, elongated pipit.

Meadow – much smaller.

Richard's

Tawny (juvenile) – slim pipit, without pot-belly of Richard's. Short hind-claw. Frequently wags tail (Richard's less so).

Richard's (juvenile) – larger than Tawny, with longer legs/tail. Stout, thrush-like bill. Very long hind-claw. Has exaggerated upright posture.

Richard's – typically gives short hover before landing. *Tawny* doesn't.

Wagtails

Yellow – most compact wagtail, by far the shortest tail, almost suggesting pipit.

Citrine and *Yellow Wagtails* – less incessant and obvious tail-wagging than other two.

Citrine – similar to Yellow, but noticeably longer tail, equal to Pied.

1st winter

1st winter

Pied Wagtail – as walks along, holds head up. Head nods more obviously than other wagtails, like miniature chicken. When perched, tail often hangs down. Slightly larger/bulkier than other wagtails, often looks plumper. Much longer tail than Yellow, but still noticeably shorter-tailed than Grey. Tail looks thinner than other wagtails.

Grey Wagtail – slimmest/most attenuated, remarkably long tail. Slightly shorter legs than other wagtails.

Grey – constantly wags tail – indeed, whole rear end. Has most incessantly moving tail of any wagtail. Noticeably delicate way of darting over rocks/along water's edge. When perched, tail tends to be held horizontal.

1st winter

1st winter

Pied – content to feed far from water. Often seen on roads/roofs.

FEEDING ACTIONS

All wagtails feed by picking items off ground or water while standing/walking; all catch insects in flight, with jump from ground or sally from perch.

Grey – often wades in shallows, just getting feet wet (Yellow and Pied Wagtails seldom wade). Habitually forages near water. Catches much food in flight, often hovering to do so. Pied and Yellow also sometimes hover, but Citrine apparently does not.

Citrine – often wades in water up to belly. Habitually forages near water.

Yellow – marked habit of feeding at feet of grazing animals (Pied and Citrine sometimes do this, Grey doesn't). Content to feed in longer grass than Pied. Often not near water.

Yellow and *Pied* make darting runs at prey seen some way ahead, often ambushing insects as these take off. ('Run-picking', not seen in Grey or Citrine.)

Black-headed (Yellow) Wagtail (distinctive south-eastern race).

Citrine Wagtail – on tundra bogs with scattered willow bushes, mountain meadows, riverbanks. More of a waterside bird than Yellow. Summer visitor to Europe, rare, mostly in east.

Male

Female

Male

Male

Grey Wagtail – on streams/rivers, especially fast-flowing ones, often in uplands.

Yellow Wagtail – mainly meadows/ marshy pastureland, with rich growth of moist grass near water. Mainly in lowlands. Summer visitor to Europe, Mar–Oct.

Yellow Wagtail (British race) .

Blue-headed (Yellow) Wagtail (continental race).

Grey – in contrast to other wagtails, often perches up in waterside trees.

Grey – far more sweeping, bounding flight than Yellow, with long tail obvious.

FLIGHT

Pied Wagtail – commonest wagtail, found in wide variety of bare, open places, including lawns, farmyards, roofs, car parks, bogs, roads, usually but not always near water. Present summer and winter.

Male

Yellow – obviously has shortest tail. Flight strongly undulating, but less pronounced sweeps/swoops of other wagtails.

FLOCKS/ROOSTS

Grey – mainly solitary and in pairs.

Pied – often sociable. Forms winter roosts of hundreds of birds, often on buildings, also in trees in town centres.

Citrine – said to have slightly stronger flight than Yellow.

Yellow, Citrine and *Grey* have song-flight, similar in style to that of a pipit.

Pied – song-flight rarely seen.

Pied – similar flight to Grey, but tail shorter.

Yellow – often in groups on migration. Forms large roosts in reed-beds on migration.

Waxwing, Dipper and Oriole

Male

Golden Oriole – flight easy/fluid, only gently undulating and ending with upward sweep.

Green Woodpecker – similar colour to female Golden Oriole, flight more slavishly undulating. Larger size, heavier build, pointed tail should be obvious.

Golden Oriole – exotic bird, thrush-like size/shape. Slim, with stout bill. Both sexes unmistakable plumage. Summer visitor, May–Aug, living in tall, broad-leaved groves of trees, often adjoining water.

Golden Oriole – very shy, leading secret life in canopy of trees, surprisingly difficult to see. Best chance is to wait patiently for birds to fly across gap, which these restless birds often do.

Female

Waxwing – flight very similar to Starling's; faster with more pronounced undulations. Wings broader/less pointed.

Waxwing – Starling-sized, but plumper, with soft texture to plumage. Breeds in remote northern forests. Feeds on insects, often performing sallies from perch to catch them in flight.

Starling

Waxwing – in winter feeds mainly on berries. In some winters, flocks move south and can appear in towns/gardens. Utterly fearless.

Dipper – at home in water. Dives in, simply walks in, also rides water on slightly opened wings.

Dipper – unique aquatic songbird. Perches on rocks/bobs up and down, white breast obvious. Plump, with short, cocked-up tail.

Kingfisher – fast, low flight. Usually avoids rushing streams with rocks.

Dipper – flies fast, direct, low over water, following stream.
Wren – similar flight, bird much smaller. Usually flies across, not along, river.

Dipper – breeds along rushing rocky streams. Often upland areas. May move downstream in winter to less torrential water e.g. weirs.

Accentors and Wren

Dunnock – small, sparrow-like bird with rounded head, thin bill, longish tail. Unobtrusive, moves along ground with creeping action/small hops. All movements accompanied with wing-/tail-flicks.

Dunnock (Hedge Accentor) – sings from open perch, with little ceremony. Often moves position after half-a-dozen phrases.

Alpine Accentor – pipit-like song-flight. Dunnock doesn't sing in flight.

Wren – lives low down near ground. Sings from fence/low bush, never from high in tree. Throws everything into loud song, bill open wide/whole body quivering. Unique shape: tiny – shortest bird in Europe, minute tail, often held vertically. Quite long, slightly downcurved bill. Abundant, hard to see. Remains inside dense, tangled vegetation, creeps about like mouse.

Dunnock – unique wing-waving display.

Alpine Accentor – much larger relative of Dunnock, size of lark. Found in barren country above 1,800m without much shrubbery. Often found by buildings (particularly in winter), feeds around snow patches. Especially on south-facing slopes.

Alpine Accentor – combines actions of Dunnock – constant wing- and tail-flicking, shuffling on ground – with more upright posture, chunky build.

Rock Bunting

Dunnock flits weakly into bushes. *Alpine Accentor* has strong, undulating flight.

Alpine Accentor – often in flocks feeding over rocks/meadows (Dunnock not sociable). Overall demeanour is like pipit, bunting or lark.

Shore Lark

Water Pipit

Alpine Accentor

Small brown birds of woodland and garden

Dunnock – size of Robin, but less rounded breast, fuller rear end, shorter legs. Distinctive creeping behaviour. Ground-loving. Doesn't hop boldly but shuffles along ground, often crouched with feet half-hidden. Wings constantly flicked at lightning speed.

Robin – usually confident behaviour. Hops, doesn't creep or shuffle, has upright posture. Often droops wings/cocks tail. Hops along grass, stops, suddenly bobs or moves on. Often in open.

Wren – tiny bill; cocked tail. Smallest brown bird in Europe. Creeps mouse-like through dense vegetation, often just above ground.

Nightingale – larger than Robin, with longer tail, but similar behaviour. Long hops over ground, stops dead, pecks, hops again. Also droops wings/cocks tail. Not usually in open.

Dunnock – slim, with fine bill.

Redstart (female) – Robin-like but has orange-red tail, constantly quivered.

House Sparrow (female) – larger than Dunnock and much fatter, with thicker, seed-eater's bill. Also shorter tail/more hopping action on the ground.

Chaffinch (female) – creeps along branches/ground. Creeping walk with slight nod of head, like a chicken. Long tail, large head with thick bill. (Compare with smaller Pied Flycatcher (*opposite*), which does not land on ground.)

Blackcap – can look Robin-like but longer/thinner, with smaller head/more horizontal outline. Doesn't normally feed on ground. Flits around in hedgerows, darting this way and that, usually within cover. Doesn't sit still for long.

Garden Warbler – very featureless, brown warbler. Behaves as warbler should, constant flitting movements within vegetation. Horizontal posture, skulking habit, hard to see. Doesn't sit still/feed on ground.

Marsh Tit – superficially like Blackcap, but smaller, with larger head, thicker neck, plumper body, shorter bill. Bold/sprightly, often at ground level. Acrobatic.

Spotted Flycatcher – small/featureless, but distinctive shape/behaviour. Large head, pointed/very broad-based bill, very long wings, short legs. Posture rather upright. (Robin is similarly brown/featureless from behind, but more podgy, with shorter wings.)

Spotted Flycatcher – very distinctive feeding method. From any height of perch, makes darting sallies out to catch flying insect before returning to same/another perch. During aerial sorties may dash, hover, sweep low to ground, often tumbling/rapidly changing direction.

Pied Flycatcher (female) – similar feeding action to Spotted Flycatcher, but smaller/less upright when perched. Compare with Chaffinch (female).

Red-backed Shrike – medium sized, long tail, predatory bill with hooked tip. Perches in open.

Blackbird (female) – medium-sized, bulky build, heavy bill, long tail. Runs neatly along lawn, stops dead, watches, runs again. Also hops along. If disturbed, makes panicky horizontal flight into nearest cover.

Song Thrush – larger than Starling and well-proportioned, with long tail. Moves around in stop-start fashion like Blackbird. Large spots on breast readily identify it.

Starling (juvenile) – smaller than Blackbird, spiky bill/much shorter tail. Walks along with waddling gait, never stopping for long, busy and bustling. Doesn't hop. Usually in small flocks, unlike Blackbird. If flocks disturbed, fly up and wheel around.

Treecreeper – readily identified by habit of creeping up tree trunks/branches, hugging them closely at all times. Long tail, thin, slightly downcurved bill.

Tree Pipit – ground-loving family of bird, but this one perches on treetops on woodland edge. Streaky, with fairly thin bill, streamlined body and long tail, which it wags up and down. Walks on ground.

Redpoll – small streaky finch with tiny bill. Hangs acrobatically from branches (usually birch) like tit.

Thrushes, Warblers and Flycatchers

CHATS

Large eyes.

Round-headed.

Small.

Long legs.

Darting or whirring flight.

Most food obtained on ground.

Plump-bodied.

Often perch upright, and regularly on rocks.

Hunting often involves perching or standing still, watchfully.

Many species perch above ground, then pounce on prey.

Often brightly coloured.

Soberly coloured.

LARGER THRUSHES

Medium-sized (larger than chats, flycatchers and warblers).

Thicker bill.

Do not use 'perch and pounce'.

Powerful flight.

Most food obtained on ground.

Strong, long legs.

Hunting often involves periods of perching or standing still.

Most food obtained in air.

Very long wings.

FLYCATCHERS

Bills very broad-based, with broad gape.

Head large and round.

Short legs.

Large eyes.

Small.

Soberly coloured or black-and-white.

Sit still and (fairly) upright for long periods.

Flicks wings, cocks tail.

Hunting involves continual aerial sallies from lookout perch.

Sometimes use 'perch and pounce' to ground.

WARBLERS

Do not use 'perch and pounce'.

Don't sit upright (except to sing), mainly horizontal posture.

Most food obtained in foliage.

Small.

Sleek, not plump.

Rarely sit still, move around constantly.

Darting, flitting flight.

On the whole, soberly coloured.

Hunting mainly by picking and gleaning.

Thrushes: Nightingales and Robin

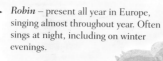

Robin – present all year in Europe, singing almost throughout year. Often sings at night, including on winter evenings.

Nightingales – summer visitors to Europe, only singing Apr–June, leaving Aug/Sept. Sing by day as much as night.

Robin – easy to see. Perches in tree to sing, halfway up or atop tree or bush.

Nightingale – larger than Robin, with smaller head, slimmer chest, longer tail. Obvious large, dark eye on bland face.

Nightingales – usually very difficult to see. Loud song is delivered from very concealed perch.

Nightingales – tend to feed on ground, under cover of thicket. Search leaf-litter/bare ground, with series of hops/long pauses. Hop along with tail raised/wings drooped.

Nightingale – when wagged several times, tail returns slowly up to resting position after last wag.

Nightingale – warmer brown than Thrush Nightingale, slightly longer tail/shorter wings. Range of habitats, including dry scrub far from water.

Thrush Nightingale – when tail wagged, no such slow return to position. Tail wagged slightly from side to side.

Thrush Nightingale – counterpart of Nightingale in Eastern/Northern Europe. Breeding sites normally confined to bushy, heavily littered, shady places near water.

Robin – often feeds in open, hopping over lawns.

Robin – small brown bird with big head/plump chest.

Nightingale – shorter wings than Thrush Nightingale, only 7 primary tips normally visible. First primary long, reaching beyond primary coverts.

Thrush Nightingale – usually shows 8 well-spaced primary tips. First primary shorter, not reaching tips of primary coverts.

Thrushes: Bluethroat, Bluetail and Bush Robin

Red-flanked Bluetail – sings while perched high in treetop.

Bluethroat – usually sings from inside cover. Occasionally sings in display-flight.

Rufous Bush Robin – usually sings from exposed perch, but also frequently in song-flight. Bird rises up/glides down in straight line.

Rufous Bush Robin – usually very skulking, takes occasional turns at flamboyance by sitting atop prickly pear cactus, bush, even wire. Takes larger prey than others on this page with heavy bill. Feeds on ground, often probes into soil for worms.

Red-flanked Bluetail – not skulking, lives in trees. Feeds by flying down from perch to catch prey on ground, then return. Also hops along ground.

Rufous Bush Robin – like tapered Nightingale; similar sized, but longer, fan-shaped tail. Quite long, heavy bill. Typically perches with tail raised over back. Pumps tail up and down, fans it, flicks wings.

Red-flanked Bluetail – plump/round-headed like Robin, but longer tail, very short bill. Constantly flicks wings/jerks tail downwards.

Robin – large head, plump body, long legs. Flicks wings, cocks tail.

Redstart – slim; long rear end. Constantly quivers tail.

Bluethroat (1st winter)

Bluethroat – slightly smaller than Robin, with longer legs. Very upright posture. Cocks/fans tail.

Male (breeding)

Bluethroat – very skulking; creeps through densest cover. Looks like slim Robin. Quick hops/runs on ground beneath undergrowth, pauses in between. Will turn over leaf-litter to find food. Doesn't probe.

Nightingale – plumper body than Bush Robin, square-ended tail. Cocks tail.

Thrushes: Chats and Redstarts

Redstart (female) – more arboreal than Black Redstart, habitually perching on branches of trees, which Black Redstart does not normally do. Goes to ground to feed, hops along, does not run.

Redstart (male) – both Redstarts have diagnostic habit of constantly shivering their rust-red tail.

Redstart – sings from tree. *Black Redstart* – sings high above ground, on roof of tall building/clifftop; Redstart never does.

Black Redstart – nests in hole in building (Redstart often does) wall (sometimes) or cave (never). *Redstart* – often (not always) nests in hole in tree; Black Redstart never does.

Black Redstart (female) – slightly larger/plumper than Redstart, generally darker.

Black Redstart – habitually feeds on ground far from cover, on rocks/ploughed fields, which Redstart usually avoids. Also often on roofs, buildings, farm machinery. Hops along ground/also runs.

Black Redstart – more inclined than Redstart to hover in front of walls catching flying insects.

Stonechat – very round crown/large head. Short wing-points.

Whinchat

Stonechat – very upright posture, no sign of leaning forward. Easily agitated bird, incessantly flicking wings/tail and calling.

Whinchat – both Whinchat and Stonechat sit up on perches in open, surveying ground below/pouncing on any prey sighted. Whinchat tends to have slightly leaning posture when perched. Less demonstrative than irritable, wing-flicking Stonechat.

Whinchat – flat crown, effect exacerbated by obvious eyebrow. Much longer wings than Stonechat, yet shorter tail.

Thrushes: Wheatears

Black Wheatear – large wheatear of Spain/Portugal where, in contrast to other wheatears, is not migratory. Found on steep slopes/cliffs in arid places; not on level ground.

Pied Wheatear – small wheatear closely related to Black-eared, but only breeding along Black Sea coast. Found in more dramatic habitats than Black-eared: cliffs, mountainsides, desolate rocky places.

Isabelline – large, pale wheatear; only breeds in extreme south-east of Europe. Requires flat, very open terrain with bare ground/ scattered rocks or bushes; essentially steppe/ semi-desert. Nests in rodent holes.

Black-eared Wheatear – small, very variable wheatear, mainly in Mediterranean; open rocky country, often hillsides, also requires bushes/trees (unlike Northern). In much of range, replaced by Northern above 600m.

Male

Northern Wheatear – by far the most widespread wheatear; only one normally found in northern half of Europe (north of southern France). Breeds in wide variety of open habitats.

Pied – in shape/posture very similar to Black-eared, slightly longer wings.

Black-eared – shorter legs than Northern, tends to perch horizontally, crouched posture. Small, light body allows it to perch on flimsy vegetation. Small/slim, longer tail than Northern, slightly smaller bill.

Black – distinctive, large, portly wheatear, with big head/heavy bill. Habit of constantly flicking and spreading tail.

Male

Female

Isabelline – larger than Northern, longer legs, slightly larger bill, broader head. Sexes almost alike. Upright stance, tail does not reach ground, wags more obviously.

Northern – female/non-breeding plumage resembles Isabelline; male distinct. Less upright posture than Isabelline, tail almost brushes ground.

Female

Male

Northern – upright, plump wheatear, with long legs.

Black Wheatear – feeds by hopping over ground/on rocks, constantly investigating/probing in cracks/fissures. Sometimes flies from perch to ground, but much less often than Black-eared.

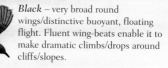

Black – very broad round wings/distinctive buoyant, floating flight. Fluent wing-beats enable it to make dramatic climbs/drops around cliffs/slopes.

Pied Wheatear – similar feeding behaviour to Black-eared, distinct from Northern in persistent habit of flying down from perch about 1m above ground, then returning again.

Black-eared Wheatear – less terrestrial than Northern or Isabelline, preferring to watch for prey from elevated perch. Does not run along ground much, simply flies down, snatches prey, returns to perch.

Northern Wheatear – two main feeding methods. Goes to ground, runs along, stops and looks, pecks, runs again etc. Also sits on low perch to watch for movement on ground, pounces down.

Isabelline – practises similar techniques to Northern, but more ground-hugging. When on ground makes longer runs on long legs, like small gamebird.

Northern – flies with flitting wing-beats low over ground.

Pied – flight as Black-eared.

Isabelline – much broader wings than Northern. Flaps more obvious, almost glides in to land.

Cyprus Wheatear – breeds only in Cyprus (present Mar–Oct), in variety of habitats, including (unusually for wheatear) woodland. Often perches in tall treetops. Smallest European wheatear, most similar in shape to Pied, but shorter wings/tail. In contrast to Pied, male/female look much alike.

Black-eared – longer tail often obvious.

Black-eared – flies with lighter action than Northern. Apparently often hovers before landing.

Thrushes: Rock Thrushes

Male

Rock Thrush – looks like cross between chat and thrush; too big for former, too small for latter – about Starling size. Long body, short tail, long bill. Summer visitor, Apr–Sept. Usually found higher than Blue Rock Thrush, above 1250m, mainly on rocky dry slopes with some bushes and trees.

Blue Rock Thrush – characteristic 'long-nosed' profile. Bill slightly longer than Rock Thrush, tail much longer, looks more 'thrush-like'. Mainly resident. Found on cliffs, man-made structures including ruins, and mountains up to 800m.

Male

Both *Rock Thrushes* mainly feed by dropping on to prey from above; low, floating flight with smooth, elastic wing-beats.

Rock – similar red tail to Redstart, but bird larger. Upright posture on rock. Long hops. Characteristic tail wag with upward flick.

Female

Female

Black Redstart – smaller bill than Rock Thrush, smaller size overall. Quivers tail. Flits.

Blue Rock – very shy; often seen at distance, perched upon rock; soon slips out of sight.

SONG-FLIGHTS

Rock Thrush – male rises from perch with slow, powerful wing-beats and begins to sing. At top of ascent, soars/sings, then plummets silently with wings spread/tail fanned. May repeat performance before landing. Having returned, sings with tail fanned/feathers ruffled.

Blackbird – much bulkier body, less prominent 'nose'. Bill thicker/shorter. Often droops wings.

Blue Rock Thrush – song-flight less frequent than Rock Thrush. Male leaps off perch, singing, usually glides upwards with wings/tail spread (not beating wings). Glides down, wings spread or half-closed, at varying angle. Upon landing, perches while wings beat slowly.

Mistle Thrush – similar upland habitats in Mediterranean region. Far larger, broad barrel-chest

Thrushes: Where Thrushes are found

Robin

WOODS – *Robin, Nightingale, Redstart, Song Thrush, Redwing, Mistle Thrush, Fieldfare, Blackbird*

GARDENS – *Robin, Redstart, Song Thrush, Redwing, Mistle Thrush, Fieldfare, Blackbird*

Nightingale

Black Redstart

BUILDINGS – *Black Redstart, Blue Rock Thrush*

MOUNTAINS – *Black Redstart, Northern Wheatear, Pied Wheatear, Black Redstart, Stonechat, Blue Rock Thrush, Rock Thrush, Mistle Thrush* (Southern Europe), *Ring Ouzel*

Song Thrush

Blue Rock Thrush

Stonechat

Ring Ouzel

CLIFFS – *Black Redstart, Black Wheatear, Blue Rock Thrush*

MOORLAND – *Northern Wheatear, Stonechat, Ring Ouzel*

UPLAND GRASSLAND – *Whinchat*

STEPPE – *Isabelline Wheatear*

Bluethroat

WATERSIDE – *Thrush Nightingale, Bluethroat*

 Redwing

ROCKY HILLSIDES – *Black-eared Wheatear, other wheatears, Stonechat*

Black-eared Wheatear

NORTHERN CONIFER FOREST – *Red-flanked Bluetail, Redwing*

Rufous Bush Robin

SCRUB – *Nightingale, Rufous Bush Robin*

Thrushes: Larger Thrushes

Blackbird – usually feeds near cover. Has less upright stance than more spotty thrushes.

Fieldfare – in common with Mistle Thrush, often feeds far from cover, usually in flocks. Has same confident hop as it forages on ground.

Fieldfare – slightly smaller and less rotund than Mistle Thrush, but has proportionally longer tail.

Blackbird – feeds solitarily among leaf-litter. *Redwing* – often feeds among leaf-litter in flocks.

Blackbird (juvenile) – spotty, much darker than Mistle/Song Thrush.

Mistle Thrush – habitually feeds far from cover (unlike Song Thrush), for example in middle of playing fields. Has most upright stance of the thrushes, moves around with bold, heavy hops.

Ring Ouzel – slightly slimmer looking than Blackbird, with longer legs, longer wings, flatter back and slightly heavier bill.

Blackbird (partial albino) – well-rounded shape, stocky.

Song Thrush – face has bland look.

Song – seldom feeds far from cover. Much more likely to be seen in small gardens than Mistle. Quite upright stance.

Redwing – strongly marked face. Slightly smaller and slimmer than Song Thrush, with shorter tail.

Redwing – often feeds in open, far from cover. More horizontal stance.

Song – only thrush that can smash open snail shells using hard surface ('anvil').

Song – small, compact thrush with well-proportioned look. Fairly short tail. Darker than Mistle.

Mistle

Song

Mistle – larger/more elongated, much longer tail. Head looks rather small for body ('just right' in Song). Very deep, 'beer gut' chest.

Mistle Thrush – very distinctive undulating flight. Gives series of a few flaps, followed by glides, with slow action, producing up-and-down flight-path. Often flies high at all times of year (Song Thrush rarely flies high).

Redwing – has fast, direct flight, but often flies high. More sharply pointed wings and shorter tail than Song Thrush.

Fieldfare – has distinctive, loose, 'messy' manner of flight. Bursts of flaps are followed by glides, sometimes with wings closed.

Mistle – in contrast to other thrushes, doesn't normally sing at dawn. Sings late morning and afternoon, often during inclement weather (high wind, rain etc.).

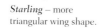

Redwing – flocks hungrily devour berries, especially haws. (All thrushes are partial to berries.)

Redwing – very similar flight silhouette to Starling. Slightly longer tail, and wings more angled back.

Fieldfare – follows much less undulating course than Mistle Thrush. Often high up, in flocks.

Starling – more triangular wing shape.

Mistle – doesn't normally forage on woodland floor, in contrast to Song Thrush and Redwing – prefers open spaces. Often remains near clump of holly or mistletoe for whole winter, aggressively defending berry source from other thrushes.

Blackbird – usually flies low into cover, with fast, fluid wing-beats. Upon landing in feeding area, often raises tail.

Ring Ouzel – flight silhouette shows off longer wings and longer tail than Blackbird. Has very fast flight, often high, usually far away.

Redwing – in flocks with own kind and other thrush species (especially Fieldfare).

Song Thrush – not in flocks (ones, twos or family parties). **Mistle Thrush** – not especially sociable; family parties only. **Blackbird/Ring Ouzel** – not especially sociable. Small parties only.

Blackbird – noisy, panicky, headlong rush for cover. **Fieldfare** – less panicky escape-flight, makes for top branches of tall tree.

Fieldfare – highly sociable; large flocks.

Ring Ouzel – very shy and cover-hugging.

Fieldfare – the only thrush with a song-flight.

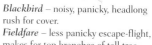

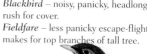

Warblers: What is a Warbler?

Warblers are all small songbirds, size of tit or smaller (except Great Reed Warbler).

Loud voice emanating from deep in bushes is often a warbler. All warblers have vigorous, spirited songs, many very distinctive. If warbling gives the sense of muttering uncertainly, under the breath, then many warblers do not warble.

Warblers are 'slippery' to watch and see well. Move around vegetation with rapid, darting movements, shifting feverishly from perch to perch. Keep well hidden, offering only glimpses.

Most thin and slender.

Often flick wings and tail nervously as go about their business.

Most species rather plain in colour – especially brown or green. Exceptions are Sylvia Warblers. Some have streaks and wing-bars. On the whole, sexes look similar.

Thin, insect-eater's bills (exceptions are Great Reed Warbler and Garden Warbler), often giving tapering shape to head.

Tend to have horizontal posture when actively moving around in foliage.

Europe empties of most warblers during winter; majority long-distance migrants from Africa.

Warblers: Arrival times in Britain

This chart shows the usual arrival times for the various species of warblers that breed in Britain. For further north in Europe, the order will be similar, but the dates will be slightly later; in southern Europe, these spring migrants correspondingly arrive earlier. Spring arrival times can be a good rough clue to a species' identity. The departure of migrants in autumn is often much more protracted.

Times given are the weeks in each month. W1 = 1st week in that month

——— Early arrivals   +++++ Peak arrivals and subsequent breeding

SPECIES	March	April	May	June
	W1 W2 W3 W4	W1 W2 W3 W4	W1 W2 W3 W4	W1 W2
Grasshopper Warbler		———+++++	++++++++++++	+++++++++
Savi's Warbler		———+++++	+++++++++++	++++++++
Sedge Warbler		————+++	+++++++++++	+++++++
Reed Warbler		———	+++++++++++	+++++++
Marsh Warbler				———++++++
Lesser Whitethroat		———++++	++++++++++	+++++++
Whitethroat		———+++	+++++++++++	+++++++
Garden Warbler		———	++++++++++	+++++++
Blackcap*	———	++++++++	+++++++++	+++++++
Wood Warbler		———	++++++++++	+++++++
Chiffchaff*	———	+++++++++	+++++++++	+++++++
Willow Warbler		——+++++	+++++++++	+++++++

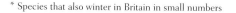

* Species that also winter in Britain in small numbers

Note: Cetti's Warbler, Dartford Warbler, Goldcrest and Firecrest can be found in Britain at any time of year.

Warblers: Types of Warbler

Cisticola ('dwells among rock roses') – absolutely tiny. Usually seen in air; incessant, up-and-down song-flight. Sings 'zit' with each undulation. In warm climates, among grass.

Cisticola

Locustella

Acrocephalus

Cisticola

Acrocephalus ('pointed heads')

Acrocephalus – group of 'Reed Warblers'. Slim, mainly brown, long bills, sloping foreheads, hence name.

Acrocephalus – seen actively moving around in stems of vegetation, hopping, climbing, often head-down. *Locustella* – creep mouse-like in vegetation, scampering, walking.

Acrocephalus – often perch prominently, especially when singing. *Locustella* – often hard to locate, even when singing, because usually perch in cover; insect-like sound hard to pinpoint.

Acrocephalus – wings straight-edged. *Locustella* – wing edges slightly curved when closed.

Acrocephalus – tails long/slim, slightly rounded tip.

Locustella (from Latin for 'grasshopper') – 'Grasshopper Warblers' similar to 'Reed Warblers', but shorter bills. Name derives from very insect-like songs.

Locustella – tails very broad, very rounded – quite different.

Acrocephalus – when singing, bills open/shut obviously. Everything thrown into song. *Locustella* – bill kept open wide, head moves almost mechanically side to side. Body often remains fairly still.

Acrocephalus – Reed Warblers have moderately long undertail coverts. *Locustella* – Grasshopper Warblers have amazingly long undertail coverts.

Acrocephalus – on ground, often hop along, cock tails. *Locustella* – run/walk on ground, not hopping.

Most birdwatchers' experience of *Locustella* warblers is of singing birds, or small, heavy-tailed bird flushed from ground/diving into cover.

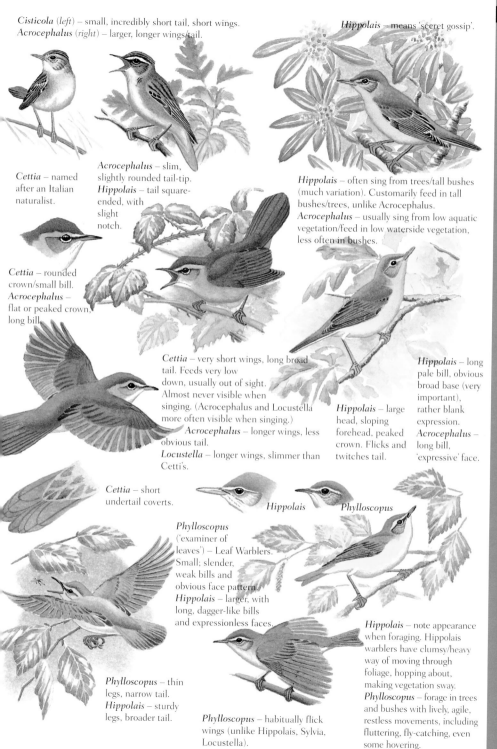

Cisticola (*left*) – small, incredibly short tail, short wings.
Acrocephalus (*right*) – larger, longer wings/tail.

Hippolais – means 'secret gossip'.

Cettia – named after an Italian naturalist.

Acrocephalus – slim, slightly rounded tail-tip.
Hippolais – tail square-ended, with slight notch.

Hippolais – often sing from trees/tall bushes (much variation). Customarily feed in tall bushes/trees, unlike Acrocephalus.
Acrocephalus – usually sing from low aquatic vegetation/feed in low waterside vegetation, less often in bushes.

Cettia – rounded crown/small bill.
Acrocephalus – flat or peaked crown, long bill.

Cettia – very short wings, long broad tail. Feeds very low down, usually out of sight. Almost never visible when singing. (Acrocephalus and Locustella more often visible when singing.)
Acrocephalus – longer wings, less obvious tail.
Locustella – longer wings, slimmer than Cetti's.

Hippolais – large head, sloping forehead, peaked crown. Flicks and twitches tail.

Hippolais – long pale bill, obvious broad base (very important), rather blank expression.
Acrocephalus – long bill, 'expressive' face.

Cettia – short undertail coverts.

Hippolais

Phylloscopus

Phylloscopus ('examiner of leaves') – Leaf Warblers. Small; slender, weak bills and obvious face pattern.
Hippolais – larger, with long, dagger-like bills and expressionless faces.

Phylloscopus – thin legs, narrow tail.
Hippolais – sturdy legs, broader tail.

Phylloscopus – habitually flick wings (unlike Hippolais, Sylvia, Locustella).

Hippolais – note appearance when foraging. Hippolais warblers have clumsy/heavy way of moving through foliage, hopping about, making vegetation sway.
Phylloscopus – forage in trees and bushes with lively, agile, restless movements, including fluttering, fly-catching, even some hovering.

Warblers: Types of Warblers

Regulus – 'little king' or 'kinglet'.

Phylloscopus – sing from prominent perches.
Regulus – sing from cover.

Regulus – tiny, wing-flicking, habitual hovering, usually in conifers.
Phylloscopus – small, wing-flicking, occasional hovering.

Phylloscopus

Phylloscopus

Regulus

Sylvia

Sylvia – 'of woods'.

Regulus – tiny, incredibly active warblers, needle-like bills/very short wings/tail, look large-headed.

Sylvia – although some small/active, movements are not as feverish as Phylloscopus. Do not hover or fly-catch.

Sylvia – skulking warblers; despite Latin name, birds of scrub/shrubbery more than woodland.

Sylvia – narrow, square-ended tail. Sturdy bill.

Sylvia – most species richly coloured, in contrast to other warblers. Sexes often look different to each other. Many have distinctive head patterns.

Locustella Warblers

Grasshopper Warbler – habitat: well-spaced, dense, low undergrowth among herbage e.g. rough grass, nettlebeds, moorland, swampy ground. Will sing from vegetation among reedbeds, e.g. bramble. Sings from plant stem, usually less than 1m above ground, close to cover. Often hard to see when singing.

Savi's Warbler – walks up to sing. (Similar Reed Warbler hops up to sing.)

Savi's – habitat: extensive tall reedbeds (sometimes other vegetation on swampy ground.) Sings from reed, often near top/in open.

River Warbler – habitat: places with low (to 2m), dense, tangled vegetation, often with young woody growth e.g. hazel/willow. Often in woodland. Not reeds. Sings from top/side of shrub, higher/more exposed than Grasshopper, 5–8m above ground.

Grasshopper – small, elongated.

Savi's – starts singing on way up to perch. Body upright, tail points almost vertically down, head turns side to side.

Savi's – larger than Grasshopper, slightly longer bill. Rounded head/thin neck make it look emaciated.

River – will sing while climbing up to perch. Head raised, bill very open, head turns from side to side, rest of body often motionless.

All three species almost impossible to see when feeding, creeping mouse-like through tangled undergrowth just above/on the ground. Savi's Warbler least shy, readily seen among reeds.

River – larger than Grasshopper, extremely broad, rounded tail.

Grasshopper – sings only once settled on perch. Body erect, head tilted up. Head turns from side to side.

Grasshopper – often uncommon, hard-to-see, summer visitor.

River – arrives mid-May. Nest near ground, often at base of bush.

Savi's – arrives mid-Apr. Nest in tall vegetation in swampy ground often just above water.

Grasshopper – arrives on breeding grounds early Apr. Nest on/just above ground, often in tussock.

Dunnock – larger, plumper, less 'tail-end-heavy'. Sings from conspicuous perch. Seen in winter. Note: if you can see it, it's probably Dunnock, not Grasshopper Warbler.

Warblers: Song-flights and habitats

The song of a warbler is a key feature; the way it sings is no less important. On these pages are some pointers as to where and when warblers sing, what they sing and whether they sing in flight.

Apart from Zitting Cisticola, all warblers with song-flights will also sing from perch.

A song-flight is a performance, with a set ritual. Other warblers occasionally sing in flight when travelling perch to perch, but this is incidental; it does not appear to be a performance.

Zitting Cisticola – flies up/down in springy flight, almost like Lark, uttering 'zit' at apex of each bound. Usually over grassland/crops.

Zitting Cisticola – tiny warbler, only one that sings in flight for long periods; doesn't sing when perched.

Olivaceous Warbler – rises vertically, turns/descends as keeps wings raised.

Booted Warbler – as Olivaceous, but lower, only to c.2m.

Hippolais – sing from tall bushes/trees. Similar songs to Acrocephalus, perhaps with more babbling quality. Less vocal than Acrocephalus. Night singing rare.

Locustella – birds of tangled undergrowth. Most singing at night.

Locustella – very downbeat performance. All have insect-like songs, performed from perch, often well-hidden, never in song-flight. Least demonstrative warblers.

Sedge Warbler – climbs to about 5m with slow wing-beats, then makes spiralling descent, singing all the while. Reed does not have ritualised song-flight.

Acrocephalus – most sing from perches, low down in marshy vegetation. Chattering song with long 'sentences', can sound very continuous. Some night singing.

THESE BIRDS SING FROM PERCH ONLY

Hippolais – Icterine, Melodious and Olive-tree Warbler.
Acrocephalus – Moustached, Reed, Marsh, Blyth's Reed, Great Reed and Paddyfield Warbler do not have ritualised song-flight.
Cettia – Cetti's Warbler does not have song-flight.
Sylvia – Blackcap, Garden Warbler, Lesser Whitethroat.
Phylloscopus – all except Wood Warbler sing from perch only.
Regulus – neither species sing in flight.

Goldcrest/Firecrest – sing from among foliage, whilst moving about. Very high-pitched songs, cyclical. Sung from conifer.

Arctic Warbler – when changing perches sometimes makes curious buzzing sound with wings.

Rüppell's Warbler (not illustrated) – ascends to as high as 10m, then zigzags down with slow wing-beats.

Phylloscopus – mainly sing from the tree- or bush-top, usually in woodland. Songs tuneful and distinctive. Only 1 Phylloscopus species has song-flight.

Barred Warbler – simple song-flight with steep climb to about 10–15m on slow, deep wing-beats, with glide down.

Common Whitethroat – rises up to 10m, then dances up/down as if on string, before final plummet. Spectacled Warbler also has Whitethroat-like song-flight.

Aquatic Warbler – makes steep silent ascent to a few metres, then fans tail/throws head up to make rapid descent.

Wood Warbler – in wood, flies along horizontal course from one perch to another 1–5m away. Only completes trilling when has landed.

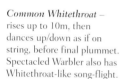

Subalpine Warbler – short, dancing, up-and-down song-flight, like Whitethroat.

Sardinian Warbler – rises just 3–4m on slow wing-beats, then glides to next bush.

Sylvia warblers usually sing from exposed perch, not normally at night. Most occur in scrubby vegetation and sing from bush-tops. Songs vary greatly; most scratchy and fast.

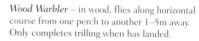

Dartford Warbler – short up-and-down song-flight to 6–7m.

The following *Sylvia* sing from perch only: Garden Warbler (*above left*), Lesser Whitethroat (*above right*), Blackcap.

Warblers: Habitats of swamp-loving Warblers

This plate shows subtly different habitats occupied by breeding Acrocephalus (and Cetti's) warblers in Europe.

Great Reed Warbler – needs large, strong, tall reed-beds, usually right by open water, often on 'islands' of reeds surrounded by water. Likes taller reeds than Reed Warbler. Widespread.

Great Reed

Sedge

Paddyfield

Reed

Sedge

Moustached

Sedge Warbler – in dense vegetation, often near reed-beds but more attached to plants next to them, e.g. bushes/rushes. Feeds low down, less dextrous on stems than Reed Warbler. Widespread.

Moustached Warbler – southern counterpart of Sedge Warbler, but present in habitat throughout the year. Mainly in reed-beds, often mixed with reedmace stands, over water. Likes areas of fallen reeds near ground.

Paddyfield Warbler – bird of reed-beds. Where overlaps with Reed Warbler, tends towards sparser reeds on landward edge. Rare: Eastern Europe, including Romania and Bulgaria.

Reed Warbler – mainly dense reed-beds. Prefers reeds at least 1m tall. Feeds mainly at middle heights in reeds. Widespread.

Cetti's Warbler – dense, tall vegetation abutting level ground, such as that made by track, usually near water. Needs areas for foraging on or near ground, so avoids vegetation growing in water. Present all year, mainly Southern Europe.

Blyth's Reed Warbler – not attracted to swampy ground at all. Bird of scrub/bush, often on edge of fields/woodland. Needs open areas next to dense bushes, feeding anywhere from low cover to tops of trees. North-eastern Europe.

Aquatic

Great Reed

Aquatic

Cetti's

Cetti's

Marsh

Aquatic Warbler – in marshlands with clumps of sedge, in vegetation less than 1m tall. More associated with sedge than Sedge Warbler. Vegetation may be in shallow water. Very rare breeding bird, East and Central Europe, especially Poland. Feeds very low down.

Marsh Warbler – in tall, rank vegetation; not reed-beds. Much attracted to nettles, meadowsweet, cow parsley-type plants, willowherbs. Avoids vegetation growing out of water. Widespread.

Warblers: Swamp-loving Warblers

Zitting Cisticola – small, plump, extremely short tail. Compact. Found in grass, makes nest of grass.

Sedge Warbler – songs interspersed with short song-flights.

Zitting Cisticola

Zitting Cisticola

Aquatic

Aquatic Warbler – smaller/slightly slimmer than Sedge. Acrobatic when holding on to plant stems, holds itself up high.

Aquatic

Sedge – throat puffed out as sings.

Sedge

Aquatic – tail very spiky, as if shredded. Characteristic tail-down, neck-up posture when singing.

Sedge – fairly rounded, broad tail. Fairly long wings/tail.

Sedge – bold, easy to see. Scolds intruder. Feeds 10–150cm above ground, catching slow-moving prey.

Cetti's Warbler – compact warbler with domed head/fine bill.

Cetti's – often on the ground, broad tail cocked.

Aquatic – shy, very difficult to see. Doesn't scold intruder. Feeds at lowest levels of thick cover. Creeps through vegetation.

Moustached Warbler – shorter, more rounded wings than Sedge; tail looks longer/broader.

Moustached – sings all year round, including mid-winter.

Moustached –

Often cocks broad tail; Sedge Warbler rarely does.

Cetti's – feeds low down, broad tail obvious. Song from cover, not from reed-beds. Similar Reed Warbler feeds from middle levels of vegetation (adapted to clinging to reed stems), and shows narrower tail. Reed Warbler sings from reeds, often clearly visible.

Great Reed Warbler – huge in comparison to Reed Warbler – thrush-sized. Long, thick bill. Very tail heavy.

Great Reed – crashes heavily among reeds.

Blyth's Reed Warbler – slim warbler, much less pot-bellied than Marsh and with flat crown. Much shorter wings than Reed and Marsh Warbler.

Blyth's Reed

Blyth's Reed – regularly cocks/fans tail (more than Reed or Marsh). Typically moves around with head/tail raised slightly. Very characteristic 'banana posture'.

Reed Warbler – long bill on spiky head. Slim.

Reed – typical horizontal posture. (Marsh often has more upright posture).

Marsh Warbler – shorter bill than Reed and more domed head shape to give slightly more bland expression.

Marsh – can look a little more pot-bellied and slightly longer wings than Reed.

Reed (as here), Marsh and Great Reed Warblers are all common hosts of the Cuckoo.

Reed – essentially reed-beds (does wander to fringing vegetation). Arrives early May.

Marsh – doesn't breed in vegetation growing out of water, so essentially not in reed-beds. Arrives very late, after cover has had time to grow, often late May/June.

Paddyfield Warbler – smaller than Reed, shorter bill.

Paddyfield – cocks/fans rounded tail (more than Reed or Marsh). Tail longer than any other Acrocephalus, exaggerated by shorter wings.

Marsh – slightly slower feeding movements than Reed. Often perches on dead stems of herbaceous plants. When agitated, very demonstrative, much scolding and flicking of wings (rarely with Reed). Sometimes raises wings while singing (not Reed). More open-mouthed, 'operatic' singing posture.

Warblers: Hippolais Warblers

The ever-tricky Hippolais warblers cause confusion with many types of warblers, as well as with each other. Look out for broad-based pale bills, square-ended tails, and habit of flicking tails. In foliage, they move with powerful hops, rustling leaves, and stretched necks to reach food, sometimes tugging at berries to dislodge them.

Melodious Warbler – South-west Europe, similar light-foliaged woodlands/bushy areas with scattered trees, usually near water. In contrast to Icterine does not like small fragments of habitat, e.g. gardens.

Booted Warbler – Mainly bird of steppelands, inhabiting bushy places, almost always near water.

Icterine Warbler – open deciduous forests/gardens, particularly of trees with light foliage, e.g. poplars, birch, alder. Tall undergrowth.

Melodious (*below*) – much shorter, less-pointed wings than Icterine. Far more skulking, doesn't usually perch in open. Flight more fluttering than dashing.

Olivaceous Warbler (*above*) – drier places than other Hippolais warblers, including bushy country, scrub and cultivations.

Icterine – long pointed wings.

Icterine – long, dagger-like bill.

Icterine

Melodious

Quite sleek, fast moving, dynamic.

Willow Warbler – much smaller than Melodious, very active, some fly-catching/hovering. Thinner bill, smaller head, obvious eye-stripe.

Olivaceous – similar to Melodious in shape, short, blunt wings, similarly skulking. (Melodious always has green/yellow colouration.) Repeated twitching of tail downwards when moving about/feeding. Other Hippolais warblers do this less often, or not at all.

Melodious – noticeably smaller than Icterine, shorter bill/more rounded head. Almost portly. Slower-moving than Icterine, remaining in same place for some time.

Icterine

Olive-tree Warbler – South-east Europe (Balkans, Greece, Bulgaria, Turkey). Open forest including oak woods, orchards, almond groves, olive groves, sometimes more bushy areas. Favours coastal regions.

Icterine Warbler – usually feeds/sings in treetops.

Olive-tree – very large, with powerful orange bill and very strong-looking dark legs.

Olive-tree – large warbler, usually forages in canopy of trees/tall bushes. Skulker, hard to see. Sings from cover, like other Hippolais warblers.

Olive-tree – powerful flight on long wings, often glides to alight.

Olive-tree

Olivaceous Warbler – flies confidently, but shorter/more rounded wings than Olive-tree; does not glide to alight.

Booted Warbler – much smaller than Olivaceous, short spiky bill/rounded head. Bill broad and orange-pink.

Olivaceous – long, broad-based bill, pointed head, square-ended tail twitched downwards repeatedly. Sings from bushes, feeds in trees.

Booted

Chiffchaff – bill shorter/darker than Booted. Bird slimmer, flicks tail down constantly.

Reed Warbler – long narrow bill, pointed head, rounded tail, not down-twitched. Sings from reed-beds, feeds mainly lower down.

Booted – looks plump. Does not flick tail down.

Warblers: Widespread Sylvia Warblers

These are the Sylvia warblers whose distribution is not centred on the Mediterranean region. Blackcap, Garden Warbler and Whitethroat are common throughout Europe. Lesser Whitethroat and Barred Warblers are more easterly in distribution.

Blackcap – most arboreal Sylvia warbler, always found near trees except on migration. Prefers to sing from high in crowns/tall bushes. Singing bird has more upright stance than Garden Warbler.

Blackcap – in winter in many parts of Western Europe. *Garden Warbler* – summer visitor only.

Garden – mostly in woodland glades with thick shrubbery/woodland edge. Usually more difficult to see when singing than Blackcap, avoids exposed branches.

Blackcap – quite large warbler, rather long-bodied/long-winged. Flat crown makes head look small.

Garden – plain face with obvious eye/surprisingly thick bill for warbler.

Garden – at nest.

Female Blackcap – on nest (Garden Warbler sexes alike).

Barred Warbler – unlike Garden Warbler, usually sings from exposed branch on top of bush. Unlike Garden Warbler or Blackcap, has song-flight.

Barred – has strong-looking feet. Often moves about slowly/heavily. Very skulking/hard to see.

Barred – large warbler, thick, pointed bill. More bulky than Garden Warbler, large head (slightly ruffled crown), distinctly heavy tail. Adults have staring yellow eye.

Barred – 1st winter.

Barred – often shares territory with Red-backed Shrike (*below*).

Garden – 1st winter.

Garden – less prominent bill/tail than Barred. Smaller head with smoother crown. Dark eye, gentle facial expression.

Blackcap – eats berries in autumn.

Barred – inhabits tall bushes with multi-layered structure, using lowest levels for nesting, upper levels for feeding. Suitable habitats often include open forest glades/hedgerows (at least 100m long).

Common Whitethroat – inquisitive. Comes to imitation of 'chearr' call. Lesser Whitethroat retiring, not coming to investigate imitations of 'tseck' call.

Common Whitethroat – conspicuous when singing short, scratchy song. Usually only warbler to use overhead wires for perching. Sings all the time.

Male

Female

Common Whitethroat – very horizontal shape, head/tail held up when moving about, more than Lesser Whitethroat.

Common Whitethroat – sings from tops of bushes, launching into frequent song-flights.

Common Whitethroat – builds nest very low down; unlike any other Sylvia warbler, often among grass stems.

Common Whitethroat – in lower scrub than Lesser Whitethroat.

Common Whitethroat – perky, with peaked crown/often trailing long tail. Pink legs, light-brown look.

Lesser Whitethroat – difficult to see, skulking warbler, usually singing from inside foliage and without song-flight.

Lesser Whitethroat – smaller than Whitethroat, much more compact, rounded head/shorter tail. Black legs, clean immaculate look.

Lesser Whitethroat – mostly in tall thickets with some trees nearby, in transition between woodland/open areas.

Lesser Whitethroat – regular habit of singing few phrases of trilling song and moving, unseen, some 100m before singing again. Much less noisy than Whitethroat.

Warblers: Mediterranean Sylvia Warblers

Blackcap – also woodland warbler. Smaller, shorter bill and flatter head (not to scale).

Orphean Warbler – large, almost as big as Barred. Longer bill, heavy head.

All these warblers live in Mediterranean region, often separated from one another by distribution. Most smaller than Whitethroat, living in various forms of scrubby vegetation.

Orphean – most tree-loving of Sylvia warblers, in deciduous woods e.g. cork oak and holm-oak, also in tall bushy areas with scattered trees. Feeds mainly in canopy, can be very hard to see.

Lesser Whitethroat – smaller than Orphean, with less tail/shorter bill (not to scale).

Female

Orphean – unlikely to be seen much at ground level. Slow and deliberate in feeding. Sings from cover of tall bushes; keeps moving from song-post to song-post.

Sardinian Warbler – common Mediterranean warbler, wide variety of habitats, including gardens, low scrub, tall scrub, trees.

Sardinian – slim warbler, short wings/long tail. (Common Whitethroat slightly larger/much plumper.) Perky, almost angry, fiery-red eye-ring. Scolds continually and investigates disturbances. Often feeds on ground, but also in crowns of trees.

Female

Male

Sardinian – sings from high perch, occasionally even overhead wires.
Subalpine Warbler – usually sings within cover.

Sardinian – shorter wings, longer tail than Subalpine.

Female

Male

Subalpine – breeds in open woodland with heathy/prickly vegetation, especially on dry, sunny hillsides. Doesn't usually occur in gardens/very low scrub.

Subalpine – bulkier than Spectacled, more pointed wings. Wags tail less. Small, slender warbler with quite long wings.

Subalpine

Rüppell's Warbler – Eastern Mediterranean (Greece and Turkey). Mainly in dry, thorny scrub with few trees, often on rocky slopes. Feeds mainly in low, open scrub, very skulking. Slower in movements than other Sylvias.

Rüppell's Warbler – slightly larger than Sardinian, longer wings/ shorter tail.

Rüppell's

Cyprus

Marmora's

Dartford

Cyprus Warbler – only found on Cyprus, in dense tall shrubbery. Particularly common in Cistus scrub.

Male

Cyprus – shorter tail than Sardinian Warbler. Shy.

Female

Sardinian Warbler – longer tail. Effervescent.

Spectacled Warbler – slightly smaller than Subalpine Warbler, shorter wings. Wags tail regularly. Slightly steeper forehead than Subalpine.

Spectacled – small warbler mainly of western Mediterranean (Italy, France, Iberia, islands, and also Cyprus). Occurs in very low vegetation, including Salicornia flats and semi-desert. Curious habit of following wheatears (or other chats), sweeping up insects disturbed by them.

Spectacled – feeds in low vegetation only. (Subalpine often feeds in trees/tall bushes, avoided by Spectacled.)

Dartford Warbler – small, all-dark, short wings/short tail, western Mediterranean and Atlantic coast to Britain. Low vegetation, heathland with gorse/heather.

Marmora's Warbler – inhabits lowest scrub of Sylvia warblers, often feeding up to 1m, spending much time on ground.

Female

Marmora's – similar to Dartford, shorter tail.

Dartford – small, keeps to cover, most often seen in sunshine. Keeps low in wet/windy conditions. Often associates with Stonechat.

Dartford – 'like Wren with long tail', often cocked.

Warblers: Widespread Leaf Warblers

Willow Warbler – Blue Tit-sized bird found in open woodlands of all sizes, especially border between trees and open country. Very much at home in small trees, bushes, scrub. Feeds at all levels above ground, sings from the top or side of a tree/bush. When singing, birds normally remain on one perch and will often turn head/body and wag tail.

Chiffchaff – feeds higher up in trees than Willow Warbler, usually perches conspicuously on treetop (often on dead branch) or overhead wire. Also sings while moving about. With each 'chiff' or 'chaff' tail wags. Often starts about half-an-hour before Willow Warbler in morning.

Chiffchaff – more bird of mature woodland than Willow Warbler, so long as the canopy is not too dense. Needs good understorey. Less at home than Willow Warbler in patches of scrub without trees. Likes oak, beech, willow.

Chiffchaff

Willow Warbler

Willow Warbler

Willow Warbler

Chiffchaff – all Leaf Warblers flick wings/wag tails intermittently; Chiffchaff wags tail much more often than others. Feeding birds appear to have nervous twitch. Movement of tail not just down, but also slightly to the side, which is unique.

Willow Warbler – not present in winter.
Chiffchaff – seen in western half of Europe in winter.

Adult

Willow –1st autumn.

Chiffchaff – smaller, more rounded/dumpy, shorter wings.

Adult

Willow Warbler – slightly larger than Chiffchaff, longer wings making it look slim/sleek. Pointed bill, usually with pinkish base. Flat crown. Legs usually paler than Chiffchaff's, a sort of pale brown.

Chiffchaff – shorter, usually darker bill than Willow. Rounded crown. Dark legs.

Chiffchaff
1st autumn.

Willow Warbler – curious habit of suddenly flying after other birds in apparent fit of fury. No others do this.

Bonelli's Warbler – very pale Leaf Warbler of Central and Southern Europe. In south of range is found in mountain forest, especially pine/oak, and with undergrowth that is not too tall/thick (e.g. bramble). In Central Europe breeds in mixed open woodlands, especially of oak, birch, beech, chestnut, with thin canopy. Bird throws whole body into song, making trembling movements, but does not have song-flight. Most song is from canopy.

Wood Warbler – mature woodlands with dense canopy, especially of oak, beech, sometimes spruce. Quite specific in requirements: good canopy, minimal undergrowth, also branches less than 3m above ground so bird can approach ground nest without too long a flight.

Wood Warbler – doesn't normally flick its wings and tail, in contrast to Chiffchaff and Willow Warbler.

Bonelli's – stubby, pink-based bill.

Wood Warbler – longer bill.

Wood Warbler – song sung from below canopy, often including short horizontal flight from one branch to next. Willow Warbler/Chiffchaff sing from exposed perch, not in canopy or in flight.

Wood Warbler – slightly larger than **Willow Warbler**, with very long wings that make tail look short. Wings often drooped slightly.

Eastern Bonelli's Warbler – birds from Balkans are slightly larger/paler, longer wings.

Wood Warbler – prefers to forage high in the canopy. Agile.

Bonelli's – 'step' on wings.

Bonelli's – between Chiffchaff/Willow Warbler in size, large head/stubby bill. Tit-like shape, shier than Chiffchaff or Willow Warbler, feeding for long periods in cover. Energetic singer.

Bonelli's – very 'clean' underneath.

Willow Warbler

Wood Warbler – large-headed/chesty. Prominent bill. Distinctive from below, tapering from broad head and chest to short tail.

Chiffchaff – shorter wings.

Warblers: Scarcer Leaf Warblers

Arctic Warbler – very far north. Among coniferous forest zone, but in birch, poplar, willow woods, usually near water.

Greenish Warbler – further south in lowland forest of oak, lime, birch.

Arctic – sings for long time from treetop perch. Erect posture, bill pointed up. When moving between song-posts, wings make remarkable buzzy sound.

Arctic – when breeding, feeds mostly in upper branches.

Greenish – more restless when singing than Arctic, frequent perch changes/some song in flight.

Arctic – migrants feed in canopy, not in low foliage. Others do.

Greenish – forages regularly at all heights.

Arctic – most dashing/dynamic of all leaf-warblers. Quick movements, strong flight, urgent manner. Quick switches in height. Hard to follow.

Arctic – slightly larger than Willow, shorter tail. Robust, flat crown. Large bill, looks snub-nosed.

Greenish – smaller, less bulky than Arctic. Rounder crown.

Greenish – much more skulking than Arctic, but also restless.

Yellow-browed Warbler

Pallas's

Greenish – similar shape to Chiffchaff. Flicks tail, but not incessantly like Chiffchaff; probably flicks wings more.

Firecrest

Arctic – long wings.

Greenish – relatively short wings.

Greenish

Yellow-browed – less hovering than Pallas's, but more regularly sallies to catch flies. Very active. Hard to see. Look for migrants among sycamore, sallow, birch.

Pallas's – often hovers like Goldcrest. Very active.

Goldcrest, Firecrest – slightly smaller than Pallas's.

Yellow-browed – unusual combination of large head/slender body.

Pallas's – shorter wings than Yellow-browed.

Warblers: Goldcrest and Firecrest

Goldcrest – in conifers, usually in canopy.
Firecrest – conifers, also deciduous bushes.
Both sing while feeding, not from exposed perch.

Goldcrest

Chiffchaff –
small but 20% larger than
Goldcrest/Firecrest.
Longer wings/tail.

Coal Tit – larger than
Goldcrest, thicker bill.

Goldcrest – tiny, short wings/tail.
Needle bill.

Firecrest –
slightly more
bulky and
heavier than
Goldcrest.
Slightly larger-
headed.
Slightly longer
tail than
Goldcrest.

Goldcrest – blank expression,
dowdy plumage. Firecrest is a Goldcrest
washed clean and glistening.

Firecrest – in display,
birds look obliquely at
each other, to show
head-stripes.

Treecreeper

Goldcrest – in display, birds bow to
each other to show 'crests'.

Goldcrest – tends to prefer feeding in canopy, in
thick branches (especially in breeding season).

Goldcrest – often
creeps up trunks like
Treecreeper. Firecrest
apparently seldom
does this. Bold and
inquisitive. Easily
attracted by 'pishing',
or imitation of its call.
Firecrest – tame but
less inquisitive.
Doesn't normally
come to 'pishing' or
imitation.

Firecrest – more often forages in
understorey, especially where both
species found together.

Goldcrest/Firecrest regularly hover as work
through foliage. *Coal Tit* hovers less often.

Goldcrest – never stops moving, exhaustingly
restless, hovers, flicks wings, moves about.
Firecrest – similar behaviour. Migrants tend to
be less incessantly restless.

Flycatchers

Spotted Flycatcher – throughout Europe in woods/forests, wherever there are tall trees/glades. Often common in gardens. Nests on ledge, often within creeper or wall, requiring sturdy support from below and good view for sitting bird. Also uses open-fronted nest-boxes.

Spotted – typical flycatcher hunting method. From lookout perch, flies out to snap up passing insect, then returns to perch, often the same one.

Spotted – tends to perch upright on exposed branches, both at top of trees/bushes, and within tall sunlit canopy. More a bird of edges than enclosed canopy.

Spotted – fast/agile flight, long wings/tail obvious. May dart sideways/upwards, swoop downwards, glide, hover, even occasionally alight on ground.

Spotted – Robin-sized upright-perching flycatcher without much plumage variation. Very elongated, slim body/long tail. Proportionally larger head than other flycatchers, fairly long, strong-looking bill makes audible click when snaps at flying insect.

Spotted – constantly makes nervous flicks of wings and tail.

Red-breasted Flycatcher – Chiffchaff-sized, very small flycatcher, quite different in shape to Spotted. Dumpy, compact look apart from long-looking tail. Relatively small and round-headed, small fine bill with yellow base, often visible from below. Rather like cross between warbler and flycatcher.

Red-breasted – mainly Eastern Europe, largely damp deciduous woods with rich undergrowth.

Red-breasted – much more secretive than Spotted, not normally perching in exposed places, preferring to remain hidden in canopy. Can be very difficult to see.

Red-breasted – although will fly-catch like Spotted, often quite content to glean insects from leaves, moving restlessly around like warbler. Other flycatchers don't do this. Even more agile/dashing than Spotted, exhibiting greater expertise at turning in tight corners. Usually makes rather short excursions. Quite readily drops to ground from low perch.

Red-breasted – incessantly flicks wings/cocks tail, often quite high over back, more than other flycatchers. Usually nests in hole in tree/wall, sometimes in foliage around trunk of tree. Uses hole nest-boxes.

Pied Flycatcher – more horizontal stance than Spotted; like Red-breasted prefers to shun more exposed perches and hunt within cover of leafy canopy, usually about halfway to treetop height. Tends to use typical fly-catching method but, in contrast to Spotted, seldom returns to the perch it has just left.

Pied – smaller than Spotted but larger than Red-breasted, a compact, plump flycatcher, with shorter looking tail than others. Has smaller bill than Spotted. Immaculately white below.

Pied – cocks tail/has unusual wing-flick, moving whole wing from shoulder. May also flick just one wing, not the other. Also perches with wings drooped slightly.

Pied – nests in holes in trees and in hole nest-boxes.

Pied – widespread in Europe, though largely missing from the South-eastern section. In mixed and deciduous woodland, especially oak woods and waterside sites.

Collared and **Semi-collared Flycatchers** – very closely related to Pied, all exhibiting similar behaviour. Best distinguished by plumage, although other pointers helpful.

Collared – male quite distinctive and more contrasting than Pied or Semi-collared. Collared and Semi-collared have fractionally longer wings than Pied, reaching halfway down tail (instead of a third). Very shy, elusive bird found only in deciduous woods, especially oak. Requires warmer conditions than Pied, in central band of Continental Europe. Feeds more in crowns of trees than Pied, seldom visits the ground.

Collared – canopy bird when breeding; migrant Collared far more inclined than Pied to hunt from low perches.

Semi-collared – said to be less shy than Collared. Found only in Balkans, in deciduous and mixed woods, mainly in mountainous regions. Least demonstrative of the three, with markedly less wing- and tail-flicking. Only reacts when under direct threat.

Semi-collared – feeding habits resemble Spotted more than Collared or Pied. Takes most of prey on wing, sallying from perch, not often from ground. Doesn't usually return to same perch.

Tits: Habitats and nesting

WET AREAS

Male

Female

Bearded Tit (Reedling) – occurs all year in large reed-beds and nowhere else. Hard to see, keeps low down in reeds.

Bearded Reedling – makes low flight over reed-tops, allowing brief views before plunging down. Flies with whirring action on straight course, trailing long tail behind like miniature Pheasant.

Bearded Reedling – nest is cup-shaped, low down in reeds.

Bearded Tit (Reedling) – often feeds at base of reeds, picking insects from water/just above. In winter, more often seen feeding perched on reed-heads, taking seeds.

Penduline – always found near water, usually in deciduous trees (willows, alders, birches) beside rivers/lakes.

Blue Tit – often feeds in reed-beds in winter. Other woodland tits don't.

Penduline Tit – tiny, with sharp bill.

Penduline – very tit-like in actions, clinging to/perching on thin outermost branches, often upside down.

Penduline – relies on presence of reedmace (typha – often wrongly thought of as bulrush) for nesting.

Penduline – nest easy to recognise. Downy and hangs from a branch (hence 'penduline') over water.

Willow – one of favourite habitats is damp woodland with swampy scrub, often beside watercourses. (More of marsh-loving tit than Marsh Tit.) Likes trees with narrow trunks, e.g. birches, willows, alders. In north of Europe, common bird of birch forest.

Marsh Tit – very confusingly named: only in woodland. Core habitat is thick, deciduous (oak, beech) woodland, often damp with lots of undergrowth. Nest is tree hole or other cavity. Uses lot of moss for nest.

Willow – excavates nest in rotten trunk of such a tree. (Marsh Tit does not excavate own nest, but will, confusingly, confiscate holes excavated by Willow Tits for its own nest.) In contrast to Marsh Tit, does not bring much, if any, moss to the nest.

DECIDUOUS WOODS

Blue Tit – mainly in deciduous woods/bushy places, including gardens. Nest mainly in tree hole.

Great Tit – found in all types of woodlands, plus bushy areas and gardens. Nest is in hole, usually in tree.

Sombre Tit – open woodland, particularly oak. Scrubby areas on mountainsides. Look for it especially in fruit orchards. Nest in tree-hole is not excavated.

Long-tailed Tit – in deciduous woods, but in south of range also mixed woodland. Requires plenty of undergrowth. Also bushes/hedgerows. Remarkable nest not placed in hole, but among low thorny shrubs or high in tree-fork. Domed, soft, covered in lichen.

CONIFEROUS WOODS

Coal Tit – prefers any kind of conifer woods. Not restricted to pure stands, also frequents mixed woodland. In Southern Europe, in deciduous forest. In winter, more catholic in habitat, sometimes found in pure deciduous woods. Nest is hole, usually in conifer. Also often near the ground, in root system of tree, or even rock hole.

Siberian Tit – ancient coniferous forest, especially pine. Likes lichen-rich branches. Nests in old woodpecker hole etc.

Willow Tit – in north of range, often found in pure conifer stands. (Marsh Tit is never found in pure conifer stands.)

Crested Tit – likes moss/lichen-rich trees, especially spruce. Deciduous woods in Southern Europe. Excavates nest in rotten tree stump.

Tits: Feeding behaviour

Great Tit – large tit; tends to feed in lower levels of bushes/trees, especially in winter. Feeds more often on ground than any other tit; especially fond of beech mast in autumn. Hacks at nuts held by foot to perch. Makes tapping like Woodpecker. Bold and tame. Common at bird tables.

Long-tailed Tit – travels along restlessly in small or large groups, never staying in one tree for long. Searches outermost twigs and branches acrobatically. From low levels to topmost branches, but never on ground. Approachable and preoccupied. Occasional visitor to hanging nut-feeders and bird tables (mainly Britain).

Blue Tit – tiny and very agile, often feeding upside down. Tends to feed in outermost branches of deciduous trees. Irrepressible, bold, tame. Seldom seen on ground, but commonly uses bird tables.

Coal Tit – usually feeds in topmost and outer branches of conifers – can be difficult to see. Small/very agile. Has shortest tail of any tit. Very fine bill for reaching into conifer needles. Regular visitor to bird tables. Often feeds on the ground.

Coal – more inclined to hover than other tits.

Crested Tit – unmistakable, but unobtrusive/difficult to see. Quiet trilling call is best locator. No loud song. Feeds almost entirely by searching lower branches. Often seen on ground. One of shyer tits, difficult to approach. Rarely visits bird tables.

Coal Tit

Siberian Tit

Marsh Tit (*near left*) – fairly regular at bird feeders (more frequent than Willow). Less shy, and noisier.

Willow Tit – in comparison to Marsh has relatively larger head. Well-developed nape muscles give 'bull-necked' appearance ('Mike Tyson' tit). Muscles are for excavating nest hole, something Marsh Tit doesn't do. Head feathering looks more untidy than Marsh. Crown feathers duller, less shiny. Almost always feeds in lower branches of trees, often close to ground, not actually on it. Not often at bird feeders. Shy. Tends to be quieter than Marsh.

Marsh – in common with Willow, feeds mostly on lower/middle branches of trees, avoiding crowns. Deals with food items with more gusto than Willow, using vigorous hammering/tearing actions not seen in that species. Often feeds in open far from cover. Typically found on plants along paths. May approach food-plants in open in long, confident flights. (Willow approaches slowly, stepwise, in short flights.)

Marsh – has neater, smaller head with longer-looking neck than Willow. Crown feathers often look shiny ('wet from the marsh').

Marsh

Willow

Willow – tail slightly rounded (central tail feathers longest).

Marsh –

Feeds on ground far more often than Willow.

Marsh – tail squarer-ended than Willow, or even slightly forked (outer tail feathers longest).

Sombre Tit – large, bulky, sluggish tit that doesn't flit restlessly from tree to tree; content to work an area thoroughly. Unobtrusive/easy to miss; not particularly shy. Has perhaps heaviest bill of any tit, used for hitting/tearing. On trunk/larger branches; not agile enough to search the outer twigs of trees. Often forages on ground among rocks. Often perches on the heads of flowers.

Siberian Tit – much larger, longer tailed, fluffier than Willow Tit, occurs in same places. Head looks large compared to Willow. Not well presented: unkempt. Feeds mainly in lower parts of trees, sometimes on ground. Often on trunks/large branches, like Great Tit or Nuthatch. Slow feeder; takes its time in each tree. Visits bird tables. Often extremely tame.

Tits: Flocks and sociability

Outside breeding season, many tits are seen in flocks, on their own or mixed in with other species of tits, plus sprinkling of Goldcrests, Nuthatches and Treecreepers. Flocks form in late summer and persist until the following early spring (Mar–Apr), when pairs split off. Flocks roam around woods/hedgerows, covering wide area each day. Not all tit species enthusiastically join flocks; number of birds in flock can be clue to identification.

Blue Tit – often in big flocks with other species, roaming around large area. Blue Tits often form core of large mixed flocks.

Goldcrest

Treecreeper

Long-tailed Tit

Long-tailed Tit (juvenile)

Great Tit – joins roaming flocks, often many individuals.

Long-tailed Tit – when not breeding invariably seen in flocks, based on families. Never seen alone. In autumn flocks can contain 20 or more birds, by mid-winter rarely more than 10. Other tits frequently join Long-tailed Tit flocks.

Coal Tit – often joins roaming flocks, in small numbers. Sometimes forms small mixed flocks with Goldcrests.

Willow Tit – south of Scandinavia, behaves as Marsh Tit, but in Scandinavia forms winter groups of 4–6 with large, but fixed, group territory.

Marsh Tit – pairs inhabit a territory all year. If mixed tit flock passes through territory, will join it as far as boundaries allow, but not further. You do not see flocks of Marsh Tits.

Crested Tit – small groups of 2–4 live in fixed territory and join flocks of other tits that pass through.

Siberian Tit – forms small flocks of 2–9 that remain in large, but fixed, territory. Often joins similar groups of Willow Tits in mixed flock.

Creepers: Which Creeper?

Some birds habitually hug tree trunks or rock faces when searching for food. Best-known are the tree-loving woodpeckers, but several smaller birds occupy a similar niche.

Woodpeckers – to move down they hop, as if using a ladder, with tail always pointing downwards.

Woodpecker – supported by stiff tail, can 'lean back' more than Nuthatch.

Woodpecker – usually much larger than Treecreeper or Nuthatch (except Lesser Spotted, shown here). Long dagger bill, tail pressed close to trunk. Has obvious forehead/neck, unlike Nuthatch.

Nuthatch – thick, straight bill; big head, no neck; chunky body; very short tail not pressed in to trunk.

Nuthatch – among tree-climbers, only these are able to climb down head first, holding on with one foot above the other. Far more erratic in movements than Treecreeper, seldom working from bottom to top but stopping and starting, running rapidly along branches, changing course frequently.

Treecreeper – bill much thinner than Nuthatch's, and curved; head relatively smaller. Tail long/held pressed in to trunk/branch. Never climb down head-first; seldom climb down at all. Often on underside of branches.

Treecreeper – often climbs up very thin trunks of small trees/saplings; Nuthatch usually avoids them. Hugs tree very close. Looks like mouse as creeps up trunk. On closer inspection makes short jerky hops. Works trunks/branches methodically, almost machine-like.

Wren

Goldcrest (*above*), *Wren* (*right*) also 'creep' over trunks and branches.

Woodpecker, Nuthatch – usually land halfway up tree or at top.

Treecreeper – habitually fly to bottom of tree trunks, then work way upwards before flying down again.

Nuthatch – often on ground. Treecreeper never goes on ground. Some woodpeckers (especially Green and Grey-headed) do.

Great Tit – often feeds on tree trunks, clinging in creeper-like fashion

Creepers: Nuthatches

Nuthatch – normally seen on tree trunks, branches or ground, rarely if ever on rocks.

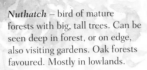

Nuthatch – bird of mature forests with big, tall trees. Can be seen deep in forest, or on edge, also visiting gardens. Oak forests favoured. Mostly in lowlands.

Nuthatch – typical view: clinging on to branch lengthwise, or holding on to tree trunk upside down.

Nuthatch – uses hole in tree (usually made by woodpecker) for nest. Usually plasters front with mud to its own ideal diameter.

Rock Nuthatch – typical view: standing with upright posture on rock. Slightly larger than Nuthatch, longer legs/bigger, slightly longer bill. Paler.

Rock Nuthatch – usually on rocks/ruins or ground but in winter does visit trees. Has tendency to 'peer' from behind rock.

Rock Nuthatch – not forest bird, but found on rocky slopes with scattered small trees/bushes. Often seen at ruins/archaeological sites. Most common between 1,000–2,500m.

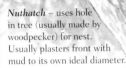

Rock Nuthatch – elaborate mud-nest placed in rock crevice, with entrance tunnel.

TWO RARE NUTHATCHES

Corsican Nuthatch – similar shape to Krüper's Nuthatch, but only found in Corsica, where no other Nuthatch species. Shy bird of pine forests at 800–1,500m.

Krüper's Nuthatch – much smaller, shorter bill than commoner Nuthatches. Lesbos/Turkey only. Found mainly in pine forest, where forages high in trees, moving around like tit. Often ventures right to end of thin branches, which larger Nuthatches do not.

Krüper's Nuthatch/ Corsican Nuthatch – excavates own nest-hole, with no plastering.

Treecreeper

Creepers: Treecreepers and Wallcreeper

TREECREEPERS

Treecreeper is more vigorous bird. Forages at more energetic rate, moving from tree to tree more quickly than Short-toed Treecreeper.

Short-toed Treecreeper – sometimes shows more 'feathery' flanks, giving hint of shorter tail.

Short-toed Treecreeper – much the more vocal of the two species. Call/song louder/more frequent than Treecreeper. Sings almost all year round; Treecreeper mainly Feb–May.

Treecreeper – shorter, more evenly curved bill. More richly coloured and contrasting than Short-toed.

Short-toed Treecreeper – fractionally longer, more 'bent-looking' bill.

Short-toed Treecreeper – hind-claw also slightly shorter (hard to see). Tends to look more 'frosted' or 'washed out' in colour than Treecreeper.

Treecreeper – far more aggressive to its rivals than Short-toed. Regularly fights/chases neighbours, behaviour rarely seen in Short-toed.

Short-toed Treecreeper – more inclined to spiral around tree trunks than Treecreeper. Shorter toe, less able to cope with smooth bark, e.g. beech trunk, so more readily takes to side branches.

WALLCREEPER

Wallcreeper – winter/female plumage – much easier to find in winter (Oct–Apr), when descends from heights/often forages on buildings/in quarries.

Wallcreeper – hops up, not down rock-faces, as if climbing a ladder. When foraging, constantly flicks wings half open (not done by any other creeper). In flight, broad wings/erratic flight make it look like falling leaf or huge butterfly. In summer between 1,000m and 3,000m on imposing sheer cliffs/rock-faces, often overhanging, particularly on cliffs with nearby streams/torrents. Often start at base of cliff-face and work up.

Shrikes

Great Grey Shrike – large shrike, long rounded tail/short wings. Mainly in Northern Europe, including into the taiga belt. Only shrike present in Europe north of Iberia in winter.

Great Grey – flies strongly, with swooping undulations if travelling for some distance.

Great Grey – perches prominently, often on top of tall trees.

Great Grey – typical shrike hunting technique: watches from lookout perch for movement below, flies down to pounce upon prey. In contrast to other shrikes, often hovers before final strike.

Great Grey – more attenuated than Lesser Grey, longer bill, longer head, longer tail. Wings proportionally shorter than those of Lesser Grey.

Great Grey (immature) – large, big-headed, plump, long-tailed shrike.

Southern Grey Shrike – very similar to Great Grey, but slightly smaller, slightly heavier bill, shorter wings/longer legs. Only in Southern France, Spain and Portugal, all year round.

Great Grey – varied diet of large insects, small mammals, reptiles and birds. Highly predatory shrike; only species that regularly pursues birds in flight, twisting/turning after quarry.

Southern Grey – perches prominently, often on wires or posts, rarely on tall trees.

Southern Grey – similarly varied diet to Great Grey, but a higher proportion of reptiles.

Lesser Grey Shrike – perches prominently; like Southern Grey avoids tops of tall trees. More upright posture than Great Grey or Southern Grey. Found mainly in Central and Eastern Europe, summer only. Selects warm, sunny places with scattered trees.

Lesser Grey – flight more direct/less swooping than Great Grey's. Mainly hunts from side of trees or bushes, about 1–6m above ground.

Lesser Grey – smaller/more compact than Great Grey with shorter, stouter bill, rounder head with thicker neck, shorter, less rounded tail. Wings proportionally longer than Great Grey, with longer primary projection.

Lesser Grey – less predatory than Great Grey and Southern Grey Shrikes, eating mainly beetles.

Immature

Lesser Grey – slightly larger and more robust than Woodchat and Red-backed Shrike, with thicker bill.

Woodchat – often perches higher than other smaller shrikes.

Woodchat – very direct flight, with lighter undulations than larger shrikes. Often 'explodes' from bush into flight.

Woodchat (immature) – slightly larger/more robust than Red-backed, with more prominent head.

Great Grey, Masked and *Red-backed Shrikes* – regularly cache food, impaling it on thorns or barbed wire. Impaling helps it to dismember larger prey. Woodchat and Lesser Grey rarely impale food.

Red-backed (male)

Red-backed (immature) – slightly more robust than Masked, shorter tail. In common with other shrikes, often flicks tail and jerks it sideways.

Red-backed (female)

Red-backed – flight undulating over long distance, but direct when between perches.

Masked – typically hunts from cover, within canopy of tree or shrub or on side branch. Often found in less open habitats than other shrikes.

Masked (immature) – smaller/slimmer-bodied than other shrikes, longer, thinner tail. Also has much thinner, stubbier, less hooked bill on smaller head.

Masked – lightest flight of the shrikes. Resembles a big flycatcher when flying after aerial prey.

Crows: Colourful Crows

Magpie – flight fluttering/unstable-looking. Bursts of wing-beats followed by stalling glides, tail dragging.

Magpie – mainly seen singly or in pairs, may roost communally. Small, noisy, excited flocks may form briefly, especially in spring.

Magpie – common all over Europe, needing both trees and patches of open ground/short turf. Often found near human habitation. Black-and-white body with long, graduated tail.

Magpie – domed nest of sticks placed at top of small tree. Familiar sight when leaves have dropped in winter. Nests well spaced – pairs are territorial.

Magpie – feeds in trees, but much at home on ground. Walks with jerky gait, also makes heavy hops.

Jay – fluttery flight, slower wing-beats than Magpie, without bursts of flaps. Makes uneven, flappy progress, seemingly making little headway despite best efforts. Over short distances, flight swooping/undulating.

Jay – pigeon-sized, with longish, square-ended tail/broad wings. Unmistakable plumage. Crown feathers can be raised.

Nutcracker – looks similar to Jay, but steadier in flight, with more direct progress. Compared to Jay looks heavy at front with shorter tail. Often flies high.

Siberian Jay – similar flappy style to Jay, but better flier, with less faltering progress. Flies with rapid wing-beats/smooth glides, undulating strongly over short distances.

Azure-winged Magpie – flight fluttering like Magpie, but easier, looser, less erratic wing-beats and smoother progress. Tail looks narrow.

Hoopoe – vaguely similar to Jay, especially in flight, but smaller/slender at front, with longer neck/bill.

Azure-winged Magpie – moves around in parties, each restlessly moving from tree to tree, one bird following another.

Azure-winged Magpie – nest open, not domed. Usually placed in crown of tree as far from trunk as possible. Breeds in loose colonies, with several nests placed in adjacent/nearby trees.

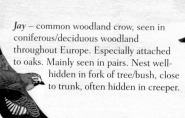

Jay – common woodland crow, seen in coniferous/deciduous woodland throughout Europe. Especially attached to oaks. Mainly seen in pairs. Nest well-hidden in fork of tree/bush, close to trunk, often hidden in creeper.

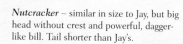

Nutcracker – similar in size to Jay, but big head without crest and powerful, dagger-like bill. Tail shorter than Jay's.

Nutcracker – in autumn collects large numbers either of hazelnuts or arolla pine.

Nutcracker – mainly in coniferous forests in Northern Europe and mountains of Central Europe. Nests in spruce trees but must have access to hazel or arolla pine.

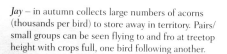

Jay – in autumn collects large numbers of acorns (thousands per bird) to store away in territory. Pairs/small groups can be seen flying to and fro at treetop height with crops full, one bird following another.

Nutcracker – nest is twig platform placed close to trunk of spruce tree. Nests very early (Mar), often completing whole cycle with snow on ground.

Siberian Jay – distinctive bird of far north, where commonest in spruce forests with much growth of black lichen, but can be inexplicably absent from places that appear to suit it perfectly.

Siberian Jay – often seen perched atop tree. Very versatile feeder; works both ground and trees, sometimes hanging upside down like tit.

Siberian Jay – small, size of thrush. Has rather loose, fluffy plumage; otherwise similar shape to Jay. Very quiet for a crow. Small parties materialise from nowhere/disappear silently. In winter inquisitive/tame, often attracted to human activity, including camp fires in forest.

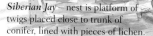

Siberian Jay – nest is platform of twigs placed close to trunk of conifer, lined with pieces of lichen.

Crows: Black Crows

Chough /Alpine Chough – small black crows, long, broad-based wings well fingered at tips. Undersides of wings often look two-toned. Small head, long bill.

Jackdaw – about size of Chough, narrower/more pointed wings with few, if any, 'fingers' showing. Shorter tail than either Chough. Undersides of wings uniformly dark. Broad neck/short bill.

Jackdaw

Chough

Alpine Chough

Alpine Chough – always seen in restless flocks, when flying resembles ashes from bonfire blowing in the wind. Often scavenges at mountain resorts for scraps.

Chough – gregarious like Alpine Chough, but often seen in pairs or small parties, too.

Chough – acrobatic flight, daring dives, twists, turns. Very distinctive mode of plunging downwards, wings held in and folded back, often holding position for subsequent steep rise. Alpine Chough has similar acrobatic flight.

Jackdaw – much smaller than Rook or Crow. Proportionally narrower wings, very short neck, much smaller bill. Rook larger than Jackdaw with longer front end. Wings long, broad, fingered.

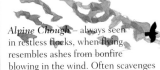

Rook (adult)

Carrion/Hooded Crow (juvenile) – bill short and thick, curved culmen. Flap on feathering on culmen fits smoothly, not bulging; no hint of white gape.

Jackdaw – nests in holes in trees, rocks or buildings.

Rook – always nests in colonies on treetops.

Carrion/Hooded Crow – not colonial: nests very well-spaced ('only one crow's-nest is found on a ship').

Raven – not colonial. Nests on cliff-ledge or tree early in year.

Rook (juvenile) – no bare skin at bill base, so extremely difficult to tell from Crow. Bill longer/more pointed, crown more peaked, flap of feathering on top of culmen bulges slightly, hint of a white 'gape'.

Carrion/Hooded Crow – more evenly broad wings; tail squared off.

Raven – usually in pairs.

Jackdaw – makes two wing-beats to every one from Rook (or Crow). Fast wing-beats, as quick as pigeon's – remember 'Slow Crow, Flap-Jack'.

Raven – huge, as big as Buzzard, much larger than Carrion/Hooded Crow and Rook. Has distinctive flight silhouette, long tail, strongly projecting head/neck, long wings, giving cross-shaped appearance. Wings broad-based/narrow-tipped, with obvious fingers. Flies with wings flexed back.

Raven

Rook – pointed head with thin bill. Wings pinched in at base, slightly more pointed and fingered than Crow's. Tail more rounded.

Rook – slightly faster, freer-looking wing-beats than ponderous Carrion/Hooded Crow, but difference very subtle.

Carrion/Hooded Crow – very slow, menacing wing-beats. Not given to aerobatics, but often soars.

Raven – slow but free/powerful wing-beats. Often rolls over in mid-flight, much given to playful aerobatics, especially in spring. Soars a great deal.

Alpine Chough – only in mountains between 1,500–4,000m, on rocky slopes/high pastures. Nests on inaccessible ledge or cavern.

Alpine Chough – wings slightly shorter, slightly narrower at base than Chough, with slight bulge on trailing edge.

Alpine Chough – on ground, wing-tips shorter than tail. Red legs, short yellow bill.

Alpine Chough – wing-tips more rounded, less obviously fingered, only 4 primaries showing. Tail longer than width of wings, pinched in at base and obviously rounded.

Chough – on ground, folded wings reach tip of tail. Red legs, long red curved bill.

Chough – wing-tips are broad and have about 6 'fingers' showing. Tail as long as wings broad, square-ended. Wings rectangular shape.

Chough – found at sea-level on rocky coasts, also on mountains. Nests in rock crevice, sea cave or building. On ground, can be distinguished from Jackdaw at great distance by probing/digging into soil (Jackdaw works the surface).

Rook – on ground, has very different look to Carrion/Hooded Crow, bare skin around bill base giving sharply peaked forehead and high crown.

Crow – typically seen in singles or pairs, but flocks do form, so the adage of 'Crow on its own, Rook in a flock' is not reliable.

Carrion/Hooded Crow – on ground, broad bill fits snugly into head, giving flat crown. Tight, well-fitting plumage. Doesn't wear baggy shorts, wears leggings.

Carrion Crow

Hooded Crow

Rook – loose plumage makes it appear to be wearing one size of feathering too many. Feathered belly makes it look like it's wearing baggy shorts.

Raven – on ground, note huge bill. Also shows loose feathering on neck.

Rook – distinctly rolling, waddling gait. Has unthreatening look. Almost always seen in groups, throughout day and year.

Carrion/Hooded Crow – direct walk/horizontal posture. Looks predatory and threatening.

Jackdaw – on ground, jaunty stride with head held up.

Starlings

Starling (summer) – common almost throughout Europe, but in Iberia only winter visitor. Plumage has metallic green sheen, with few spots. Throat smooth, legs reddish-pink.

Starling (winter) – very spotty.

Starling – in evening, may gather in enormous flocks to roost in reed-beds, bushes, on buildings. Prior to settling down, often flies in huge, amoeba-like formations in sky. Flies on relatively straight course (slight undulations) on distinctly triangular wings.

Starling – effervescent bird with spiky bill, short tail, continuous waddling walk. Almost always seen in flocks, moving across lawns/ probing into soil.

Starling – often perches on TV aerial, singing with wings half-flapping.

Starling – nests in hole in tree or building, not flying far to collect food for young.

Starling (juvenile) – browner than adult.

Spotless Starling (winter) – looks rather uninteresting/dark.

Rose-coloured Starling – shorter, blunter, more curved bill than young Starling.

Blackbird – superficially similar, but longer bill/tail. Hops/runs across lawns, standing stock still in between. In pairs or alone.

Rose-coloured Starling (summer visitor) – rare breeding bird in Eastern Europe. Unmistakable.

Rose-coloured Starling – groups follow locust swarms. Breed mainly in rocky places.

Spotless Starling – nest site usually in building (sometimes tree/rock crevice). Birds feed young mainly on beetles, which may require longer commuting journey to find.

Spotless Starling – juvenile far darker than other juvenile Starlings.

Spotless Starling (summer) – resident in Iberia, Corsica, Sardinia, Sicily only. Like Starling that has had oil poured over it, often looks messy/unkempt. Has longer feathers on throat, usually has brighter pink legs.

Sparrows

MALES

Spanish Sparrow – boldly marked, looks big.

House Sparrow – often grubby.

Tree Sparrow – small, neat and trim, shorter tail, more rounded head. Variety of habitats, including towns. Nest is usually in hole in tree.

Spanish – often far from people, in bushes, trees, marshes. Not in large cities. Only found in warm, humid areas. Nest usually in vegetation, but often in large nest of stork or raptor.

Spanish – notable for gathering in huge flocks (tens of thousands), especially at the roost. Also migrates (in the east) in dense flocks. Neither habit typical of other sparrows.

Spanish – very slightly larger than House, heavier bill.

Tree – no female plumage, sexes alike.

FEMALES

Spanish (*above*) – additional characteristics that work on some individuals: longer gape than House, reaching to eye; more curved cutting edge to upper mandible; slightly more pronounced crown, peaked head, longer wings.

Rock – upright posture, legs obviously showing. Huge bill, larger than House Sparrow's, on broader head. Bold and stripy.

House – habitually squats down, loose breast feathers partially covering legs. Smaller head/bill than Rock Sparrow, plumage less patterned.

Rock (*above*) – rocky hillsides and mountains. Nests in rock cavity.

House – marginally smaller/more compact than Spanish; no obvious streaks on breast. Always associated with people and buildings, from farmyards to major cities. Nest usually in crevice in building.

Rock – in flight undulates strongly, unlike other sparrows.

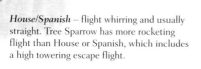

House/Spanish – flight whirring and usually straight. Tree Sparrow has more rocketing flight than House or Spanish, which includes a high towering escape flight.

Seed-eating bird families

Finches for most part build immaculate cup-shaped nests out of finer materials, often including plant down. Usually sited in bushes.

Finches often have pleasant, rambling songs (mainly mixtures of calls), sung by colourful males, often in flight.

Sparrows don't sing well; utter series of chirps, albeit with some gusto.

Buntings have short, not rambling songs, rarely in flight.

Sparrows build untidy domed nests out of grass, often stuffed into hole.

Buntings build nests low down, often in grass.

Greenfinch (female) – same size/similar shape to House Sparrow, but much more strongly forked tail.

Male

Chaffinch (female) – smaller bill than House Sparrow, more peaked head.

House Sparrow (female) – tail weakly forked.

Dunnock – very thin bill, mainly eats insects. Not usually sociable, just ones and twos. Slimmer than sparrow, more rounded head. Characteristic mouse-like creep/'shuffle' along ground, but also hops. Many movements accompanied by nervous-looking wing/tail-flicking, out of character for any finch or sparrow.

Chaffinch (female) – far more streamlined than sparrow or Greenfinch, with long wings and, especially, long tail.

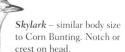

Buntings as a rule have longer tails than sparrows and finches.

Reed Bunting – longer tail than similar House Sparrow; distinctive habit of flicking/spreading tail, which sparrow doesn't do.

Common Waxbill – tiny finch-like bird with red waxy bill. Introduced to Iberia, where rare.

Linnet (female) – small and streamlined, with tiny grey bill; long, well-forked tail.

Finches feed on ground, on herbs, in trees; found in many habitats.

Buntings feed mainly on ground; prefer open habitats.

Sparrows feed on ground and on herbs; also catholic in habitat requirements.

Corn Bunting – habit of hovering for a moment before landing.

Sparrows have fairly straight cutting edge to bill, and even-sized mandibles.

Buntings have S-shaped cutting edge to bill, which points down as nears eye; mandibles of different sizes.

Common Rosefinch – blunter bill/longer tail than sparrow, beady eye on bland face. Far less effervescent, more skulking.

House Sparrow (female)

House Sparrow – thicker bill than Reed Bunting (*top left of page*).

House Sparrow (female)

Yellowhammer – similar in shape to Chaffinch, but longer tail with deeper fork.

Skylark – similar body size to Corn Bunting. Notch or crest on head.

Corn Bunting – round head, heavy bill. Larger/streakier than sparrow.

Finches: Finches and their food plants

Bullfinch – feeds from trees/herbs, not often on ground. Partial to tree buds, including oaks and fruit trees (can be a pest); also ash seeds, herbs such as nettles.

Serin – feeds mainly on ground. Favourite foods: grass seeds and those of ground weeds, including dandelions.

Hawfinch – feeds in treetops/on ground (not on herbs). Favourite seeds are hornbeam, beech, wild cherry, elm, maple and oak. In Southern Europe, also feeds on olives.

Chaffinch – feeds on ground/in trees, not from herbs. Takes wide variety of seeds, including beechmast. Also many insects in summer, gleaning foliage and even catching flies in air.

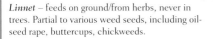

Brambling – feeds on ground/in trees, not from herbs. In winter a specialist on beechmast, and strongly associated with beech woods.

Linnet – feeds on ground/from herbs, never in trees. Partial to various weed seeds, including oil-seed rape, buttercups, chickweeds.

Redpolls – feed mainly in trees, but also on herbs and, less often, on ground. Strongly associated with birch, but also feeds in alders in winter.

Goldfinch – feeds mainly from herbs, less often in trees, rarely on ground. Strong attraction for thistles and members of same family, e.g. burdocks, dandelions. Feeds in alder trees with Siskins and Redpolls. Also (mainly males) feeds on teazel.

Twite – feeds on ground/from herbs, not in trees. Takes grass seeds and, in winter, feeds on seeds of saltmarsh plants (feeds closer to seaward side than other finches).

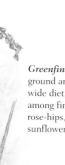

Greenfinch – feeds from ground and on herbs. Has wide diet, but is unusual among finches in taking rose-hips, yew fruits and sunflower seeds.

Siskin – mainly feeds in trees, very seldom on herbs; on ground when favoured seeds have fallen (e.g. late spring). Favours spruce in breeding season, alders and birch seeds in winter.

Citril Finch – mainly on ground, but also from cones in spruce and pine trees. Feeds on grass seeds in alpine meadows. In Corsica is associated with tree-heath scrub.

Crossbills – only from trees, not from herbs and not on ground (although come to ground to drink). The species specialise on cones of different conifers (see p242).

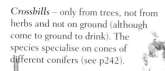

Pine Grosbeak – feeds from trees and shrubs. Favours buds and shoots of spruce trees. Unusually for a finch, eats a lot of berries, especially rowan.

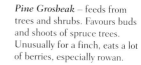

Common Rosefinch – feeds on ground, in bushes and from herbs. Has no strong preferences.

Finches: Finches in flight

Pine Grosbeak – its flight is a cross between that of a large finch and of a small thrush. Obviously long-tailed, and with powerful, bounding leaps and drops.

Several finches also perform aerial song-flights, often describing a circle or figure-of-eight at constant height. When displaying, the wings are beaten slowly, in the manner of a bat. In the Serin, the bird rolls from side to side as it flies along. Other finches with commonly seen song-flights: Crossbills, Twite, Redpolls, Greenfinch, Siskin, (Goldfinch occasionally).

Bullfinch – fast-flying, with undulations not as deep as those of, say, the Hawfinch. Plump, but not front-heavy, and square-ended tail is not unusually long or short.

Bullfinch – not in tight-knit flocks. Birds tend to follow each other in 'single file'.

Hawfinch – extraordinary silhouette – so front-heavy as to give the appearance of effort to keep the bird from plunging down; also short tail. Wing-beats are super-fast and the bird flies with deep undulations. Often flies very high, above treetop height. Quite often just 1 bird will be seen.

Greenfinch – chunky finch with powerful undulating flight. Shorter tailed than Chaffinch, and with deeper up-and-down flight.

Crossbills – chunky finches with fairly short tails. Typical undulating flight of 'average' finch. Can look very heavy-headed, especially if the crop is full of food. Tend to fly high, above treetop height, usually in flocks of 5–20.

Chaffinch – long, elegant silhouette; slim with long tail. Flight undulating, with long, but moderately shallow sweeps. Alights on the ground with fluttering flourish.

Brambling – slightly shorter tail than Chaffinch, with a more obvious notch to it, and the bird has a more bouncy flight. Flocks tend to be tight-knit, often more so than Chaffinch flocks.

Linnet – in tight flocks, often rising up in skipping flight over the fields before landing again rapidly. When mixed feeding flocks of finches and sparrows are disturbed, flying Linnets separate out into their own group.

Linnet, Redpoll, Twite, Siskin and **Goldfinch** – light, airy, bouncing flight. Flocks are packed so tightly, and so co-ordinated that the birds appear to be attached by thread.

Redpoll – often flies high over; slightly more bouncing flight than similar Linnet, but has shorter tail.

Twite – flocks often fly far away when disturbed. It looks noticeably longer-tailed than Linnet.

Goldfinch

Citril Finch – skipping flight, but noticeably long tail.

Serin – very airy, skipping flight with deep undulations – quite a ride!

Siskin – flocks feeding in trees often burst out as one, in spectacular 'cascade', then wheel round and often land again in the same tree. Looks long-winged and medium-tailed.

Finches: Various Finches

Female

Bullfinch – never the finch for large and/or noisy flocks. Quiet, bush-haunting species, only found in small, dinner-party sized gatherings (up to 10).

Male

Bullfinch – does not normally feed in open, or on ground. Stays in cover, often difficult to see.

Hawfinch – notoriously difficult to see; tends to take flight at slightest disturbance and make for treetops, where remains for long periods. Even when not disturbed, lives secret life in canopy, unnoticed. Also a quiet species, hard to locate by sound.

Hawfinch – identified by shape alone. Outsize bill – almost looking too large for body – together with huge neck, plump body/short tail. Looks like cross between finch and parrot.

Male

Redwings

Hawfinch – often feeds among leaf-litter on forest floor. Look for it among flocks of birds, e.g. Redwings.

Pine Grosbeak – has curved upper mandible that might recall Crossbill, but bill of Crossbill dominates its head, whereas in Pine Grosbeak looks comparatively small. Colour scheme (male reddish, female greenish) mirrors that of Crossbills. *Parrot Crossbill* has equally chunky body, but is much smaller/far shorter tail.

Pine Grosbeak – largest finch, size of small thrush. Quite thickset, with very distinctive fluffy plumage.

Pine Grosbeak – often in moderate-sized flocks feeding on berries in winter, when can be astonishingly approachable/tame.

Female

Chaffinch – slim, long-bodied, long-tailed, elegant finch.

Male

Common Rosefinch – another finch in which male is red-coloured (acquired only in its second year – see p241). Smaller than Pine Grosbeak and Crossbill, not associated with conifers. More 'normal' finch-like shape than Crossbill, with longer tail and stubby, but not crossed, bill. Skulking.

Common Rosefinch – typical upright posture when singing, very open-mouthed.

Female

Chaffinch – often looks more horizontal than other finches when perched, although tail sometimes droops.

Chaffinch – moves along ground with distinctive tripping walk, head nodding like miniature chicken; also hops.

Male

Brambling – similar shape to Chaffinch, but shorter-tailed and less elongated.

Female

Two-barred Crossbill – shaped like Chaffinch, superficially similar in plumage, but head broader/tail shorter.

Brambling – often less noisy than Chaffinch. Both these species gather in flocks in woods/fields, often mixing together. So, to find a Brambling, it is best to search among flocks of Chaffinches.

Female

Bramblings

Chaffinch

Chaffinch

Male

Brambling – more obvious fork in tail. Head seems slightly larger than Chaffinch; bill slightly thicker.

Finches: Predominantly green Finches

Finches that sit on wires: Serin, Greenfinch, Linnet, Goldfinch, Twite and, sometimes, Chaffinch and Brambling. By and large, other finches don't.

Serin – smallest of Europe's green-coloured finches, about Blue Tit size. Large head but tiny stubby bill – imagine it has flown into something and squashed its bill.

Male

Serin – very restless, fast-moving bird.

Serin – main habitat is woodland edge and gardens. Sun-loving bird, commonest in Mediterranean region. Particularly fond of sitting on tops of conifers, especially Cypresses.

Juvenile

Female

Serin – usually feeds on ground, where has creeping gait – difficult to see the hops. Similar Siskin is usually in trees.

Siskin – longer wings/more colourful tail than Serin (*above*).

Siskin – slightly larger than Serin, with smaller head/much thinner bill. Longer wings that appear to reach part way down tail.

Siskin – often in flocks feeding in trees, hanging tit-like from seed cones (not behaviour associated with Serin or Greenfinch).

Female

Siskin – often by streams and lakes.

Male

Siskin – essentially forest bird, especially when breeding. Favours spruces. More northern/montane than Serin.

Female

Male

Greenfinch – large, stout, sparrow-like finch with broad head. Large, oddly pale bill/frowning, slightly fierce expression.

Greenfinch – when perching looks very upright, accentuating large head/short tail.

Greenfinch – very common bird of parks, gardens, woodland edge.

Crossbill (female) – chunky/bull-necked. Bill always looks large and, if seen well, is diagnostic.

Greenfinch – often feeds on heads of herbaceous plants, which tend to be avoided by Siskin and Serin.

Citril Finch – juvenile.

Crossbill – clambers among coniferous branches, often using bill for support in manner of parrot. Longish wings, short tail.

Citril Finch – slim/long finch, with longer tail than any other on this page. Considerably slimmer and smaller than Greenfinch. Longer bill.

Citril Finch – finch of mountainous regions (above 700m) in Central Europe. Mainly in coniferous forest, often commutes to nearby meadows to feed. In Corsica, occurs in scrub above tree line.

Citril Finch – often near mountain huts. In winter, occasionally visits alders and birches.

Citril Finch – seen feeding on conifer cones, doesn't hang upside down like Siskin.

Finches: Predominantly brown Finches

Female

Linnet – always nervous, not allowing close approach, especially when in flocks. Common, breeding in all kinds of open habitats.

Linnet – bill tiny, short/grey, body slim. Tail longer than on many finches, but not Twite.

Twite – the 'Mountain Linnet' breeds in upland pastures/hills, in cool, windy, wet climates – uncommon. Found in dunes and saltmarshes in winter.

Linnet – at most times of year has plain appearance. Colourful male in spring is spectacular, but not usually representative of species.

Twite – definitely longer tail than Linnet, giving more tapered look. Also slimmer.

Redpolls – smaller than Linnet and Twite, more compact, shorter tails.

Twite – seeing the head is often the key to identifying species. Bill is as small, if not smaller than Linnet's, but often yellow (male's in breeding season grey). Head slightly smaller, looks fluffier. Face lacks any of the Linnet's 'powder spots' or eyebrow, looks warmly coloured.

Lesser Redpoll – small/dark.

Mealy   **Arctic**

Redpolls – first clue is that these streaky brown finches are feeding in birch trees. In contrast to Linnet and Twite, hang from branches in manner of tit.

Arctic Redpoll – overall fluffy plumage (may look almost globular); dense feathering on thick neck (especially nape), giving slightly front-heavy look; dense feathering on underparts, giving fluffy appearance on ample belly undercarriage (similar to lark); dense feathering on face, making bill appear absolutely tiny/eye small. Face has 'pushed-in' appearance, consequently forehead is steeper than Mealy Redpoll.

Redpoll – larger than Lesser Redpoll and with 'frosted' appearance.

Male *Mealy* in spring.

Mealy   **Arctic**

Common Rosefinch – females/1st-year males brown. Featureless brown finch, larger/heavier than Linnet or Twite, less likely to be seen in large flocks.

Male

Common Rosefinch – in complete contrast to many brown finches, skulking and hard to see.

Common Rosefinch – look for somewhat swollen bill/beady eye. Looks front-heavy, with ample head and long tail.

Crossbill – juvenile is heavy finch with broad bill (takes a few months before diagnostic crossing of mandibles develops). In conifer trees, in contrast to most other birds on this spread.

Chaffinch – female long-tailed, elegant finch. Lots of white in wings and on tail-sides.

Goldfinch – can look brown, but colourful plumage makes it easy to identify. Bill sharply pointed/pale.

Goldfinch – juveniles have unpatterned head.

Trumpeter Finch – rare finch of hot, semi-desert areas of Spain. Small, tame, readily identifiable. Very small with comparatively large head/enormous bill.

Male

Female

Trumpeter Finch – ground feeder, creeps along. Looks rather plain/ordinary until bill seen.

Finches: Crossbills

Finches of coniferous woodlands, adapted to feeding on seeds from cones.

Various points to note when separating *Common Crossbill* and *Parrot Crossbill* given here, but note that bills of females/young of both species slightly smaller than those of males. In most *Common Crossbills* tip of lower mandible can be seen peeking above upper mandible, but never in *Parrot Crossbill*. Lower edge of *Parrot Crossbill*'s lower mandible bulges, but doesn't in *Common Crossbill*.

Parrot Crossbill – bigger head on much thicker neck. Bill looks more bluntly tipped, because upper mandible curves more strongly down.

Male

Species differ in tree species from which they feed. Acrobatic when feeding, using bill as third limb.

Parrot Crossbill – often noticeably larger/heavier, can at times suggest even Hawfinch in its bulk.

Parrot Crossbill – shows more obvious pale cutting edges to mandibles.

Common

Parrot

Female

Scottish Crossbill – bill of intermediate size and shape.

Said to form smaller flocks than other Crossbills.

In north, *Common Crossbill* favours spruce, *Parrot Crossbill* favours pine. *Parrot Crossbill* less common, makes fewer migratory movements south of taiga breeding range.

Juvenile *Common Crossbill* drinking.

Parrot Crossbill – bill as deep as long, often melting seamlessly into curve of flatter crown. *Common Crossbill*'s bill longer than deep, so forehead looks steeper and more obvious.

Two-barred Crossbill – usually has less robust bill than Common Crossbill on smaller head. Longer tail.

Two-barred Crossbill – favours larch trees. Also often feeds on rowan berries, which other crossbills rarely do.

Buntings: Snow and Lapland Buntings and Snow Finch

Snow Finch – looks trimmer than Snow Bunting, with more upright posture. Often flicks longer tail upwards. Often in flocks, look like snow flurries when birds fly.

Snow Finch – actually a sparrow. Resembles Snow Bunting, but smaller/slimmer, much larger bill. End of tail square, not forked.

Snow Finch – only on high mountains (1,900–3,100m) in Central European ranges. Often seen feeding at ski resorts and along roads.

Snow Bunting – when breeding, Arctic–Alpine species of bare, rocky places. Very unlikely ever to cross paths with Snow Finch.

Snow Bunting – head of breeding male has been described as snowman with coals for eyes/nose.

Lapland Bunting – on mountains and tundra. In contrast to Snow Bunting, avoids bare, rocky places – prefers low shrubbery.

Snow Bunting – gathers in flocks that move forward in leapfrog fashion, back birds flying to front, themselves then being flown over.

Lapland Bunting – thicker bill than Snow Bunting.

Snow Bunting – spends most of time on ground, where walks/runs with belly slung low/feathers partly covering legs.

Skylark – more hesitant style of flight, often hovering before landing.

Male

Female

Snow Bunting

Lapland Bunting – very ground-hugging.

Lapland Bunting – similarly strong flight. In shape resembles Skylark, but has shorter, clearly notched tail, narrower wings, shorter front end.

Lapland Bunting

Skylark

Buntings: Brown Buntings

Little Bunting – flicks tail nervously like Reed, but seldom spreads it. Also given to wing-flicking. Shorter tail than Reed. Furtive.

Little – small/more compact than Reed, with proportionally longer, more sharply pointed bill with straight-edged culmen, giving snubby-nosed look.

Rustic Bunting (*below left*) – smaller than Reed but larger than Little. Bill resembles Little, with straight culmen making it look sharply pointed. Bill also slightly longer/heavier than Little's or Reed's. Crown usually looks ragged/peaked.

Female

Male

Reed Bunting – has habit of continuously flicking/spreading tail.

Reed – medium-sized bunting with small bill. Culmen slightly curved. Slightly more rounded crown than Little or Rustic.

Rustic – shorter tail than Reed. Flicks tail. Usually seen alone (Reed and Little sociable).

Winter

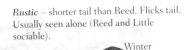

Lapland – larger than Reed, Little and Rustic Buntings, with heavy build, including larger head. Has combination of very long, sharply pointed wings/short tail.

Rustic – requires more trees/bushes than Little, but still found in boggy parts of taiga forest, especially where main forest trees interspersed with birch and willow. Feeds young on freshwater invertebrates.

Lapland – ground-hugging, skulking bunting with short legs. Flies off for miles when disturbed.

Little – northern taiga, in open areas within spruce or birch forest with some undergrowth, usually beside water. Scarce.

Little – tends to resemble finch with light, undulating style.

Reed – usual undulating flight like many small seed-eating birds, but has characteristic hesitant, uneven style. Lands as soon as possible in cover.

Rustic – more determined, less hesitant flight than Reed.

Reed – in South-east Europe, Reed Buntings much larger than North-western counterparts and have big, heavy bills. Always requires thick vegetation growth on very wet soils, so usually found in marshes and reed-beds (also heaths). Common.

Ortolan – bill slightly longer than Cretzschmar's.

Ortolan – slim, medium-sized, pinkish-brown bunting with obvious eye-ring/pink bill. Very rounded head, no hint of crest. Found in sunny habitats over much of Europe. In Southern Europe, often in mountainous regions.

Cretzschmar's – bill shorter than Ortolan's, with culmen angling down more sharply to point. With close view, cutting edge of bill drops steeply down as reaches gape.

Cretzschmar's – very similar to Ortolan; little smaller/shorter tail. Found only in Balkans and Greek Islands, usually close to coast, favouring rocky/scrubby hillsides below 1,350m.

Corn Bunting – has large head/very big bill.

Rock Bunting – distinctive, medium-sized bunting with short wings/long tail. Tends to look rather sparrow-like. Often sings from high perch such as tall tree. However, feeds on ground, often at roadsides. Quiet, unobtrusive.

Cretzschmar's – perhaps most terrestrial bunting, almost always seen on ground. Usually sings from rock, never tree. Quite tame.

Rock – as name implies, associated with rocky areas, especially on upland slopes with scattered trees/not much vegetation. Found up to about 1,900m.

Corn – strong undulating flight. Distinctive tendency to hesitate before landing, fluttering for a short time.

Ortolan – often sings from bushes/trees and may even forage within them. However, like most buntings, still feeds mainly on ground, especially on short turf. Shy.

Corn – largest/most plump bunting, very similar in shape to lark.

Corn – often perches on wires/posts, making it a conspicuous bird of extensive arable areas. Often flies from wire to ground with legs dangling in display.

Buntings: Yellowish Buntings

MALES

Yellowhammer – fairly large, long-tailed species common almost throughout Europe in farmland with hedgerows/woodland edge – any dry, sunny habitat with lots of rich vegetation. Very upright when singing.

Yellowhammer – quite showy species, easy to see, perching on top of bushes, trees, wires, feeding out in open on fields.

Cirl Bunting – slightly smaller than Yellowhammer, often perches less prominently, making it tricky to locate a singing bird. Mainly in south of Europe, in similar habitats to Yellowhammer, but prefers smaller fields surrounded by few tall trees, avoiding most open habitats.

Yellowhammer – sings for longer part of year than other small birds, right into Aug.

Yellowhammer – flies with long undulations; looks longer-tailed than Reed or Cirl Bunting.

Cirl

Black-headed Bunting – larger, more hefty bunting than Yellowhammer. Summer visitor to South-east Europe, in dry country with scattered trees/dense, tall bushes.

Cirl Bunting – very secretive, hiding away in bushes/trees and feeding quietly on ground, almost disappearing in grass.

Black-headed – flies powerfully with fluent undulations, lacking usual hesitation of bunting.

Black-headed – similar song-flight to Corn Bunting, flying along with quivering wings and dangling legs.

Yellow-breasted Bunting – smaller than other yellowish buntings, but well built. Rare breeding bird of far North-east Europe (Finland, present only in mid-summer), breeding in tall grass meadows with scattered bushes, usually near water.

Black-headed – sings as vigorously as Yellowhammer but remains on its breeding sites only from May–July.

Cinereous Bunting – hardly deserving of label 'yellowish'. Big, long-tailed bunting found only on a few Greek Islands. Found on barren rocky slopes.

Black-headed Wagtail – this form of Yellow Wagtail has similar plumage pattern to bunting, but much slimmer with longer, narrower tail and fine, not thick, bill.

FEMALES

Male buntings are easy to recognise, but females offer plenty of possibilities for confusion.

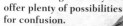

Black-headed Bunting – big, not very streaky bunting, with long body, long tail, heavy grey bill. Longer neck than Yellowhammer or Cirl Bunting. In comparison with other yellowish buntings, also has very long legs.

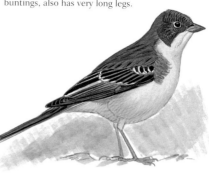

Yellowhammer – longer wings/tail than Cirl Bunting, making it look more elongated.

Cirl Bunting – slimmer/more compact than Yellowhammer, with flatter head/more hunched appearance.

Reed Bunting – size as Yellow-breasted but smaller bill with curved culmen.

Yellow-breasted Bunting – small but sturdy, short tail contributing to compact look. Quite long, stout pink bill with straight-edged culmen.

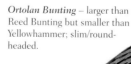

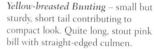

Cinereous Bunting – dull, featureless bunting, larger than Yellowhammer but smaller than Black-headed. Relatively long tail/large pointed grey bill with straight culmen.

Ortolan Bunting – larger than Reed Bunting but smaller than Yellowhammer; slim/round-headed.

Recommended reading

The following titles were consulted frequently during the preparation of this book, and are recommended for anyone wishing to delve further into the subjects of bird behaviour and identification.

Bang, P. & Dahlstrøm, P. 2001. **Animal Tracks and Signs.** *Oxford University Press.*

Beaman, M. & Madge, S. 1998. **The Handbook of Bird Identification for Europe and the Western Palearctic.** *Christopher Helm.*

Birding World. *Ornithological Magazine* (monthly).

Birdwatch. *Ornithological Magazine* (monthly).

Bird Watching. *Ornithological Magazine* (monthly).

British Birds. *Ornithological Magazine* (monthly).

Bruun, B., Delin, H., Svensson, L. & Singer, A. 1986. **The Hamlyn Guide to Birds of Britain and Europe** (Revised Edition). *Hamlyn.*

Cramp, S., Simmons, K.E.L. & Perrins, C.M. 1977–94. **The Birds of the Western Palearctic** (Vols 1–9). *Oxford University Press.*

Hammond, N. & Pearson, B. 1994. **Hamlyn Bird Behaviour Guides: Waders.** *Hamlyn.*

Harris, A., Shirihai, H. & Christie, D. 1996. **The MacMillan Birder's Guide to European and Middle Eastern Birds.** *Macmillan.*

Harris, A., Tucker, L. & Vinicombe, K. 1989. **The MacMillan Field Guide to Bird Identification.** *Macmillan.*

Harrison, P. 1983. **Seabirds: An Identification Guide.** *Beckenham.*

Hayman, P. & Hume, R. 2002. **The New Birdwatcher's Pocket Guide to Britain and Europe.** *Mitchell Beazley.*

Hayman, P., Marchant, J. & Prater, T. 1986. **Shorebirds.** *Croom Helm.*

Holden, P. & Cleeves, T. 2002. **RSPB Handbook of British Birds.** *Christopher Helm.*

Del Hoyo, J., Elliott, A. & Sargatal, J. 1992–2002. **Handbook of Birds of the World** (Vols 1–7). *Lynx Edicions.*

Hume, R. & Pearson, B. 1993. **Hamlyn Bird Behaviour Guides: Seabirds.** *Hamlyn.*

Hume, R., Wallace, I., Rees, D., Busby, J. & Partington, P. 1990. **Birds by Character – The Fieldguide to Jizz Identification.** *Papermac.*

Jonsson, L. 1992. **Birds of Europe with North Africa and the Middle East.** *Christopher Helm.*

Kightley, C., Madge, S. & Nurney, D. 1998. **Pocket Guide to the Birds of Britain and North-West Europe.** *Pica Press.*

Madge, S. & Burn, H. 1988. **Wildfowl: An Identification Guide to the Ducks, Geese and Swans of the World.** *Christopher Helm.*

Ogilvy, M. & Pearson, B. 1994. **Hamlyn Bird Behaviour Guides: Wildfowl.** *Hamlyn.*

Sibley, D. 2000. **The North American Bird Guide.** *Pica Press.*

Snow, D.W. & Perrins, C.M. 1998. **The Birds of the Western Palearctic** (Concise Edition, Vols 1–2) *Oxford University Press.*

Svensson, L., Grant, P.J., Mullarney, K. & Zetterström, D. 1999. **Collins Bird Guide.** *HarperCollins.*

Glossary

Arm – the inner wing of a bird, nearest the body (before the carpal joint).

Bowed – bending downwards, or arched down.

Breeding – the plumage that a bird exhibits during the breeding season, including for the pre-nesting stages when it is trying to attract a mate.

Carpal – the area where the front edge of the wing kinks (the 'wrist') is where one finds the carpal joints. Sometimes there are marks here called carpal patches.

Carrion – the flesh of dead animals.

Chick – a general term for a non-flying young bird, usually with fluffy, downy plumage.

Crepuscular – active in the twilight (at dusk and dawn).

Culmen – the upper section (mandible) of a bird's bill.

Cup-nest – a kind of nest of basic, open design, somewhat similar to a shallow cup.

Dabbling – working the bill at the surface of the water to acquire food.

Diagnostic – especially important for making an identification (diagnosis).

Display – a posture or series of ritualised postures used to convey a message such as threat, appeasement or courtship.

Diurnal – normally active by day.

Eclipse – a special plumage worn by certain male birds to camouflage them when they are moulting their flight feathers.

Fingers – the effect of the primary flight feathers appearing spread and well-separated at the end of an open wing, as if they were fingers at the end of a human hand.

First Winter – a bird in its first winter of life, having hatched the previous breeding season; also referring to the plumage it shows at this time. The following spring the bird will moult into First Summer plumage.

Fledgling – a young bird that has left the nest and has its first set of feathers.

Flush – the act of causing a bird to fly away in alarm.

Gape – the fleshy corner or inside of the beak, often brightly coloured.

Gleaning – searching over and picking from a surface such as a leaf.

Glide – a type of flight in which the motion is forwards but the wings are not repeatedly flapped.

Gonys (Gonydeal Angle) – the ridge along the bottom of a bird's lower mandible. It often angles upwards towards the tip.

Graduated – broad at the base but gradually getting narrower towards the end.

Habitat – the type of place in which a bird lives e.g. marsh, wood, lake.

Hand – the outer wing of a bird, beyond the carpal joints, away from the body.

Hover – flying 'on the spot', maintaining a steady position in the air by flapping.

Immature – any stage between juvenile and adult, including both the bird itself and the plumage it exhibits.

Juvenile – specifically, a bird that is wearing its first full set of feathers, having lost the downy plumage of a chick or nestling.

Lek – a gathering of male birds at a communal display ground, or arena.

Migration – any movement of a substantial part, or a complete population, from one place to another.

Morph – different colouration within an interbreeding population unrelated to geographical range.

Nestling – a young bird that has recently hatched and is still confined to the nest. Once it has left the nest it is called a fledgling.

Nocturnal – usually active only at night.

Non-breeding – any plumage adopted by a bird for purposes other than breeding (and which is significantly different from breeding plumage).

Perch and Pounce – a common feeding technique of many types of bird, involving the prolonged watching of the ground from a perch, followed by a quick flutter down to catch any prey sighted.

Phase – *see* Morph.

Picking – taking an item in the bill directly from a surface (e.g. mud), usually using sight to find it. *See* Probing.

Predator – any animal that might kill and eat the bird, its eggs or young.

Primary – one of the main flight feathers on a bird (*see* 'parts of a bird' diagram in the Introduction).

Primary Projection – on the folded wing, the distance that the primaries project beyond the tertials (see 'parts of a bird' diagram in the Introduction).

Probing – using the bill to search for food items below a surface, by immersing it into a substrate.

Quartering – a slow, forward movement in flight low over the ground.

Race – *see* Species.

Raptor – hook-billed birds of prey, excluding owls.

Roost – a site where one or more birds sleep, not necessarily at night. The term can also include gatherings of the birds themselves.

Scavenger – an animal that eats the meat of dead animals, and often also various items of rubbish.

Second Winter – a bird (or the plumage it acquires) during its second winter of life. This plumage is moulted the following spring to reveal Second Summer plumage.

Secondary – one of a tract of flight feathers that forms the trailing edge of the wing (*see* 'parts of a bird diagram' in the Introduction).

Skulking – birds that customarily hide deep in vegetation and are difficult to see.

Soar – a type of flight in which the movement is upwards (often in a spiral) but the wings are not repeatedly flapped.

Song-flight – a ritualised flight following a more or less specific pattern, uttered to an accompaniment of song, made for the purpose of proclaiming a territory.

Species – a recognisable type of bird, usually breeding only with its own kind. A subspecies (or race) is a recognisable population of birds, usually living in a particular geographical area, which may interbreed with a similar population where the two meet.

Stitching – a series of probes in quick succession, giving the impression of sewing.

Stop-Run-Peck – a sight-feeding technique, involving standing still and watching for the movement of prey, followed by a quick chase and grab of any prey sighted.

Taiga – a broad habitat zone, found in Northern Europe, defined by large, unbroken areas of coniferous forest.

Territory – a bird's defended space, protected for its own use for feeding or, more usually, breeding (or both).

Trailing edge – the back or hind edge of a wing.

Towering – flying upwards very rapidly, often to a great height, in order to evade danger.

Tundra – a broad habitat zone found in the very north of Europe, defined by large areas of low-growing, often damp vegetation without trees.

Undulating – a very common mode of flight in which the progression can be seen to be up and down. A few flaps are followed by the closure of the wings, followed by a few flaps, and so on.

Index